letters from GOD

If God wrote you a letter everyday for a year,
what would He say?

IVAN TAIT

Scripture quotations marked AMP are from The Amplified Bible, Old Testament
copyright © 1965, 1987 by the Zondervan Corporation. The Amplified Bible, New
Testament copyright © 1954, 1958, 1987 by The Lockman Foundation. Used by
permission. All rights reserved.

Unless otherwise indicated, all scripture quotations are from The Holy Bible, English
Standard Version® (ESV®). Copyright ©2001 by Crossway Bibles, a division of
Good News Publishers. Used by
permission. All rights reserved.

Scripture quotations marked KJV are from the Holy Bible, King James Version
(Authorized Version). First published in 1611. Quoted from the KJV Classic
Reference Bible, Copyright © 1983 by The Zondervan Corporation.

Scripture quotations marked MSG are taken from The Message. Copyright ©
1993, 1994, 1995, 1996, 2000, 2001, 2002, 2003 by Eugene H. Peterson. Used by
permission of NavPress Publishing Group. Website.

Scripture quotations marked NASB are taken from the New American Standard
Bible®, Copyright © 1960, 1962, 1963, 1968, 1971, 1972, 1973, 1975, 1977, 1995
by The Lockman Foundation. Used by permission.

Scripture quotations marked NIV are taken from the Holy Bible, New International
Version®. NIV®. Copyright © 1973, 1978, 1984 by International Bible Society.
Used by permission of Zondervan. All rights reserved.

Scripture quotations marked "NKJV™" are taken from the New King James
Version®. Copyright © 1982 by Thomas Nelson, Inc. Used by permission. All rights
reserved.

Scripture quotations marked RSV are taken from the Revised Standard Version of the
Bible, copyright © 1946, 1952, 1971 by the Division of Christian Education of the
National Council of the Churches of Christ in the USA. Used by permission.

Scripture quotations marked TLB are taken from The Living Bible copyright ©
1971. Used by
permission of Tyndale House Publishers, Inc., Carol Stream, Illinois 60188. All
rights reserved.

Published by
What Matters Publishing House
What Matters Ministries and Missions
PO Box 62820,
Colorado Springs, CO 80962
International Standard Book Number (ISBN):   978-0-9893060-5-8
Design and Layout: What Matters Ministries and Missions

Printed in the United States of America

I dedicate this book to my daughters.

Bethany, Kindra, and Abbi, you wrap me in the sunlight of your love and affection and hold my heart in your hands.

Introduction

Words can make us or break us. It is a self-evident truth that the right words, spoken at the right time by the right person, can change our world! These defining moments occur when we listen with our hearts and not our heads. Have you ever realized that words have the power of life and death? Proverbs 18:21 confirms this, saying, "Death and life are in the power of the tongue and those who love it will eat its fruit" (NKJV). I remember meeting my stepfather for the first time as a young boy. The words he spoke over me as he took his knuckles and repeatedly struck me on the top of my head echoed in my ears long after he shouted them. "Your father didn't want you and neither do I, you little..." he roared. Those words pierced my soul and marked me as an illegitimate, unwanted child. I suffered under that verbal abuse for many years. It encased me in shame and guilt, paralyzing my self-confidence and stealing my potential. But I also remember at the age of eight, my mother holding my hands after a basketball game, looking into my eyes, taking my face and telling me that I was her favorite child, that I was her gift from God. With her words she saved me from utter destruction, giving me a glimpse of light in an otherwise dark, ungodly, and monster-invaded room.

Words can start wars and end wars. They can mend the invisible wounds of our hearts. They can change the ugly, vain imaginations of the heart into songs of joy and laughter. The sound of words can be like music to the weary soul. They can be like a well of life and a spring of hope or they can imprison, enslave, and torture us for years. How much more can the words of God the Father carry power to change, heal, and inspire us to wholeness, greatness, and love!

Words can make a soul grow wings and strengthen them with wind causing us to soar into our destinies. The right words can heal our wounds, open our blind eyes, repair our broken hearts, and inspire us to greatness. Words are food to our spirit and water to our mind. Words can change a worm into a prince, a fool into a genius, and a failure into a hero. The power of words cannot be measured for good or for evil. One word can lift the weight of the world off our shoulders. It can shake off the clouds of darkness or depression engulfing our hearts. Words are pillars of strength. They are the solid rocks on which we stand against the winds, rains, and floods of life. Jesus said, "The words that I have spoken to you are spirit and are life" (John 6:63, NASB). Isaiah 55:11 tells of the strength of God's spoken word, "So is my word that goes out from my mouth: It will not return to me empty, but will accomplish what I desire and achieve the purpose for which I sent it" (NIV). We see this in action in Genesis 1:3. God said, "Let there be light," and it was so! God literally holds the entire universe together by the power—the glue—of His word.

As you read this book, I encourage you to be like Jeremiah who said, "Your words were found, and I ate them; and Your words were to me a joy and the rejoicing of my heart" (Jer 55:11, AMP). Read these letters from God. They will be medicine to your soul creating immunities against ugliness and evil, building a fortress of faith in your mind, and surrounding you with an ocean of God's love. God's words are the last word on every subject of life. Open your heart and let the light shine in. Redefine every day of your year with a life-giving letter. Dream as big as God dreams, love as wide as God loves, walk as tall as God walks and let your soul soar!!

Ivan Tait

...my heart stands in awe of your words. I rejoice at your word,
as one who finds great treasure.
Psalm 119:161 NKJV

The words of the Lord are pure words,
like silver refined in a furnace on the ground,
purified seven times. You, oh Lord, will keep them;
Psalm 12:6 ESV

How sweet are thy words unto my taste! yea,
sweeter than honey to my mouth!
Psalm 119:103 KJV

Every word you give me is a miracle word,
how could I help but obey?
Break open your words, let the light shine out,
let ordinary people see the meaning.
Psalm 119:129 MSG

A word fitly spoken and in due season is like apples of
gold in settings of silver.
Proverbs 25:11 AMP

The Spirit gives life, the flesh counts for nothing. The words I have
spoken to you, they are full of the Spirit and life.
John 6:63 NIV

Jesus answered by quoting Deuteronomy: "It takes more than bread to
stay alive. It takes a steady stream of words from God's mouth."
Matthew 4:4 MSG

Everyone then who hears these words of mine and does them will be
like a wise man who built his house on the rock.
Matthew 7:24 ESV

January 1

In Noah's Ark

Genesis 7:1
Go into the ark, you and your whole family…
NIV

In Noah's ark, I placed the world. In Noah's ark, I set all My promises. In Noah's ark, I placed all My hopes and dreams of a new world and a new beginning. In Noah's ark, I laid out My plans for the human race. In Noah's ark, I held the heart of the world: every animal, every beating heart, every good wish, and all My blessing. Today is no different. I have placed in you My new Noah's ark, all the essence of who I am. I have withheld nothing from you. I have placed My Son in you. All the treasures of the universe lie in you, in the person of My Son. You need nothing, you lack nothing, and you will miss nothing.

The hopes of the world are in you. The dreams of the world abide within you. Steer your way through the floods. Land on My mountain. Step out and begin to build, plant, and grow a new life with Me as the seeds of your possibilities come into reality.

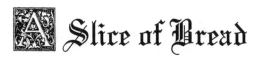 Slice of Bread

Deuteronomy 15:4
Save when there shall be no poor among you...
KJV

Look for the poor and hungry souls of the world. Give them a slice
of your love. Keep them alive by your constant generosity. Give from
your heart, not from your duty or religious goodwill. A slice of love
bread carries unseen nutrients and healing properties. Share your life
with orphans; shelter them and educate them. They are your diamonds
in the rough waiting for the expert jeweler to polish them and bring
out their glorious colors and brilliance. I love orphans and widows. I
am their Father. I give them to you so you will never be without pure
purpose and divine love. The poor, lost, and forsaken are the highway
to My heart. They lead you into My arms. They place you in the center
of My will. They protect you from the devil's counterfeits. They open
your eyes to truth and pure religion. They yoke you to Me and keep
you connected to My heart. Love them; see Me. Love them; be Me.

atisfying Companionship

Psalm 25:14
The secret [of the sweet, satisfying companionship] of the
Lord have they who fear Him,
AMP

I reveal Myself to those who fear Me. I reveal My secrets and open My hands gladly to those who tremble at My Word. I look to and depend on those who trust Me unconditionally. I am always ready to answer the questions of your life. There are depths to My love that I want to reveal to you, entire oceans of untapped spiritual and natural resources. My love heals and builds the areas of your life that have been broken. This love will clothe your spirit and preserve your heritage. It will define your family and color your world. There is a relationship that you and I can have, a sweet satisfying companionship that makes all other relationships work. This companionship adds life where death has been, meaning where nothingness has dwelt, and peace where strife and turmoil have ruled. A satisfying companionship is what I offer you. If you accept this, our journey will begin anew. Blessing, gifts, insight, and life shall all be yours for life.

hen You Wake

Psalm 17:15
As for me, I will continue beholding Your face in righteousness, I shall
be fully satisfied when I awake, beholding Your countenance.
Author's Paraphrase

When you wake, I wake. When you wake, I am already there waiting for your heart to reach out to Me. I stand by your bed with My arms outstretched, calling you by name. I have My hands full with gifts for your day, destinies, blessings, and assignments. No day is wasted with Me as your guide. I have a full life prepared for you. There will be no permanent life-altering mistakes in your future and no disasters of the Spirit life. Your waking in the morning hours will be a time of joyful expectancy when you unravel yourself and claim your inheritance. The life of the Spirit begins. Never neglect life. Never forget it, lose it, or pass it by. Stop and drink My life through prayer, worship, and thanksgiving. When you wake, a song of victory will begin. It will announce your waking to all My enemies, and they will flee.

Maneuvering through the Rapids

Psalm 107:29
He hushes the storm to a calm and to a gentle whisper, so
that the waves of the sea are still.
AMP

Take your time traveling through life. Don't rush, panic, or get in a hurry. Calm down. Eat My word like healing candy. Rest in My promises. Hide your heart in My faithfulness. Tune your heart to the high notes of true love, exceeding faith, and pure holiness. Live as a conqueror in the midst of wolves, goats, and snakes. Maneuver through the rapids of life. Keep rowing; never take your oar out of the boat. Others around you will quit, jump ship, and abandon their oars, but you are called to live in the calm where peace reigns—where you can hear the sound of all living things around you, never distracted by the noise of troubled waters around you, never fearing that your boat will sink, always moving forward, always seeing the light ahead of you, never looking back, never fearing, doubting, or trembling at the unknown. Safety is your word. All of your life you will be safe. Danger is safety to you because I control the rapids, waves, and winds. I am your rudder. I will bring you safely home each time. Rest in this and flourish.

rue Escape

2 Timothy 2:26
They will escape out of the snare of the devil and do the will of God.
Author's Paraphrase

Total freedom is your destiny. There is no partial escape with Me.
Because you do My will faithfully, you will escape your past. The
you of yesterday will never rise again. The mental monument of the
world will crumble before your eyes. The former loves of the flesh
will dissolve. Like butter in a skillet, your old tyrant masters will
crawl away like fangless snakes looking for a hole to hide in. Every
torturous, alluring power will lose its seducing, captivating power.
All of your losses will be abundantly replaced. My soul and your soul
will meld together; we will become inseparable. Our minds will think
the same, our hearts will beat as one, our spirits will commune in the
sweetness of life. You shall be the source of true blessing to the lonely
soul. True escape is true surrender when all you ask becomes one with
all I am. Escape from the world, and escape into Me. Every divine
escape leads to a divine discovery where you find the treasures of your
destiny. Each treasure revealed leads to a new equipping and a new
intimacy with Me. Escape from yesterday. Dive into your future.

Finding Your Pulse

Matthew 6:21
For where your treasure is, there will your heart be also.
KJV

Life has a way of stealing passion from people—good passion, energizing passion. Many people are dead men walking. Even though their mouths are moving and their hearts are beating, they have lost their true pulse, the reason for their true existence, that miracle part of them that lets them know they are alive. I know where to find your pulse—that place where you feel totally alive, where breathing is easy and every step is a joyful expectancy that something good is going to happen. From this day forward, you will live in perfect harmony with your God-given pulse. I created it, I gave it to you, and I will keep it beating. Always take your pulse. Make sure it is beating in unison with Mine. Then all your dreams will come true. My heartbeat is tangible. My pulse is filled with miracles. Take your pulse daily. Check it with My heartbeat. Let it speed up or slow down in harmony with Mine. Then you will always be at the right place at the right time, seeing rightly, hearing rightly, doing rightly. Blessing after blessing will appear at your doorstep announcing My arrival.

ifted Up

Acts 3:7
And He took him by the right hand, and lifted him up: and immediately his feet and ankles bones received strength.
KJV

When I touch someone with My power, they are forever changed. Anything that does not change you for the better does not originate with Me. It is time to be lifted out of every crippling circumstance and weakening thought. I will leave no part of you untouched. I will take you from the place you are at now, and I will transfer you into a place of amazing influence. Your abilities to help people are about to increase. Don't doubt My goodness. Don't hesitate to believe what I am saying. Your trust in Me is your bank account number. When you trust Me unconditionally, your bank vault opens. Yes, it is time for you to see My mighty power work on your behalf. The time is near for My return. Occupy your place of influence in Me and never relinquish it to anyone. Now take My hand and let Me put you in your place of destiny.

ct Like Clay

Isaiah 64:8
We are the clay, and You our potter; and
we are the work of Your hand.
NKJV

Act like clay and not like a rock. Clay has no voice of resistance and no sound of rebellion. Clay is soft and pliable to move, shape, and form. Clay has the hope of change built into it. It is the picture of potential. Anything can be done with clay. It has no limitations on it, only the limitations of the potter. Clay can become the dream of the potter. Clay is the vision manifest of its potter. It is the voice of the potter's heart. Clay speaks for the potter. It represents the intentions and hopes of its potter. Clay has no permanent flaws. In a second it can be re-made and re-created. If it does not work, the potter can change it. It cries out possibility. It screams adventure. It is the complete fulfillment of the potter's life. All of His love is poured into the clay, and all of His hope is lavished on His clay. The potter holds nothing back. No amount of pressure, strain, or pain can lie endured for the sake of the potter's dream. Oh, be My clay. Stand still. Wait for My touch. It will change you. It will form your heart and cure your deformities. Trust My touch. Rely on My perfect intentions for you. You were born to be My clay, so act like it, and I will add magnificence to your destiny as My clay.

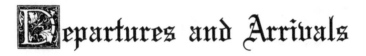epartures and Arrivals

Deuteronomy 28:6
Blessed shalt thou be when thou comest in, and
blessed shalt thou be when thou goest out.
KJV

Life is full of departures and arrivals. There are times for leaving and times for arriving. Don't try to change the departures or the arrivals. It is necessary for your destiny. Sometimes you need to walk away from certain types of relationships. There are people who will begin as friends but will turn into dangerous liabilities. You must be willing to depart. There are always new beginnings waiting in the wings of your life. Don't fear leaving a bad situation. Don't hesitate departing from an unfruitful life or a dead field. Give yourself the right to arrive at My will. Arriving and departing are healthy when done in My will. Each departure brings a new revelation of My blessing. You cannot arrive at My new doors of opportunity if you are stuck in the past. You cannot enter into My evolving plan for your life if you refuse to leave the old plan. My will is a moving, evolving, enlarging will. I am a moving God. I don't stand still. Leave your past. Bury it. Never revisit the ghosts of yesterday. Enter My will, discover My plan, and arrive at My house. Live here, dwell unhindered, and arrive at life.

Learned Contentment

Philippians 4:11
For I have learned how to be content in whatever state I am.
Author's Paraphrase

There is a school of contentment all of My soldiers must go through. It is imperative that My soldiers have no areas left within them that can be sold, bought, or bribed with any outside pleasures or stimulations. A God-soldier must first be disciplined in the habit of holiness. This allows him to grow stronger each day. Your habits build a house for Me to dwell in. Second, a soldier must be untouchable by all the forces of evil. No amount of emotional, mental, or spiritual torture can break My soldier. A God-soldier must master the area of learned contentment whether in the cold or heat of life. My soldier remains steady and faithful. He perseveres through hardship with joy and a smile. He walks without a limp in his attitudes. His stride is unhampered by inconvenience, personal discomfort, or sacrifice. My soldier learns this holy art and becomes a master of contentment. In this way, he or she is fully trustworthy and able to be trusted with all the riches of My kingdom.

The Gift of Thirst

Psalm 42:2
My inner self thirsts for God, for the living God.
When shall I come and behold the face of God?
AMP

Your thirst for Me is My gift to you. Your thirst leads you into My courts, and it places you before My throne. Your thirst allows Me to fill your heart with My love and glory. Deep inside of you are "Grand Canyons" of need and desire, all of which I can and will satisfy.
Your thirst is your GPS to Me. It will find Me even through storms, tornadoes, or hurricanes. As long as you remain thirsty you will never be lost. Your hunger calls to Me in the night watches. It calls out My name even when you sleep. Hunger defines you; it explains you to Me. It unlocks My heart to you. It reminds Me of your need and love for Me. No reserve, no regret, and no retreat is the cry of a thirsty soul.
I promise you that I will quench as much thirst as you have. Thirst honors Me. It places Me on the throne of your heart, and it eliminates My competitors for your heart. It makes Me Lord of your will and Author of your life. Thirst and be satisfied. Thirst, and I will be satisfied.

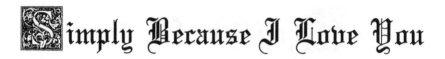imply Because I Love You

Proverbs 15:6
In the house of the righteous there is much treasure: but in the revenue of the wicked is trouble.
KJV

There are many places in which there are hidden and buried treasures. I know the location of these places. I know where all buried spiritual treasures are. I am the one who buried these treasures. They are buried so that My people who truly love Me and who have pure motives can find them. I have the map with the exact directions to the treasures. I know you are no longer interested in vain glory, ego, pride, or empty and vain pleasures of the flesh. I will give you the treasure maps. Your heart's desires will be granted. No begging or pleading is necessary. These are your treasures that I have reserved for you simply because I love you. I want you to use what you need and give the rest away. Help the hurting, bind up their wounds, and put eye salve on their blind eyes. Cherish the abandoned souls. Protect the victimized. Hide the forsaken and restore the vanquished minds of the helpless travelers. Give where there will be no return. Sow yourself, and I will keep your seed flowing. You will never lack seed to sow and riches to reap.

 Am Listening

1 John 5:14
And this is the confidence which we have in Him: that if we ask
anything according to His will, He listens to and hears us.
AMP

Don't ever doubt that I am interested in hearing your prayer requests.
I love the sound of prayer. Prayer is My symphony; it is My sanctuary
of beautiful music. Heaven is filled with the fragrances of pure prayers.
They are the flower gardens of heaven. One pure, sincere, unselfish
prayer is like the smell of a thousand beautiful flowers to Me. I love
your prayers; I long to say "yes" to them. I practice answering prayer.
It is My daily food knowing you need Me and that you are relying on
Me, knowing that because you trusted Me, I will now fix that which
was broken. Restoring the lost, healing the sick, and liberating the
prisoners brings Me great joy. I live to surprise you with outrageous
answers. I live to give you new and awesome convictions and to open
your eyes to new truths and fresh ideas. Never doubt My goodwill.
I am listening. Now, start talking.

ew Chains

Jeremiah 40:4
And now, behold, I loose thee this day from the chains
which were upon thine hand…
KJV

Breathe in the clean air of freedom; no one will harm you again. You will never hear the rattle of your chains dragging behind you. My freedom is permanent. The family chains hiding your DNA will be dissolved. The chains of the mind will shatter. The chains of bad habits will melt before you like snow in the sun. You will never need to look back; nothing is following you. I have separated their tentacles from your very soul. Your insides have been reconstructed and your heart, soul, and spirit are forever transformed. Now your chains are chains of mercy and truth, love and power. Wear these chains every day; show them off. Chain as many people as you can to these chains, for they are everlasting chains of heaven. You are now a slave of love. Your heart has been circumcised, your spirit purged, and your emotions healed. Now you are ready to take your place in My army. Strap your weapons on, mount your horse, and blow the trumpet. Charge the enemy's camp and rescue His captives. Loose them and heal them. This is your true destiny to unleash heaven on hell's captives and let the sound of freedom reign throughout the earth.

The Key to My House

Hebrews 4:16
Come boldly to the throne of grace, that we may obtain
mercy and find grace to help in time of need.
NKJV

Do not hesitate drawing near to Me. Approach Me with your intentions. Draw near to Me with your hunger. Embrace Me with your honor. Stay near to Me—inseparable, undividable with your single heart. Look inside My eyes. Can you not see the ocean of love? Can you see how much I desire to bless you and give you unlimited access to Me, that you might run toward Me? Notice My arms are outstretched to you, waiting in holy anticipation to see you surrender to My will, waiting to clothe you in the garments of an overcomer, anticipating your rise to wholeness. I have been waiting to hear the sound of your dreams knocking on the door of My heart, for I promise you that I will grant them all to you. I have told everyone you are coming. Sit awhile at My table, dine with Me, open up your heart to Me, and let Me soothe your pain. I have told the watchmen at the door to let you have the key to My house. It's yours. Come and see Me any time you wish; I am never too busy for you. Look deep into My face, and you will find that after awhile you lose sight of this troublesome world. Let Me take the rags of religion off of you. Take your new clothes and put them on; they match Mine. They have no wrinkles, no spots, and no stains. They are pure white, washed in the Son, gleaming with hope. Remember, I am your safe place. I am your heart's home.

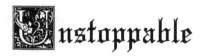nstoppable

Acts 5:39
But if it be of God, ye cannot overthrow it…
KJV

I am unstoppable. I cannot be dethroned, overpowered, or pushed out of the way. My position as Supreme Ruler of the world is permanent. I have absolute and unchangeable power over the universe. All three worlds are under My power. Everything on earth, under the earth, and in heaven above are under My domain. I am your personal Bodyguard, Builder, and Doctor. I am in the process of building you an indestructible life—a life secure and covered with impenetrable armor. This life will be a shelter to the victims of Satan's army, a hospital for the broken and sick, and a restoration center for those who have fallen into the hands of life's thieves. Your life will carry the mark of Calvary, the crucifixion touch. That is one who has crucified his old life and habits and embraced the Prince of life from this sacred place of sanctification. You will rule over the enemy forces and demonic influences around you. Dwell in My mind and life, and you will be a chain-breaker and life-giver your whole, unstoppable life.

The Sound of a Growing Heart

Philippians 2:13
For it is God which worketh in you both to
will and to do of his good pleasure.
KJV

When you are near Me, can you feel your heart growing? The
movement inside you is your growing heart, growing with every
heartbeat of love and mercy you give to the needy. Let it beat, and
it will grow to the size of My heart. Can you imagine fitting the
whole world in your heart? Loving every living thing, being so full
of goodness that all evil flees from you? This is the evidence of My
presence. My heart in you will respond to My whisper; no screaming
is necessary. There are no loud quakes in order to get your attention.
No trouble, calamity, or breakdowns necessary. Just one touch from
My hand and scales fall off, demons flee, and circumstances are
fixed. When I am done with you, there will be no division of any kind
between you and Me. We will be as one. The sound of a growing heart
will be like music to you. You will live to love and love to live. Grow
into Me. I am all yours.

In the Quiet Place

1 Chronicles 4:40
And they found fat pasture and good, and the land
was wide, and quiet, and peaceable.
KJV

The quiet place is your place of refreshing. Come to it; let it heal you and strengthen your heart. Let it open your eyes to see the truth of life. Come and bring no falseness or pretense with you—no insecurity— because these are eviction notices. I don't stay where I am not wanted. Tear your tortured emotions out of your heart. Rip doubt out of your mind and stand in My quiet place in honesty. This way there will be no hindrances to your prayers. Dive headlong into My presence. Let it become your soul's medicine. Come in and don't be afraid. I am waiting with open arms. I never break an appointment; don't break yours. When you linger in My quiet place, you will be permanently transformed. Each day you will grow stronger and wiser. Build your house here; it is where I live. Accept no torment, torture, or anxiety; they must never be tolerated. Declare your territory to be peaceful, safe, and good. This is where you will always find Me waiting.

Branches of Your Will

Matthew 26:39
And he went a little farther, and fell on his face, and prayed, saying,
O my Father, if it be possible, let this cup pass from me:
nevertheless not as I will, but as thou wilt.
KJV

Learn to prune yourself. The branches of your will are forever yielding
fruit. Be revealed! The true you is waiting to come out. Prune your
soul, your spirit, your choices, and then your destiny will manifest.
Send your roots deep into the soil of My will. Let them linger long in
the life-giving nourishment that comes from abiding in Me. Find your
birthright and become a warrior. Live your dreams with Me. Leave the
old, withered parts of you behind. Don't try to re-graft yourself into
the old life. It is a dead, dried-up past. Instead, drink My lifelike water
and let your soul take wings. Grow. Become strong like the oak and
flexible like the palm tree. Become powerful like the cedar and stay
planted in My courts. Live a long, healthy life on My rain. Spread your
lifelike branches so that others may find a home in you. One will, one
life, one destination.

All the Pieces of You

Psalm 139:16
Thine eyes did see my substance, yet being unperfect; and in thy book
all my members were written, which in continuance were fashioned,
when as yet there was none of them.
KJV

I sought you and found you hiding deep within the chambers of your heart, undisclosed and undiscovered with all the pieces of you hiding from life—true life, real life, My life. You were lonely, wandering, lost, disconnected, and unwanted. But no more. Now I am your Hiding Place. I have hidden you in the cleft of the rock—safe, secure, and protected. No ugliness can reach you. No strange or unwelcome voices can confuse you. There will be no strange, unwanted conductors playing on the strings of your heart, for I desire to be your life's Conductor, Director, and Planner. I will find the music of your life and bring it out. You don't know it yet, but living inside of you are symphonies of music to move the lost hearts of lonely souls toward Me. I will lead you first by My hand, then by My voice, and finally by a whisper. Then you will know all the purposes for which I created you. I have found all the pieces of you, and I am putting them back together day by day until you are ready to be displayed—totally whole, totally equipped, and totally Mine.

 Offer You Me

Jeremiah 31:3
The Lord hath appeared of old unto me, saying,
Yea, I have loved thee with an everlasting love: therefore with
lovingkindness have I drawn thee.
KJV

I offer you Me: unlimited, unconditional, and unrestricted. Take Me for yourself, for I have already taken you. I live in a place of absolute trust. I rescue the unqualified, and I repair the discarded. My constant love is flowing toward you; it will lead you to your knees. There is a place of surrender that contents your soul and removes the troubling emotions. So completely will you be healed that your courage will erupt and your warrior spirit will overpower your enemies, ripping off their masks and exposing their traitor's hearts. Notice that your pain dissolves in My hands. The viruses of the soul cannot survive in My presence; they are extinguished in an ocean of love. Stand inside of Me and lay yourself on My altar. Surrender to My all-consuming presence and live untouched by evil.

The Sand Under Your Feet

Matthew 7:24
Therefore whosoever heareth these sayings of mine, and doeth them, I
will liken him unto a wise man, which built his house upon a rock.
KJV

The sand under your feet will always shift, so stand still. I will blow
it away. You were not born to stand on any ground but solid ground.
There is a Rock that never moves. It can endure all tests, all shifting,
and all attacks. This Rock is your Rock. It is solid, secure, stable, and
dependable footing for you to build your life on. Never has this Rock
been known to break, move, or be overwhelmed by any flood, wind, or
storm. I last forever and because you build your life on Me, you will,
too. Now you can live in this new place of security. Feel the breezes
of life taking you to spiritual places that you have never seen before.
Scale the impassable mountain. Open the sails of your spirit and let Me
fill you with the winds of heaven's love. Stop and look around. Notice
where I have taken you; it is far beyond your own reach and potential
and into a land you were always born to occupy. You have seen your
last sandcastle. Now your house is built on the Rock.

 Am Passing By

Matthew 9:22
Daughter, be of good comfort; thy faith hath made thee whole.
And the woman was made whole from that hour.
KJV

Be on the watch! I am passing by! Do not miss Me! Make sure you tie your heart to My harbor. Do not be found at your enemy's dock. He will burn your boat, and your journey will be over. I have maps for you to read and journeys for you to take. Get busy preparing yourself, and your boat for your trip. Fill it with gas and oil and provide food and provisions for your journey, the journey of your life. It is a journey that leads you to Me—all of Me. It is time to look up and read the map written on your heart. Look inside your heart with sincerity, and it will never deceive you or mislead you. I am waiting for you at your journey's end, and I have your treasure in My hand. Do not fear the uncharted waters that you will cross, for they have all been crossed before. They are good waters full of light and adventure. Remember, I am waiting. Never forget that although there may be many places you could go and many places you could end up, I am your destination.

urn

John 2:17
And His disciples remembered that it was written,
The zeal of thine house hath eaten me up.
KJV

Burn with Me, burn for Me, and burn through Me! Burn the world up
with My message of love and forgiveness. Burn with holy zeal, and
My love will consume every part of you. Let the coals of fire from
My altar fill the lantern of your heart. Burn, burn, burn! Live burning,
talk burning, sleep with a burning heart, and walk with burning feet
that scream out for the truth. The fire from My altar will consume
your family with salvation's songs. Never take your eyes off of the
fire; never let it go out. Never let the flame die down to a smoldering,
unperceivable light. Never live far from its warmth. It is the fire that
the ghosts of your past fear. They tremble at raging love, blazing
holiness, and unconditional goodness. They cannot bear all-consuming
praise, honesty, or pounding convictions. Burn now, burn here,
burn forever.

A Hungry Soul Moves Me

Matthew 5:6
Blessed are they which do hunger and thirst after
righteousness: for they shall be filled.
KJV

Beware of the soothing sound of prosperity and success. They are the
blessings that can swallow your soul and seduce your imagination.
They can quickly turn into two poisonous serpents. One promises what
only I can deliver, and the other convinces you that you don't need
Me. Both are deathtraps to your spirit. Hunger for Me with all your
strength. Open your soul like a mighty sail, and let Me fill you with
the winds of righteousness. Let Me lift you from the dungeon of legal
pleasures and take you where very few have ever traveled. This place
is a secret place, and only the hungry can go there. Know this: It is the
hungry soul that moves Me. Hunger causes My Spirit to boil and burn.
It compels Me to answer you and grant your requests. Stay hungry,
live hungry, and cultivate hunger.

I Give All Myself to You

Luke 5:20
Man, thy sins are forgiven thee.
KJV

I forgive you for everything, even the things that you cannot forgive yourself for. I embrace you in your pain. I turn to you when you cry out. I need your company. Every hour I see you, even in the jungle that surrounds you. I hear your heart beating in the night. I remember everything about you when everyone else forgets. I free you from the old, rusty chains of the past. I cherish you like a newborn. I watch over you in battle. I restore your joy in the morning. I comfort your loss and listen to your desires even when they make no sense. I strengthen you for the journey. I favor you with open doors. I adopt you as My own. I spare you from judgment. I heal every disease. I hide you from the raging storms of life. I protect you from yourself, and I love you with an everlasting love that cannot be extinguished. I give all Myself to you unrestrictedly.

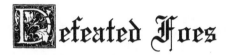efeated Foes

Revelation 12:10
For the accuser of our brethren is cast down, which
accused them before our God day and night.
KJV

This is your heritage: to win, to defy your former masters, to stare at them while they lie defeated on the ground unable to rise again, and to stand in the power of your convictions, unmovable and resolved to conquer. This brings Me glory. My servants who wear the martyr's crown spoke plainly and lived plainly. They loved not their lives even unto the death. This kind of dedication makes one invincible. These are the hearts of heaven's heroes. They had the courage of a Lion and the blood of a King as their weapons. You have the sword of power in your mouth and an undivided heart. This is the real you, the champion I have created! A lion's heart, a lamb's nature, and the soul of an eagle that soars and conquers; this is your destiny.

My Word Is Your Key

1 Samuel 9:27
But stand thou still a while, that I may
shew thee the word of God.
KJV

They who renounce Me with rough words are already lost. They have crucified Me again. They have nailed Me and My love to a cross of intellectualism, which is built on lies and distortions. Man's imaginary children are spawned by doubters and unbelievers. They believe they can stand toe to toe with Me and outargue Me in their ignorance, but you are gifted with greater wisdom and knowledge, greater insight, illumination, and understanding. You will answer their questions with My wisdom and insight. You will turn those with sincere hearts toward truth. With My Word you will unchain the intellectual prisoners who long for saving knowledge; it is your key to unlock their jail cells and let them go free. Turn the key in the lock of their hearts and walk them out of prison.

et Me

Revelation 3:20
Behold, I stand at the door, and knock: if any man
hear my voice, and open the door, I will come in to him, and
will sup with him, and he with me.
KJV

Let Me fill you with heaven's nectar. Let Me pour some heavenly wine on you to soothe your aches and pains. Let Me surround you with heaven's secrets. Let Me give you your true nature and rename you according to your potential. Let Me unclog your ears from the lies the world has told you so you can hear Me sing songs to you that heal and reshape you. Let Me give you a new heart—one that is easily moved and provoked by Me. Let Me hold your heart in My hands so it is still like a newborn child in its mother's arms, never forgetting the touch of love. Let Me show you things the angels dream of seeing. Let Me into the secret rooms of your heart where even you dare not go. Let Me reach unreachable, untouchable parts of you. Let Me fix the damaged parts of you. Let Me into your life to tell your story far and wide. Let Me give you a voice to speak My mysteries and delights so all the world will want to stop and listen. Let Me be your life.

 A New Heart

1 Samuel 10:6,9
The Spirit of the Lord came upon Saul and he stood up and
turned around and God gave him another heart.
Author's Paraphrase

If your heart does not love what I love or need what I need, if your heart does not want to seek Me early, desperately, and forever, if your heart does not thirst for My courts or desire to forgive the unlovely people, then give your heart to Me, and I will give you a new one exactly like Mine. I desire for you to feel the love I have for the poor, wretched, discarded souls of the world. I desire that you see through My eyes and that you are consumed with love and empathy for everyone. The heart I am prepared to give you will never betray you by wanting or longing for anything illegal, illegitimate, or dangerous. It will guide you into truth by loving truth. It will lead you to wealth, honor, and riches by its humility. A new heart is available to you any time yours is broken. Keep it clean, nourish it with truth, and strengthen it with My sacred food. It will make you great upon the earth. A man without My heart is an empty shell. My heart will lead you to My paths like a light in the woods. Trust My heart without reserve, without retreat, and without regret. Take time learning the sound of your new heart. Its sound will be like the sound of choirs shouting and rejoicing over heaven's victory. From now on, you will follow Me. Learn the voice of your new heart.

The Quiet Storm

Mark 4:39
And he arose, and rebuked the wind,
and said unto the sea, Peace, be still...
KJV

Is a storm dangerous if its rage does not hurt you? This is why I am called a Shelter from the storm because you can be in the storms of life and they won't hurt you. I am the perfect Shield from all of the dangers of life. I can protect you from the hidden, unexpected storms. I can protect you from the sudden storm that comes quickly without warning. I can protect you from every kind of storm that life may bring. The storms listen when I speak. They are like a baby silenced by the touch of its mother. The only thing you will feel in any storm you experience is quiet and calm. When you are fully trained in the management of storms, you will teach others to manage their storms.

You will become a storm forecaster, a storm silencer, and a storm master. Speak My name with authority. Believe that what you say can change the weather of people's lives, and it will.

he Beholding

John 12:21
Sir, we would see Jesus.
KJV

Keep your eyes fixed on Me, and your heart will be freed from all smallness. See who I am and what I can do. All sin is defeated. The beholding of Me is the greatest need you will have. To behold Me is to know Me, and to know Me is the eternal goal of your life. In beholding, failure's voice will disappear forever, and your insurmountable mountains will shrink before your eyes. In beholding, the confusion of your life will become as clear as looking through the microscope of heaven. In beholding, your life's ugly memories will change to My victories. In beholding, beauty will reveal itself to you and embrace the most tender parts of your life. In beholding, your dreams will become realities and your desires fresh dishes of manna each new day. Open your heart each morning, and your God-eyes will open and behold the glory and greatness of your future with Me. You are not a seer or a dreamer by accident but by design. You will never see in gray again. No filters are necessary for your true life. No false murals need to be painted; your real life is here. Your destiny's Light has appeared; His name is Jesus. Behold Him and live. I give dreams, and I make dreams come true. No one else has this power. Only I can give a dream and then bring it to pass. First you dream about knowing Me. I am your first dream, your life dream. Finally, you become a dream-giver, helping others find their dreams. When you look up after many years of loving and seeing Me bless others, all your dreams will be reality.

y Hands

Matthew 8:3
Jesus put forth his hand and touched him and said, Be thou whole.
Author's Paraphrase

My hands are specially designed to heal the damage of your life experiences. There is no wound or break that I cannot heal. I see with X-ray vision. My hands can reach through the past, present, and future. I can reach through the years of your past and repair every breach in your spirit and soul. My hands are not subject to time. They pass through time like water through a sieve. My hands restore instantly. They reconnect every part of you that is floating in the air. My hands formed you in your mother's womb. I will put you in a safe place. I will make My repairs and then I will anoint, appoint, and release you into the world. There you will be a builder of broken lives, a repairer of broken bridges, and a bringer of hope, faith, and love. Your abilities will double every year, and you will live in a state of constant amazement. Enjoy, enjoy, enjoy! Take your time, don't be anxious, and don't get in a hurry. Everything must be done right. I cannot leave you half-formed. I completely finish what I start. I am incapable of leaving you or yours unblessed. The riches of My blessing will be yours until the end of your journey.

 Can See the Future

2 Corinthians 4:7
We possess this precious treasure in human vessels that
God's power may be seen in us, through us, and for us.
Author's Paraphrase

I am not wasting My time with you. Every minute I have ever spent chasing you and influencing you has been worth it. I believe in who you are becoming. I will persuade you concerning My power in you and My ability to make you a high achiever and a life changer. I can foretell the future, and I see you as a great general in My army leading My soldiers into war. The secret of your power is in cherishing the treasure that I have placed within you, which is Christ in you, the Hope of Glory. Don't believe the voice of the serpent. Plug your ears when he speaks. Open your heart and let Me pull the treasure out. Let Me show you what having heaven living inside of you is like. There is a day of victorious shouting coming for you because of the new discoveries you are about to make. You will look into the Holy of Holies, and your life will never be the same again. I can see your future, and it makes Me smile.

Beauty for Ashes

Isaiah 61:3
To console those who mourn in Zion,
To give them beauty for ashes...
NKJV

I start with nothing. You may not understand everything right now, but what I am doing in certain areas of your life is reducing you to ashes. Only when all human effort is abolished can I begin a divine work within you. I cannot use anything that comes from your flesh. I cannot use anything that was born in the cradle of self. I can only use the pure, uncorrupted gold that is within you. So relax and trust what I am doing. Let the reducing process continue. Know this: The end result will be beauty—pure, clean beauty. Beauty in your heart, thoughts, and motives. Beauty in your walk with Me, beauty in your personality, and beauty in your service to Me. Don't linger around the ashes. Dwell on the beauty. Let it be your covering. Spread it everywhere.

he Architect

1 Corinthians 3:9
For we are God's fellow workers; you are
God's field, you are God's building.
NKJV

I am your personal Life Architect. I have finished the blueprints for your life, the master plan. Every room of your life has already been designed. I know the size of every piece of furniture and where it goes. I have not forgotten anything. I am a Master Builder. Nothing I design falls apart; it cannot be knocked down, torn down, or wrecked. No storm can destroy it, no flood can drown it. It is virtually indestructible, and there is no one who can damage it. I have painted it with completely resistant paint that never wears out. It never has to be repainted. One coat is all it needs. The plumbing and electricity will never wear out, rust, or fail. Yes, I am very proud of where you are headed. My design for you is flawless. Everyone who sees it will want the same design. Enjoy every brick, stone, and board I add to you. Don't resist when I cut, carve, or replace something. Just stand there and receive My perfect touch. Let the world marvel at My handiwork.

arked

2 Corinthians 9:8
And God is able to make all grace abound toward you,
that you, always having all sufficiency in all things, may
have an abundance for every good work.
NKJV

I have marked you for the whole world to know you are Mine. In the past when you lived without Me in your life, you were filled with lonely, empty places. Your soul was like a sieve; everything went right through you. You had a lonely heart and a battered spirit, but now everything has changed. My grace has changed you. Now your labels are: sufficiency, ability, achievement, and success. These are the words that will mark your life forever, not inadequacy, failure, or loss. Never underachiever! No! I am marking you. I am putting My stamp of approval on all of your endeavors for Me. Grace will always follow you everywhere you go. Now you are needed, wanted, valuable, and indispensable. You are marked by My love. Everyone in heaven, earth, and underneath will know it. Now your name will carry My honor.

Take the Chisel

John 15:3
You are already clean because of the word
which I have spoken to you.
NKJV

My Word is like soap for your soul. As you eat it, it will clean your innermost parts. As you feast on it, it will recreate your whole being. Eat My Word like candy today. Snack on it all day long. Wrap it around you like a warm heating blanket on a cold, winter day. My Word has special powers that nothing else has. It works wonders for those who trust it and live by it. Lay on it like a bed, rely on it like the air you breathe, live on it like the food you eat. It will keep you healthy, healed, and whole. Turn to it when you are worried. Speak it when your mind betrays you. Trust Me in this, for I know what I'm talking about. You are no longer weak or immature. You are a full-time student of Christlike living, and all you need to know is written in My Word. Now take daily baths in My Word, and the smell of the world will never be on you. Eat it like vitamins, and your heart will never get sick. Meditate on it, and you will never be poor. My Word will protect you and make you fearless and unashamed. Now take the chisel and engrave it on the heart of the world.

nbroken

Luke 10:33
But a certain Samaritan, as he journeyed, came where he was.
And when he saw him, he had compassion.
NKJV

Others in your life have seen you broken and bleeding, robbed of your dignity, stripped of your value, and they ignored you. I will never do that to you. I cannot do that to you. I refuse to ever do that to you. I see you; you are not invisible to Me. I see every wound from father, mother, and friends. I feel your pain, and I declare holy war on it. Lay there for awhile. Let Me bandage your wounds. I have special healing oil with your name on it. It works perfectly on you, and it will restore, repair, and recreate your organs. First your heart, then your soul, and finally your spirit. Lay there still; don't move. When I am done, you will be perfectly whole and sound. No part of you will be broken, bleeding, or dysfunctional. I am Healing. I am Health. And I am Well-being. When this day is done, you will see the world in a different way. There will be no clouds, no traitors, and no snakes. All that you will see is you and Me living life together, unbroken and unabandoned.

 nbroken Fellowship

1 John 1:7
If you walk in the Light of My truth as I am in the Light,
we have unbroken fellowship with one another, and the blood of
Jesus Christ cleanses you from all sin and guilt.
Author's Paraphrase

You are not guilty! Say that to yourself. How good it feels to be forgiven. Relish the light on your clean heart. Enjoy a clear conscience and bathe yourself in the healing power of being right with Me. This is your spiritual sauna. When you dwell there, your stress leaves, your muscles relax, and your headaches never return. I have made you and designed you to live in light with no dark secrets and no buried memories. Everything tormenting has to go. You are a light bringer. You will chase away people's ghosts. You will never break rank with Me. Always ask Me questions. Don't leap before you know I told you to. Your fellowship with Me will make you great. Your free-flowing wisdom will open many impossible doors, and your sincere love will win you many friends. Live long in My blessing and give it all away.

 Giving Yourself

Isaiah 58:10
And if you give yourself to the hungry and satisfy
the desire of the afflicted, then your light will rise in
darkness and your gloom will become like midday.
NASB

Everybody needs and wants the same thing: peace, love, health, and happiness. They think that things, places, or people can give those to them, so they chase empty tombs with false faces all their lives, always disappointed with the results. I want you to invest yourself in the things I'm invested in. I build My church, I feed the hungry, I rescue the orphan. I save the lost, I cure the sick, I relieve the widow. I love the unlovely. I comfort the hurting. I provide for the poor. I clothe the naked, and I release the prisoner. I restore the lost and educate the ignorant. I empower the weak, fulfill the dreamer, and cure the leper. I open the eyes of the blind and put a song in the brokenhearted. I lift the rejected. I am in all for all. Feast on Me and give yourself to this hurting, lost, miserable world. Giving yourself is the only way to find yourself.

The Root Ax

Psalm 145:14-15
The Lord upholdeth all that fall, and raiseth up all
those that be bowed down. The eyes of all wait upon thee;
and thou givest them their meat in due season.
KJV

Don't worry about anything. You cannot fail Me when you keep turning to Me. Just be patient. Trust in My power to change you. I don't modify your behavior; I transform your character. I don't chop off your branches; I pull out your roots. It is the bad roots I'm going after. I have a special root ax; it can cut any root no matter how big or old. It has never failed, and when it severs roots, they remain severed while new, healthy, godly roots grow in their place. I love you, and that is why I am showing you everything that could hurt you and getting rid of it. Now you're positioned for true happiness. Now you will see the light from My lampstand. Now your trials will end, warfare will cease, and failure will disappear. Dreams are now being fulfilled. Your family will be saved, your health will grow stronger, and your checkbook will never bounce. Trust My character while I create yours.

My Welcomed Guest

Psalm 121:7-8
He keeps you from all evil and preserves your life. He keeps
his eye upon you as you come and go, and always guards you.
TLB

I will keep you wherever you go. Safety is My name. I will be your
Bodyguard, your soul's Guardian, and your spirit's Protector. I will
deliver you from those who make excuses and neglect My holy life.
I will keep your energy high. I am your Compass and your Map. I
know where you need to go, and I know the shortest way to get there.
I am your Lamp, your Flashlight, your Spotlight, and your Ever-
Living Torch. I will provide for your journey. I will keep the lions
and predators at bay. Remember, I am never inconvenienced by your
needs. I thrive on taking care of you. I delight in the sound of your
rejoicing. I am your Watchman, and you are always My welcomed
guest. I never forget your face, your voice, or your name. I have them
engraved on My heart and there they will stay forever. No evil will
ever befall you. This is My promise to you.

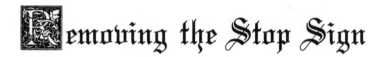emoving the Stop Sign

Isaiah 40:2
Your warfare is over, your iniquity is cleansed, you
will receive a double portion of joy for all of your misery.
Author's Paraphrase

People are addicted to struggles. They get hooked on the adrenaline
of drama. They cannot live without it, and they go from one drama to
the next, believing it is what makes them know they are alive. This
lie has ruined the lives of many of My children. Your inner warfare
ends today! You will get closure and find inner peace for your personal
struggles. Your unresolved conflicts will disappear. The confusion will
clear up instantly, and the stop sign in your life will be removed. The
red light has turned green. It is time to get back the years and months
you have missed out on. Look in your pockets because they are about
to overflow with blessings. In days past you had nothing to offer, but
now you are the giver, you are the paymaster, and you are the one
writing checks for the church, orphans, and widows. You are the one
at peace handing out wisdom and seeing the solutions to the problems
people face. Never again will you be in the prison of torment. That
jailhouse has been burned down. Go forward.

atching Over You

Isaiah 49:10
They shall neither hunger nor thirst; the searing sun and
scorching desert winds will not reach them any more. For
the Lord in his mercy will lead them beside the cool waters.
TLB

How black can the human heart be? How desperately wicked? No one
knows the full extent of how far men fell from My grace and love.
But I have reversed the effects of the fall. All curses are broken, all
needs are met, and all hunger and thirst have been provided for. Just
know this: I am watching over you, and I will not let anyone deceive
you with enticing words of man's philosophies. I will protect you
from corrupting, immoral influences. The deceivers with their many
appealing masks will never be able to pull the wool over your eyes.
You will not end up broke and empty-handed. Instead, you will find
yourself by beautiful springs of living water where you can go every
day and drink until all your thirst is quenched. Only when your thirst
for Me is quenched can you quench other people's thirst. I need you to
know that since the day you were born I have been watching over you.
It is what I do because I love you.

 ut of the Lion's Mouth

Amos 3:12
I will take you out of the mouth of the lion, piece by
piece, and heal the wounds of the predator's teeth.
Author's Paraphrase

Throughout your life, the predators have ripped off of you pieces of
your life. They have chewed on you as if you were a bone. They have
ripped your arms, legs, and heart out, but I have a healing, restoring
touch. One touch and what was lost, stolen, or taken is restored.
Can you believe this? Can you trust Me? If you can, the miracle you
have been waiting for will be activated. I know the mouth of your
lion; it is weak and rotten. His teeth are an illusion; his growl a hoax.
Everything you have ever lost will be given back to you in better shape
than before. You will recover your discernment and see the invisible
treasures of heaven. You will deliver the blind from their darkness. You
will carry My cross to a lost world. Darkness will flee when you speak
My Word, and I will give you a special miracle shovel to dig wells for
the thirsty. All this because you are a vessel of honor. No losses for
you again; only perpetual gain and true safety.

 ome to My House

Luke 8:41
And behold, there came a man named Jairus, and he
was a ruler of the synagogue. And he fell down at Jesus' feet and
begged Him to come to his house.
NKJV

Come into My house. I will give you My address. Don't stand outside
the door; walk in. I have many wonderful secrets to reveal to you. Visit
Me, and I will visit you. I am coming to your house. I will cleanse it
from all generational leprosy. Every room will be clean, every door
anointed. The walls will have holy paint that is disease-healing and
disease-immune. I will repair the broken and cracked door. I will
remove the mold and mildew. Not one speck of dust will remain. The
walls will cry out salvation, the doors will praise Me, and the floors
will speak of My mighty deeds. Take a seat and relax. Let Me do a
complete makeover. When I'm done, the shouting will start. The old
memories people have left in you are fading away like a fog. My wind
will blow them away. Every evil word ever spoken will be broken.
Words that are invitations to the enemy will be no more. I will clear
out all the intruders who try to bring their trash and leave it at your
door. There will be singing and praising coming to your house.

Becoming Clay

Jeremiah 18:6
Look, as the clay is in the potter's hand,
so are you in My hand...
NKJV

When I formed you, you were lost in a maze of confusion. You had no destination, future, or hope; your priorities were twisted and selfish. Your heart was filled with the arrows of your abusers, and your mind was infested with self-cannibalizing thoughts. Your heart was broken and afraid. Every part of you was disconnected and in disunity. You cried out from the deepest part of your heart, and I heard you. I reached out My Hand and lifted you from emptiness. Now you must become clay—soft, pliable clay, a lump with no hardness or resistance in it. I want to make you My instrument of power. I want you to always allow Me to change you any time I need to. Therefore, remain as My clay. If you do this, the world will be yours; all you can imagine I will grant you, and your deepest dreams will come true.

The Watchman's Trumpet

Ezekiel 33:6
But if the watchman sees the sword coming and does not blow the
trumpet, and the people are not warned, and the sword comes and
takes any person from among them, he is taken away in his iniquity;
but his blood I will require at the watchman's hand.
NKJV

Do not be a people pleaser. Do not sell your soul for people's approval.
Telling the truth in love is the only thing that can save people. You are
responsible for the truth you know and for all truth that is available
to you. Give it to people as medicine. Those who know the Truth
and hide it, change it, or withhold it will be accountable to Me. You
are given a gift of knowing the Truth. Blow the watchman's trumpet.
Never cheat a person from the Truth. When you speak, I will be
with you. I will fill your words with life and healing. I will give you
wisdom that will leave people speechless, and your words will be like
a lifesaver thrown to a drowning world. Save all who you can with the
Truth. Blow that trumpet; let it sound throughout the land. Let Truth
reign. Give people a chance to be free by introducing them to the
pure Truth.

 nly Forward

Exodus 14:15
The Lord said to Moses, "Why do you cry to me?
Tell the people of Israel to go forward.
ESV

Go forward. No more looking back for you! Put your hand to the plow, move your feet, and go forward. I know you, and I know your past. Listen to Me lead you to your heart's desire. With Me you will never lose ground or territory. Go forward, go forward, go forward. Hear My trumpet and learn what it means. I have volumes of books with secrets to reveal to you. Your prayers are heard, your promises fulfilled, your mind persuaded, your power released, and your praise will light up heaven. Praise at all hours and in all moments and circumstances. I keep you from deceivers and conmen. I preserve you and keep you from falling. Just do one thing for Me: Go forward—only forward. Lay aside the backbreaking burdens and overwhelming weights. Lay aside the distractions of your past pleasures. Forget yesterday's ghosts. Turn your back on every temptation, and I will make your crown glorious. I am making you without a reverse in your engine. Do not look back, for your destiny lies ahead of you. Now stand up and move forward, always and forever forward.

With Open Hands

Matthew 13:8
But others fell on good ground and yielded a crop:
some a hundredfold, some sixty, some thirty.
NKJV

Remember the life you once lived when your ground was dry and cracked, your tongue craved water, and your stomach always felt empty. Even when it was full, I made you dissatisfied. I brought divine discontentment into your life to save you from a life of worthless living. You are good ground now — soft, broken soil, easy to move, pliable, and without rocks. You are tender, hungry, and thirsty for My sacred seeds of life. It is time to bring forth harvests. It is time to reap your blessings. In some areas you will reap thirtyfold, in some sixtyfold, and in others a hundredfold harvests! No more waiting or struggling. Your harvest is ripe and ready. Your work, family, and personal life will all change after today! I command your seed to produce. I curse bad seeds and limited harvests. Your harvests will be unreasonable and super abundant. You will see your expected harvests and hold them in your hands. Rich fields and bumper crops will flow. You will experience a life of fullness and be saturated with fresh water every morning. Your personal life will manifest the signs of being blessed by a loving Father. Everyone will know it is harvest time for you. They will run toward your warehouse, and you will unlock the door to their futures. Give them all the provisions they need. Don't hold any good thing back from them. For in doing so, you guarantee your own abundance. See Me standing here with open hands.

 Feasting on Me

Psalm 107:9
For He satisfieth the longing soul, and filleth
the hungry soul with goodness.
KJV

Your hunger is the architect of your blessing. Long for, hunger, and yearn for My Word today. I will remove another veil. This veil is holding back truth, much-needed truth. No one can satisfy your soul, for it is tuned to Me. All other sources of gratification are empty imitations. They are counterfeits hopelessly trying to fill the hollow places of your God-designed soul. Open your soul, and I will fill it today—not with empty desires but with perfectly made soul satisfaction. There will be no more unnecessary thirst, longing, or hunger. I will give you dreams in the night to inspire you to create. You will find yourself laughing in victory and singing in joy. Your life will magnify Me. Weeping and sorrow will disappear from your family because your time for reaping has started—reaping your long-awaited dreams, prayers, and hopes. All that will be left is shouting and rejoicing. Remember, I made you, and I know what you need. I have designed you to be happy only with Me at the center of your life. There is great power in being centered, satisfied, and hungry all at the same time. This is the secret to life: feasting on Me all day long.

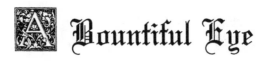

A Bountiful Eye

Proverbs 22:9
He that hath a bountiful eye shall be blessed;
for he giveth of his bread to the poor.
KJV

I have brought you to this place in your life in order to add to you the missing pieces of your life. Now is the time to open your hands. Give something away today. Make sure it costs you something. It is ordinary to give leftovers or unneeded pieces of you; however, your prosperity is hiding behind your generosity. Give away respect, love, and money, and My Spirit will chase you down and bless you with unreasonable blessings. I will make you an object of My compassion today. When you wake, a blessing will greet you. When you rise, a blessing will shake your hand. When you start your day, a blessing will lead the way. As fast as the blessings come, give them away. This is what I want you to do today: Be a giving soul. I will fill your life with divine connections and opportunities. I release your gifts through generosity and goodness. Look for your praying companions and godly friends, people who polish your pearls and lead you to the cross. This is a good life, a blessed place, and a holy purpose.

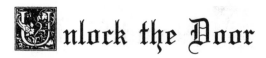nlock the Door

Luke 16:10-11
He that is faithful in that which is least is faithful also in much: and
he that is unjust in the least is unjust also in much. If therefore
ye have not been faithful in the unrighteous mammon, who will
commit to your trust the true riches?
KJV

Lift up the everlasting doors. Your will is what I want from you, not
words, ideas, customs, or rituals. I want the lock on your heart opened!
Let Me in! Lift up the doors so that I can truly reach you and help
you today. This day is a day of intimacy. There will be no resisting,
pushing Me away, ignoring My Holy Spirit, or getting distracted.
Simply open your heart and discover Me. Then, your troubles will
vanish, and you will see My face clearly. I do not want you to get
discouraged with the delayed answers in your life. You must learn to
trust Me unconditionally; only then can I trust you and release to you
the true riches of life. These are the riches of body, soul, and spirit.
Life is about to get very good for you. I will paint a new canvas for
you with all the right colors in it. Faithfulness is your new name. Be
faithful to everyone. Be faithful mentally, emotionally, spiritually,
and morally. Let kindness be your personality's face. Live free from
frustration by not being owned by anything other than Me. Let Me be
your obsession, and I will commit everything I have and everything I
am to supporting you and fulfilling all of your dreams. Now, you will
see clearly.

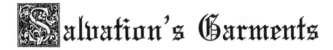alvation's Garments

Isaiah 61:10
I will greatly rejoice in the Lord; my soul shall exult in my God,
for He has clothed me with the garments of salvation; He has covered
me with the robe of righteousness.
ESV

Put on your salvation garments. Wear them with godly pride, for it is your salvation garments that protect you from Satan's scorpions, leeches, and snakes. Your salvation garments are your free pass into My presence, righteousness, healing, cleansing, and acceptance. Wear love as your armor. Wave your shoes of peace for the world to see.

Your decisions either clothe you with Me or strip you of Me. My salvation garments are priceless; they cannot be bought with money. They must be given as a gift and only given by Me. Your salvation garments terrify your enemies. They strip them of their courage. They weaken their resolve and break their bones. Dress to kill the devil! Choose your clothes carefully, for your enemy will point you toward his fake garments stained with the blood of wrecked lives and lost children. They look good on the outside, but they carry fatal, incurable diseases. This is not for you. You will see the great works of goodness I will do. You will meditate on peace and be far from terror. You will show others what I can do for them, and you will never decrease. Your fate is increasing daily. Your house is full of treasure that cannot be stolen from you. Don't receive an accusation against yourself. Your robe automatically repels unrighteousness and protects you from Satan's poisonous arrows. Dress to kill the useless and unprofitable.

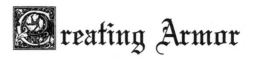reating Armor

Colossians 4:6
Let your speech at all times be gracious (pleasant
and winsome), seasoned [as it were] with salt, [so that
you may never be at a loss] to know how you ought to
answer anyone [who puts a question to you].
AMP

Your mouth is full of waiting miracles. Say what I say. Let your words harmonize with My will, and My words will be like spiritual penicillin, healing all germs, viruses, and bacteria of the soul. Your words are your weapons. They create a throne for Me and wave My scepter of power over your life. Wash your words, and your heart will be established. Allow your words to prepare your destiny. I have sacrificed everything to make sure you succeed in life. Embrace My instructions, for each lesson adds another piece of armor to you. I give you the purity blessing, the unity blessing, and the holy activity blessing. With these you're guaranteed to reign in life. Who can stop your forward motion? No one. Not now. Not ever. Words are like swords or medicine; you use them to heal the broken-hearted. Don't ever let your words curse you or enslave you. Set the world on fire with faith-filled, love-ruled words.

The Fields Are Waking Up

1 Kings 18:41
Then Elijah said to Ahab, "Go up, eat and drink; for
there is the sound of abundance of rain."
NKJV

Now is the time of revival, not tomorrow. Fall on your knees now, begin to humble yourself, and turn from every attitude and action that displeases Me. Rain will then begin to fall. Every piece of dry ground will begin to soften, and the dead fields will begin to produce harvests of plenty. Shout to Me, for the drought is over! It's time to plow the softened ground. Prepare your heart to receive My incorruptible seed that can grow anywhere with or without water, and with or without care. My seeds are programmed to produce and cannot fail. They will accomplish what they are sent to do in your life. It is time to stop and look around. You will see that the one seed has now filled your entire field. Thousands upon thousands of producing, life-giving, germinating seeds are around. You are a rain-maker. You turn the deserts into gardens, the waste places into springs and wells of living water. Take the dead, forsaken souls you meet and throw them into My healing rain. Let it rain, pour, and shower every day. The fields are waking up.

repared Triumphs

Proverbs 12:11
He who tills his land shall be satisfied with bread, but he who follows
worthless pursuits is lacking in sense and is without understanding.
AMP

Abandon idleness in your natural and spiritual life. Begin to work and
sow seeds today and for the rest of your life. The blessing is waiting
for you, hiding behind your discipline. Godly habits are the source
of your supernatural harvests. Never be lazy. Never compromise the
integrity of your life. Know that I am for you today and have prepared
your triumphs. I have made you a skilled warrior. The battles you fight
today are already won. The work you do is already successful, and the
people you serve will be set free. I am training you to win. Remember,
you are part of a new family. Trusting Me is the key to everything
good. Hard work with great faith will change the world. Your
consistency will pay off. You were born to know Me, to live for Me,
and to work for Me. Never doubt it. Never look for another harbor. I
am what you want and need. I am all you need, morning, noon, and
night. I am the pot of gold at the end of the rainbow. I have already
prepared your triumphs. Every day and everywhere there shall be the
sound of triumph.

ormed in the Hands of Love

Isaiah 64:8
But, now, I am your Father; you are the clay, and I am your Potter;
and you are the work of My hand.
Author's Paraphrase

You are not the product of the pain, rejection, and hurt of your past life. Your past has now become your path to life, love, joy, and power. No one from this day forward has the power to drag you, pull you, drive you, or enslave you back onto that path—that place where no light shines and only shadows live. That place is now a graveyard. I have filled that graveyard with the bones of your painful and hurtful memories; you will never see those bones again. You will never hear the sound of those dangerous days and dangerous people walking toward you. They will not say "I love you" and then never speak to you again. Now I have placed you in a new place, in the cleft of the rock. There I will hide you and keep you from all danger and harm. You are standing on solid rock. Do you think there is anyone in the universe who can move you from the place where I have placed you? There is no one. I rule the Heavens, and I rule the earth, and I rule you. I am in control of everyone in your life. I will orchestrate them to help accomplish the dreams you know in your heart you were born to fulfill. I will add all the colors to your life that you need, every shade will reflect My will. Every single day you will smell the fragrance of my presence. You will be surrounded with a garden of faith. Raise your hands to Me in worship when you sense the fruit of my Spirit.

You shall never be in a desert. You shall never be in a drought. You shall never go through the situations that many people go through because they do not have the patience to listen to Me. They do not wait for Me to speak. In haste, they do what they want, but that is not the heart I have given you. Your heart is that of a child's, my child's. It is tender, soft, and easily provoked by My voice. A whisper is all you need from Me. And from this day forward, you will always be able to hear Me. You will always be able to see Me. You will never, ever feel alone. I promise you that every time you come into the secret place My face will be revealed to you. My song will resound in your spirit. I am doing these things so that you will become My spokesperson. You will become like a mirror that reflects My face of love, My voice of comfort. Your hands will drip with My anointing oil of healing. Your voice will be filled with the merciful kindness that I have for all of humanity. Dwell in Me. Marinate in My love. Saturate your faith in My Word. Sing it, write it, speak it, live it, and become who you were always meant to be.

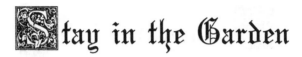tay in the Garden

Genesis 3:8
And they heard the voice of the Lord God
walking in the garden in the cool of the day…
KJV

Go to the quiet place and stay there until you hear My voice. I am waiting to talk to you. I am longing for your company. The time for praying is now. No more thinking, worrying, or stressing. Release everything to Me. Release every care. By the time you're done, it will all be worked out. Today is a stress-free day. Sing, rule, acquire, give, protect, bless, tend, trust, and fly. Today let Me lead you to a healing, healthy place. Let Me strengthen your convictions; they are the source of all your victories. Let Me tune your heart to beat exactly in rhythm with Mine. I am your sure Rock and Foundation. Stay in My garden and flourish. Don't look at the other gardens around you. Don't smell other people's flowers. Their smell is seductive and hypnotic. They look and feel genuine but will wither and fade. What I am giving you has My touch on it and is therefore indestructible. My Voice is My gift to you. It is your Comfort in the storm, your Shelter from troubling rains, and the Healing for your heart and soul. One Word from Me, and everything changes forever. Stay in the garden.

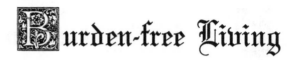

Burden-free Living

Psalm 55:22
Cast thy burden upon the Lord, and He shall sustain thee:
He shall never suffer the righteous to be moved.
KJV

Let Me remove the burden from your shoulders. Let Me lighten your load. I see the stress. I hear the voice of your heart. I am here for you always. The times of illumination are here. I want you to see things the way I see them. Everything in your life will be filled with light and understanding. No confusion or cloudiness—just pure, simple clarity. I am separating you from the corrupting influences that pursue you. I will resurrect fields of love and compassion. The relevance of your life is multiplying. Your search for significance has arrived. The manifestation of My Spirit in all areas of your life will be visible to the naked eye. The parts of you that are still not surrendered to My will are now changing. The softness and pliability I was looking for is now in your heart. You are now Mine. I know I can trust you to obey My instructions and hold My sacred gifts in your hands. Your back will never break, your shoulders never droop. Your spine will be like a piece of steel, strong and able to support you all of your life. You have seen enough trouble for one life. Let Me show you where to rest, unwind, and be refreshed and encouraged. You are free. Live and act that way. Hold this gift tightly.

Pull Up Your Anchor

1 Peter 2:9
But you are a chosen race, a royal priesthood, a holy nation, a people
for his own possession, that you may proclaim the excellencies of
Him who called you out of darkness into his marvelous light.
ESV

Living inside you today is My life. You are not normal. You are not
like everyone else. You have been handpicked for divine purposes.
You are spiritually unique and gifted. Many of your gifts are still
dormant but ready to emerge. I am your Promoter. I will guarantee
your growth and success. Fatal diseases will stay away from you. The
tyrants of your life will fall, and you will receive a spirit unable to
be provoked. You need some alone time with Me—with healing and
solitude. Let Me teach you how to relax. There is great strength in rest.
In this place of restoration, you will find what you are looking for.
Here is where My divine purpose will begin to emerge from a peaceful
heart. Accomplishments that you never dreamed of will follow you.
Because of My wounds, yours will vanish. I will form Myself in
you, and I will build you a mansion that no thief can steal. You are a
producer of blessings. You're not meant for idleness. I made you to be
like Me. Unless you're creating something, you'll never see all that I
have planned for you. I want to form Myself in you. When I am done,
you will look just like Me. Don't doubt it; embrace it. Let it take you
down the river of My will. Let it carry you out into the ocean. You
don't belong with those who play it safe. You're a sailor. Pull up your
anchor, and I will do the rest.

Your Past Is Forgotten

2 Corinthians 5:17
Therefore, if anyone is in Christ, he is a new creation.
The old has passed away; behold, the new has come.
ESV

Your past is forgotten, and your failures are erased. Nothing you have
done will stop the wonderful plan I have for you. You will experience
a new life. Refreshment and encouragement are your daily portions.
No more looking back! Put your hand to the plow and do not stop,
for the victory is yours. There is a Lamb whose blood cries out
for souls to cleanse and purify. This blood will be your song to the
world—cleansing streams of divine power, peace, acceptance, divine
protection, and a holy entrance into My house. People will come
in multitudes to the sound of My blood's voice calling them to the
cleansing stream. All your questions will be answered, and the steps
of your feet will become strong, steady, and secure. The serpent's head
will fall, and your sword will be dipped in the blood of My enemies.
Don't remember your yesterdays. Fix your eyes on the banner I have
given you. Don't gather yesterday's boulders; they will break your
back. Don't let regret put a noose around your neck. You are meant to
change the world. You're different. Believe it, and it will do its work.
"Purified," "Holy," and "Power" are your banners. Wave them for
everyone to see, and watch your family and friends run toward Me.
Remember, your past is forgotten.

Take My Coat

1 Corinthians 13:7
Love bears up under anything and everything that comes, is ever ready to believe the best of every person, its hopes are fadeless under all circumstances, and it endures everything [without weakening].
AMP

Dress in Me, and you will act like Me. Put on love, joy, and peace like a new garment. There is a new level of divine love that is being released to you. Those who have offended and frustrated you will no longer be threats to your peace but are actually sent to introduce you to your true self. It is a baptism of love that is coming your way. You will be filled with all of My fullness. No one will have power over you. If you want nothing from people and see Me as your Source, you will find yourself set free from their power. Stand by and watch Me destroy all doubt and frustrations in your life. I am setting you in a place of immunity from the lusts of the flesh, the pride of life, and the deceitfulness of sin. Your mouth will be a weapon of deliverance, your heart a refuge for the fatherless, your mind a hiding place for My goodness, and your hands a place of healing. There will be no sweat, no thorns, no curses, no bruises, and no war for you. Take My coat; it is a coat filled with the power of My unconditional love. Your life is My masterpiece. You will look at what I have done in your life, and you will fall on your face and worship Me. No one will ever control you again with these flaws and imperfections.

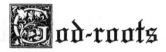od-roots

Ephesians 3:16
That He would grant you, according to the riches of His glory, to be
strengthened with might through His Spirit in the inner man.
NKJV

A river of strength is coming toward you. It will wash away all the
trash and mental and emotional mildew that you have experienced in
your life. Your strength will be doubled. Your inner man will step to
the front of your life. Never fear your old self; it has been crucified and
is unable to resurrect as it is dead and withered. Now, your God-roots
are taking over, and your spiritual tree is loaded with imperishable
fruit—fruit that others want, need, and crave. You are a fruit-bearer.
Sinners will come to your tree for love, joy, and peace. My fruit in
you is ripe and ready to be consumed. I clothe you in My best robe
now. No fig leaves, no animal skins, no stained garments. Now you're
strong and dressed in Holy Light. I have worked hard to get you to this
place of transparency. If you reveal yourself to Me, I cannot hold back
any of My blessings. You are like a bulldozer tearing down Satan's
strongholds. You won't need special attention anymore. Stand tall and
stand strong. The enemies' gates are crumbling.

nhindered

Psalm 27:1-2
The Lord is my light and my salvation; whom shall I fear? The Lord is the strength of my life; of whom shall I be afraid? When the wicked, even mine enemies and my foes, came upon me to eat up my flesh, they stumbled and fell.
KJV

There is a sweet, unhindered communion that comes when you choose to live in My cleansing light. There are no strange voices. There are no disturbing emotions, no addicting desires; only the warmth of the sound of My voice coursing through the highway of your heart. Leave the old voices and sounds behind. I will give you a name among My servants, faith that stops the hoards of hell, and a witness to turn the hearts of the unfaithful back to Me. Conversations will begin to manifest in your family. A sweet, unhindered communion will be between us, and you'll have the power to serve Me until I call you home. I will translate you into My presence every time you say My name, and I will pin another medal on you to show you how proud I am of you. I have a storehouse of love rewards waiting for you. Light will follow you. Wisdom will speak for you. Salvation will show up wherever you go. No one will bother your peace. You will never be intimidated by anyone. Their faces will present no threat to you. You are a piece of sold out, determined steel for Me. I say it; you do it. End of story.

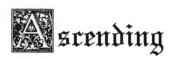scending

Psalm 15:1
Lord, who shall abide in thy tabernacle? Who shall dwell in thy
holy hill?
KJV

Ascending is your trumpet call; reaching up to Me is your day's assignment. Don't hesitate to move into My passion and My presence. Drink My love like a sweet nectar. Separate yourself from worldly people. Walk in self-denial, holiness, and moral purity. Let grace be your sword, gentleness your banner, and tie humility to your personality. Embrace tenderness, zeal, and passion. Speak with the voice of mercy and long-suffering. Stand immovable in My faithfulness and My uncompromising convictions. Nothing shall separate you from Me. I will show you the path to My Holy Hill—the place where I live and the saints walk. This is your home, too. This holy place is not for visitors; it is only for residents. No one else is allowed. Don't grow tired of being good. Never cease walking in integrity. Don't ever listen to the educated liars. They have blinders on their eyes. They will not take them off. Look at Me, for My face is the map to finding the Holy Hill.

he World

1 John 2:15
Do not love the world or the things in the world. If anyone loves the
world, the love of the Father is not in him.
ESV

There is a battle that everyone must fight. If you choose life and
reject the death traps of the world, the seductive spirits of Satan, and
resist the bribes and false promises, you will be anointed with power.
Love will flow freely from My heart to yours. I will put Myself on
display for you. Never again will you find yourself in chains. I want
to show you the beautiful life of grace and truth. Your life is destined
for greatness, exploits, battles won, new territory claimed, peace on
all your borders, knowledge of the Holy, and seasons of happiness.
All of these will I give you for being single-hearted, honorable, and
honest. The world knows how to seduce; it knows the songs the human
heart loves. Its desire is to enslave, addict, and overpower you. Each
time you resist, you get closer to Me. My face becomes clearer, and
everything comes into focus. Don't believe the lie that tells you you're
missing out on a lot of fun. Remember the world will make you pay
with your soul. I restore your soul from the damage of the world. I am
your Father. My Love is now in you. Let it out.

our Portion

Proverbs 12:7
The wicked are overthrown and are not, but the house
of the [uncompromisingly] righteous shall stand.
AMP

I rebuke everything coming against your family! It will not touch you. I rebuke the spiritual attacks against your family and those you love most. The territory you have lost is very important to Me, and it will be recovered. Every area of failure will be turned into victory. The devil is defeated, and I am on the throne! Prepare yourself for a season of growth and progress. Look toward Me, lean on Me, live in Me, and all My words will come to pass. Divine encounters, revival, and breakthroughs are your portion. My gracious consolation will follow you day after day. If you resist the lies and arrows of doubt, no one will be able to stand before you all the days of your life. I am the portion of your life. I give you everything you need to reign in this life fully loved, fully equipped, and fully discovered. This is the truth of your life. Eat your full portion of life.

Completely Soaked

Zechariah 10:1
Ask ye of the Lord rain in the time of the
latter rain; so the Lord shall make bright
clouds, and give them showers of rain,
to every one grass in the field.
KJV

You are going to ask Me for rain. You are going to call upon Me for showers of blessing in the day of your planting, for I cause your seed to grow. I cause the storm clouds to cover the land and a downpour of blessing to feed your seeds. You are destined to have an abundant harvest. Can the devil steal it from you today? No! Can evil men steal it from you today? No! Can jealous people steal it from you today? No! Your harvest is secure in My hands. It is time you began to reap hundredfold returns! Prepare yourself for the downpour of heaven. My rain produces power to draw people out of their pits, to lift them up and set them on the Rock, and to release to them the songs of salvation. You will continually be watered in the midst of a crooked and perverse generation. Stand up. Lift your heart in your hands to Me and get completely soaked in the rain.

The Embrace of Brokenness

Luke 22:19
And he took bread, and gave thanks, and brake it,
and gave unto them, saying, This is My body which is given
for you: this do in remembrance of me.
KJV

You are My bread if you embrace My brokenness. I will be able to share you with the hungry world. Because you believe in the death, burial, and resurrection of My Son, you will walk in regular and consistent communion with Me. You will walk in unbroken fellowship with Me. Everything will come into focus. My Spirit will be over you, on you, and upon you. The Holy Spirit will go before you. We will protect you from behind and guard you on both sides. Because you are walking in communion with Me and because you have continual trust in My will for your life, you will live in the power of the resurrection. Today, you are washed in the blood of My Son. I have forgiven and forgotten all of your sins. You have a new beginning and a new open door. Start over today. Celebrate all the facets of Jesus. Celebrate the washing and cleansing of His holy blood. No accusing finger can stand before you. Your life is saved from destruction, secured from spiritual invasion, satisfied with blessings from above, and anointed to live fully and unconditionally surrendered. Don't fear the embrace of brokenness.

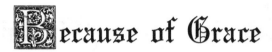ecause of Grace

1 Corinthians 15:10
But by the grace of God I am what I am, and his grace to me
was not without effect. No, I worked harder than all of them - yet
not I, but the grace of God that was with me.
NIV

You are who you are because of the grace I have given you. It will
never run out, wear out, or disappear. All day long you will feel the
supernatural ability of My Spirit. You will feel so much grace that you
will be able to produce an abundance of good works for Me. When
you look all around, you will see My grace at work in your life. Don't
be afraid. Don't feel insecure or be tormented by the words of the devil
or the words of people who do not listen to My voice. Stand on the
Rock and declare grace, grace, and more grace! Tell yourself that My
grace empowers you to overcome sin and to succeed where you have
been a failure. It allows Me to reign and sin to fail. It repaints your
self-portrait and rewrites the endings of every chapter of your new life.
Grace moves you from the home of death to the home of life. It fills
the empty lakes and rivers of your soul. It renews and reprograms your
mind to believe in My wonder-working power. Live free from every
encumbrance. Enjoy life's blessings by surrendering to My divine
influence on your heart. Let it be manifested in your lifestyle.

 Am Your Windmill

Psalm 115:14
The Lord shall increase you more and
more, you and your children.
KJV

Your family has been targeted for multiplication. First, your finances will increase through good investments and obedient giving. Second, your family unity will be strengthened to the point of becoming indivisible. Your minds will be as one. Your vision will become clear. Your future will be established as you multiply and begin to see increase in your bank account. No rust, no thieves, no squandering. I am locking up your fortune and keeping it safe for you. The true riches of love, grace, and health will start knocking on your door. I am your Windmill. I am forcing life to flow from Me to you. While others may live with aching hearts, you will have continual increase and peace. They drink sour milk, but you drink the honey from the Rock. Remember that even thunderstorms help the crops. Because you love Me, I will reverse anything negative that tries to come your way. I am your Windmill. Hear the sound of a new wind.

ut of Darkness

Colossians 1:13
Who hath delivered us from the power of darkness, and
hath translated us into the kingdom of his dear Son.
KJV

You have been especially chosen by Me to be a royal priest in your
household, a citizen of a holy nation, a child of Mine. You have been
snatched out of darkness and translated into My kingdom. All day
long you will praise Me and honor Me with your behavior, words,
and lifestyle. My Spirit and My glory will rest on your head. Not one
single, hostile alien shall come upon your spirit today; no abuse shall
touch you. The devil will be hindered and will not come near you
today. You shall walk as one arrayed in the garments of a victorious
priest. Doors will swing open today. People will be kind to you and
show you favor. Trials and testing will be like water flowing off your
back, and you will be energized by the strength of My words inside of
you, burning like fire in your bones. The life you need is the inward
life of wealth. When My kingdom reigns inside of you, you are at rest,
victorious, and fulfilled. Without it you are a wanderer in a dry, hot
desert. Because you have My knowledge, you will live in a constant
state of holiness filled by love, driven by faith, supported by hope, and
surrounded by peace.

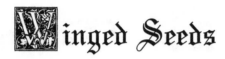 Winged Seeds

Genesis 8:22
While the earth remaineth, seedtime
and harvest, and cold and heat, and summer and winter,
and day and night shall not cease.
KJV

Since the day you were conceived, I have been faithfully sowing My winged seeds into your heart. I need you to understand what a winged seed is. It is not a normal seed that is simply grown where it is planted. Winged seeds are able to fly and spread themselves. They have the power to grow in more than one place at a time. These special seeds will start to germinate inside of you now. Today, they will begin to fly, and the result will be multiple harvests showing up at your door. Oh, the blessing that I have prepared for you and the overwhelming goodness that is going to overtake you! No more empty days without a harvest or blessing to brag about. I am bringing your blessing boat in. The winged seeds are being released, and the fields are becoming ripe for the harvest. Thank Me daily. This is the heart sprinkler that waters the seeds. Laugh, sing, and praise. This is the sunshine that will grow the wings of your seeds.

asted Days Reclaimed

Romans 13:12
The night is far spent, the day is at hand: let us therefore cast
off the works of darkness, and let us put on the armour of light.
KJV

When you feel as if you've wasted a lot of time, lost a lot of days, and regret grips your soul, remember that I can reclaim the wasted days and nights of your life. A wasted day is a tragic event in heaven. Each day is a gift with tasks and assignments in it. It must be done, accomplished, and fulfilled. One day is all I need to change the world. I will teach you to redeem the time, to polish a day like an undiscovered pearl. I have placed a miracle in every day. Each day holds a dream. Once it's lost, a new one takes its place. Never take for granted the hours I have given you. Use those hours to learn from Me, grow into Me, and strengthen your convictions. I am going to do a quick work of recovery so no day is lost and forgotten. Rededicate yourself to becoming a producer of life. Create, invent, learn, appreciate, advance, move upward, and live without limits. There are many more days on the way for you to enjoy. Drink a day like it is the nectar of life. Enjoy every smell, fragrance, and the beauty of My creation. Before you know it, everything will be restored.

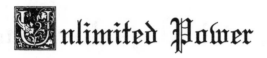nlimited Power

Luke 4:14
There Jesus returned in the unlimited power of the
spirit – and his fame spread through the whole region.
Author's Paraphrase

Let Me clothe you in My power. The power for living a godly life
shall be your milk. Power to see impossible miracles shall follow
you around. Your godly clothing shall be the power of loving the
unlovable. Your shoes shall be covered in the power to journey well.
Your sword shall be the power to receive harvests from dead fields.
Fasting and prayer shall be your shield and banner. No area of defeat
shall be able to conquer you again. Your ring shall be the power of the
blood covenant I have made with you through My Son's sacrifice. Your
foes shall be terrified because of the power I release in your life. I will
saturate your ground with seed-producing power—power to preach
My message, power to be a hero to the hopeless, and power to have
fruitful seasons and times of refreshing from the Lord. Your mornings
will be quiet times of intimate power to see into the spirit world of
angels. You will live untouched by evil. My plan shall hold you like a
hand in My grip of love.

Under My Care

Psalm 121:7-8
He keeps you from all evil and preserves your life. He keeps
his eye upon you as you come and go and always guards you.
Author's Paraphrase.

Relax; the dogs are outside your gate, and they can't get in. I will keep
you safe wherever you go today. I will cover you with My hand, and
it will be your shield. Safety is My name. I will be your Bodyguard.
I will keep the violent away from you. I will blind their eyes so they
can't see you as you walk by. I am your soul's Guardian. The soul
thieves will never be able to touch your soul when they reach for it.
Their hand will slide off because of the anointing oil on your soul.
Your soul cannot be stolen, and it will never be sold. I will deliver you
from those who make covenants with ease and pleasure, who cease
being profitable servants. I will keep you as the apple of My eye and
at the very center of My attention. You will never be out of My light
even for a moment. I am your guardian. I assign Myself to guarantee
your arrival in heaven without spot, blemish, or scratch. You will have
no more scars after you are under My protection. Live free of fear and
care. Enjoy waking up and going to sleep. Remember, you are under
My care.

 ith Me

Genesis 39:2
The Lord was with Joseph in everything he did.
Author's Paraphrase

I will never leave you. I am incapable of abandonment. Everyone who has ever left you has left their rejection mark with you, but I will leave My love mark on you. When you're good, bad, present, or absent, I am with you. In every trail of life I am with you. I will be there for you as whatever you need Me to be. When you need a Father, I am there. When you need a teacher, a guide, or whatever the moment calls for, I am yours from the beginning of your life until you close your eyes to meet Me. I am with you. Wrap your faith around these words today. Let them heal all the memories of loss and loneliness you have ever felt. Take this healing love and spend your life spreading it around. Do to others what I have done to you. Your wholeness is hiding in your love walk. Your power is hiding in your faith walk. Your destiny is hiding in your obedience. Stand still in My will, and your promotion will step forward.

Touched by Heaven

Acts 4:13
When they saw the boldness and unfettered eloquence of
Peter and John and perceived they were unlearned, they marveled
and knew they had been with Jesus.
Author's Paraphrase

When you are touched by heaven, all momentum switches in your favor. You are no longer the one carrying the world on your shoulders. You are no longer depending on your talents, knowledge, or abilities to make your dreams come true. Now, My power flows through your life. My power flows through your words and actions, silencing the skeptics and critics. Because you spend intimate time with Me, it will be visible to the naked eye. For every moment you spend in communion with Me, another level of power will manifest in your life. Take time each day to be alone with Me. Find a solitary place away from everyone where the outside world cannot reach you. Live alone for a few hours a day. Make time. It's critical to your future and legacy. Never underestimate the power of being with Me. Let My Spirit rub off on you. Let it resonate your dreams and heal your personality. Let it unfetter your soul and untie the thoughts of your heart. Peace, power, and triumph are yours when you are touched by heaven.

These Nailed, Pierced Hands

Luke 24:39
Behold my hands and my feet, that it is I
myself: handle me, and see; for a spirit hath not flesh
and bones, as ye see me have.
KJV

These nailed, pierced hands of Mine are all that the world needs. My hands can calm the raging storm of the soul. They can quiet the invisible ache of any heart. These hands framed the world and stretched out the blanket of the universe. Yes, My nailed, pierced hands have healing powers. They can raise the dead heart and waken broken love. They can cleanse the leper of his flesh-eating disease. They can open the eyes of willfully blind people and open the ears of the deaf. There is no problem these nailed, pierced hands cannot cure. Fall on your knees, for bended knees summon My hands to love and restore. Trust My nailed, pierced hands; they cannot fail, harm, or defile. They are guaranteed to bless. Present yourself at My throne every morning, for My blessing from these nailed, pierced hands, and you will prosper all the days of your life.

The Riches of Grace

Hebrews 4:16
Draw near to My throne of grace with boldness, that you may receive mercy and find grace to help you in your time of need.
Author's Paraphrase

Don't fall for the grace heresies that make you completely unaccountable and irresponsible for your life and actions. Remember, My grace does not enable sin to reign; it enables you to reign. My beautiful, powerful, and matchless grace is My divine influence poured upon your heart and reflected in your lifestyle. Love My grace. Lean into it. Depend on it. Clothe yourself with it. It can accomplish what you cannot. The riches of My grace will now be poured out on you. People will see it now by the way you love them unconditionally, how you endure trouble, how you can resist temptation, and how success and favor follow you around. My grace will make the pleasures and temptation of the world loathsome in your eyes. My grace will cause your heart to be untouchable by evil. Your relationships will begin to flourish beyond explanation. Live in My grace. Swim in it. For those who look to My grace always see Me looking back.

The Homeless Seed

Ecclesiastes 11:1
Cast your seed upon the waters, you will find it after many days.
Author's Paraphrase

Seeds need direction. A seed is lonely and homeless until it is given a task to accomplish. Direct your seed. Put it on the right course. Give it a destination. Aim it with purpose. Don't aimlessly allow your seed to sit on hard, unreceptive ground dying or being blown away by the winds of visionless men. Attach your seed to vision. The field you plant in yields to you its harvest. Bad fields, bad harvest. Bring a large bag with you everywhere you go because these seeds are not your normal seeds. These seeds I am giving you multiply supernaturally when they are sown. Sow a seed and watch it reappear in your bag. I give seed to the sower. I have made you a strategic sower of supernatural, immortal seed. These seeds will never die, wither, or run out as long as you keep sowing. When you send them, they will go out as one and return with an army. Sow, sow, sow; reap, reap, reap. Do it faithfully, daily, and consistently. Do it with joy, gratitude, and expectation. Live like you will never run out of seed. Become the biggest sower you know. Never keep, hoard, or hold back your seed. Let go of what is in your hand, and I will let go of what is in Mine.

The Heart

Ezekiel 11:19
And I will give them one heart, a soft heart, and I will put a
new spirit within them, and I will remove the stony heart, and give
them a heart easily moved by my spirit.
Author's Paraphrase

I will make your heart so soft and teachable, so sensitive to My every whisper that even a hint will sound like a shout to you. No more bad decisions. No more wrong turns and dead ends. No more unwise entanglements. No double-mindedness or unsure reasoning. Your new heart comes fully equipped with a voice detector. It can detect My voice anywhere among the other strange voices of life. It functions on Spirit-oil, and it thrives on My presence. It lives to be touched by My love, and it can last 120 years without malfunctions. Give My heart in you its way. Let it guide. It is equipped with a road map to Me. Your days of confusion are over. Your days of happiness have started. The heart of wisdom, love, and integrity is yours. A bionic heart beats in your chest that is built to endure good times, bad times, and unclear times. Turn your will toward Me. This keeps your heart in My hands and recharges your 120-year battery.

The Footsteps of the Past

Exodus 14:13
The Egyptians which have pursued you and
tormented you will you see no more.
Author's Paraphrase

The family demons that sometimes whisper their wishes and desires in your dreams, trying to work their way back into your life, will be expelled forever from your family. Nothing damaging physically, spiritually, or emotionally will pass through your family ever again. You are free. The footsteps of calamity and threats are vanishing from your mind. Your mind will no longer be your tormentor's playground. I am burying the monstrous corpses once and for all. The very memory of the ghosts will be like smoke blown away by the wind. Freedom is your reward for loving, obeying, and serving Me. With this freedom comes power, strength, and spiritual insight. You are now baptized in usefulness, covered in relevance, and surrounded by miracles. Live a worthy life you can respect. Come to Me worshipping. Bring a worshipping will. Surround yourself with like-minded friends and like-hearted soul winners. Fill heaven with the souls of the forsaken and enjoy your freedom.

The Buttered Road

Job 29:6
Your steps were washed in butter and the
rock poured out rivers of oil.
Author's Paraphrase.

Your path is one of smoothness. I have sent out My road crews, and their job is to clear the road of all stumps, dead trees, and broken branches. They will fill the ditches, level the unleveled ground, and then pour butter on the road. Butter is My preferential treatment. You are treated like a VIP. Your needs are met, your requests granted, your desires anticipated, and your dreams created. Your road leads to your destiny. Every turn has been planned, every stop fully supplied, and all those on this buttered road alerted to your coming. I do this so I can speak to the rock of oil. When it sees you coming, it will begin to pour out not trickles or oozing but rivers of oil. Oil is My healing power for all areas of life and for all travelers on this road. It will be your job to pour as much oil on travelers as you can. Let the oil do its job, and sit back and watch broken lives be transformed before your very eyes.

oyalty

Proverbs 10:22
The blessing of the Lord, it maketh rich, and
he addeth no sorrow with it.
KJV

All men and women on earth are born spiritual orphans. They are born lost, unloved, and unwanted by nature. They are born sick of heart and diseased with the seed of sin, death, and destruction. Their lowliness is already in place, and their sorrow already waiting. They need a King to intervene, and this is what I have come to do. I have come to take their inherited rags and replace them with the wealth of a King and make everyone royalty by adoption. Therefore, I command riches of every kind to invade your life. Be anointed with the robes of a prince or princess. Be saturated in your very soul with spiritual wealth, emotional wealth, and relational wealth. I am healing your mind, your will, and your emotions with My blessing. My blessing is now yours. It will cleanse your life from all sorrow. Stand there and feel My hand on your head now. Receive the power of My virtue flowing into you, repairing, restoring, and equipping you for life. Remain where you are, and My blessing will also remain.

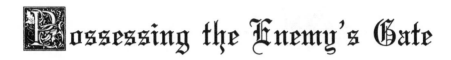ossessing the Enemy's Gate

Genesis 22:17
…And your seed will possess the gates of your enemies.
Author's Paraphrase

The enemy has always hated your family and the potential of your family. The gates of hell that have been prepared against them have failed. There are no gates left to harm you. Know this: Your enemies will be possessed; their gates will be your family's trophies. What conquered past relatives and past generations will not conquer your family. Your children, natural or spiritual, will open the gates of your enemies. All the spoil hiding behind those gates will be yours and your children's. Come to the gate destruction meeting. Watch Me melt the gates and retrieve the gold buried within the gates. I will extract all the jewels and precious stones that are covered over by rust and dust. They will shine again. These jewels represent stolen treasure of past generations. Your family will never lack again. Grace will flow again. Love will be your pillow, mercy your blanket, and faith your hands. Your walls will be called salvation, and the doors of your house praise and thanksgiving. You will strike at the heart of poverty and deliver the spoil to the poor. You will see My face in the wee hours of the morning to remind you of this tie around your neck, and you will pass it on to your descendants.

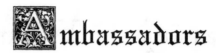mbassadors

2 Corinthians 5:20
Now then we are ambassadors for Christ, as though
God did beseech you by us: we pray you in Christ's
stead, be ye reconciled to God.
KJV

I have called you as an Ambassador of Unity. Your special gift will be
to bring unity where there is strife, contention, and division. As you
walk in unity with My plan and My will for your life, you will see this
gift growing and expanding inside of you. Don't fear any intimidator
or aggressive controller. Through My gift in you, you will dismantle
their weapons, and they will stand naked before the truth. The truth
will be your sword; love, your chains; and mercy, your song. Lay hold
of these weapons that are arms of power and watch Me change people
and situations. Watch Me heal homes, families, and broken lives. You
should prepare yourself for this unifying thread to flow in every area of
your life. Stand in your gifts. Do not flinch, blink, or hesitate. Run at
your fear. Stomp on your doubts. Crush your hesitation and take hold
of eternity's hand. Let it lead you to your Promised Land. Allow the
milk and honey of My will to saturate your heart and heal your soul.
Now, turn and do likewise to others.

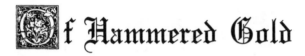

Of Hammered Gold

1 Peter 1:7
That the trial of your faith, being much more
precious than of gold that perisheth, though it be tried
with fire, might be found unto praise and honour and glory
at the appearing of Jesus Christ.
KJV

Do not be confused over the trials that come upon you sometimes. There is a rescue plan in place. I am never caught by surprise by your unpredictable circumstances. I know everything that will happen to you, and I have already prepared an exit for you. Life is full of surprises for everyone, but because you are with Me, they have no ability to harm you. Be still. Embrace My patience, and it will steer you softly through the waters of life. Don't forget that you are a piece of fine, expensive gold. Let the hammer do its work. When I'm done, you will be extremely valuable and desired by people who are covered in worthless dust, grime, and mud. I am making you a special vessel of Mine. You will have My special touch that only a master metalworker can impart. Your journey leads to Me, your value leads others to Me, and your hammer marks tell the world that I love you.

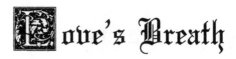

Ephesians 5:2
And walk in love, as Christ also hath loved us,
and hath given himself for us an offering and a
sacrifice to God for a sweetsmelling savour.
KJV

When you stand at the crossroads, choose life—the life of love, not of bitterness. No one on earth can escape this crossroads and neither can you. Choose love, and My love will breathe on you. It will fill your life with healing, goodness, and warmth. Kindness will embrace you every day. Goodwill will be your constant companion. Negativity will disappear like an unwanted fog. Your vision for life will step forward. Your enemies will no longer intimidate you. You will never lose sleep or have anxiety attacks. No more headaches, heartaches, or unresolved issues. When love breathes on you, you begin to live. Stop, take a deep breath of love, and begin to sing, for your new victories are on the way. Forgive all sins against you. Pardon the person who will never change their behavior. Release yourself from the power of their imperfections and permit yourself a new and uncluttered emotional life. Live freely.

ife Injections

2 Thessalonians 2:17
May the Lord strengthen, comfort, and make you
steadfast and unmovable in every good work and word.
Author's Paraphrase

Come into My hospital. Let Me encourage you with good news of
good things to come. Let Me refresh your spirit and awaken good
desires in your heart. Let Me hook you up to My IVs and rehydrate
you again. Let Me fill your arteries with life-giving water, the kind that
restores your soul. Let Me unclog your arteries from life-threatening
doubts. Let Me cleanse your blood from all infectious diseases, and
let Me give you life injections. These injections are not available at
any other hospitals, just Mine. They are supernatural health injections.
They make you super-human, able to do the impossible and able
to endure beyond reason. They make you able to love beyond the
expected and to love above the circumstances of the world. Life
injections cannot be bought or sold; they can only be given by Me at
My hospital. Only I have access to them, and I have chosen to give
them to you. So come and live the healthiest and wealthiest life that
man has ever known.

ngel Armor

Jeremiah 1:18
I have made you a protected city and an iron
pillar and brazen walls – none can harm you.
Author's Paraphrase

You are encased with impenetrable armor. You will not have any more
weak spots. Your armor is made of angel steel. The angels wear this
special armor. Never again will you be found wounded and bleeding
on the side of the road. Every weapon your enemy possesses is
powerless against angel armor. His spear, arrows, and cannons will
bounce off of you. His accusations, torments, and deception will melt
before you. His cruelties, seductions, and bribes will appear weak,
powerless, and empty. No temptation will distract you from God. No
enticement will reach your heart. Every scheme will reveal itself, and
you will not fall into any enemy traps. Rejoice all day long that I am
your shield and your armor. Wear your angel armor with pride and
respect. Trust and depend on Me, and none will betray you.

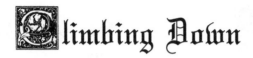limbing Down

Micah 6:8
He hath shewed thee, O man, what is good; and what
doth the Lord require of thee, but to do justly, and to
love mercy, and to walk humbly with thy God?
KJV

Climbing up the ladder of life; this imaginary ladder is the all-consuming dream of selfish men. I have not called you to climb up but to climb down. You see, with Me the way up comes on your way down. Yes, down into humility, compassion, and selfless living, giving, and goodwill. When you prefer others above yourself and allow them to take the glory or credit, then you are on your way up. When you empty your pockets for the poor and when you sacrifice your agenda for the promotion of others, you have arrived at Me. I am your Reward and your Constant Prize. I give you Me. I give you total access to My power, secrets, and gifts. I unleash heaven on your family and send My gatherers to rescue all the stray sheep in your fold. Therefore, climb down and rise up.

 reamers Never Die

Joel 2:28
And it shall come to pass afterward, that I will
pour out my spirit upon all flesh; and your sons
and your daughters shall prophesy, your old men shall
dream dreams, your young men shall see visions.
KJV

A dream is the sign that I am still alive in your heart. You can change the world with the right dream. Never let people and their negativity, doubt, and pessimism steal your dreams. As high as you can dream, I can take you. Your dreams are the wings of your faith, and I ride on the wings of faith. If you want to be where I am, dream. If you want to live in My abiding presence, keep dreaming. I will add all the other ingredients that your dreams will need. I will add desire, discipline, and wisdom. I will lay out your dream plan, which is that piece that all dreamers must have. I will explain every step of the plan to you. No stone will be left unturned. All the wisdom and motivation you will need to succeed will be there. I need you to do the dreaming, and I will do the explaining. Remember, dreamers never die.

nduring

James 5:11
Behold, we count them happy which endure…
KJV

Your heart will not quit on you. Your spiritual times will not be tiresome. I have placed My eternal battery in you. It never wears out or runs out. It is the power that keeps the universe going day after day, year after year, and life after life. It cannot be stopped. This power lives inside of you. I have everything you need to endure every trial and test that life may throw at you. You can relax and lean on Me. Rest your shoulder in the hand of My promises. Drink these promises like life-giving water. Let them rearrange your thoughts and adjust your attitudes. Let them enrich you with the wealth of eternity's wisdom and understanding. When you refuse to be provoked and instead you stand still and wait for the negative emotions to pass, you give Me a chance to fill you with power, strength, and peace. Then, you can endure rejection, hardships, irritations, and rude, selfish, and inconsiderate people. And you will be ready to be truly trusted and used by Me.

Finding Your Harp

Psalm 137:2
We hung our harps by the willow trees.
Author's Paraphrase

Don't ever let anyone steal your praise and worship harp. Guard your harp as your most prized possession. Never lay it down because of verbally critical and abusive people in your life. Never throw it away because your heart does not match your song. Sing, and your heart will follow your harp. Build Me a house with your praise. Your harp calls to Me; it summons Me and draws Me near to you. I will build a throne above you, a listening throne, where I sit and you minister to Me. I love the sound of your free-will worship. It is the totality of My purpose in your life. Your harp is your weapon. When you play it, demons flee. The atmosphere is filled with angel's songs. The invisible hosts are summoned. They follow My throne, surrounding Me with worship in harmony with your harp. Know this: As long as you play, you will never sing alone. Play your praise harp. Let it ring loud and clear. Let the whole earth be filled with My glory.

Give Me Your Ear, Fastened to the Door

Exodus 21:6
Then his master shall bring him unto the judges; he shall also
bring him to the door, or unto the door post; and his master shall
bore his ear through with an aul; and he shall serve him for ever.
KJV

When people are ready to surrender all to Me, they go through a holy ritual. They place their ear on the door post, and their master bores a love hole in their ear symbolizing the free-will, life-long commitment to Me. This act of undying love is the liberating sign of total freedom by total surrender. I love you, and you love Me freely without force, threat, or blackmail—no manipulation or bribery involved. All these nullify our relationship. True love is the mark of our relationship. Genuine affection, true communication, sincere love, intimate bonding. Exclusiveness; you are only Mine, and I am only yours. Freedom of Spirit, unrestrained worship, and unconditional commitment. Take this life, and rule with it. Rule the Enemy, conquer the flesh, vanquish the world, and live above fear. Give Me your ear, and I will give you My heart.

 ealing Rivers

John 7:38
He that believeth on me, out of his
belly shall flow rivers of living water.
Author's Paraphrase

I am the Thirst Quencher. I love thirst. It is a sign of deep and true love for Me. Whatever your thirst asks for, I can quench. Some thirst I remove and some I satisfy. But the purpose of your thirst for Me is that I can open the healing rivers within you. Hiding within your spirit man are the healing rivers of My love, joy, and peace. They are for you to enjoy. The river of revelation, trust, and power are for others to benefit from. The rivers of worship, purity, and surrender are for Me to enjoy.

You see, there are three harvests of healing rivers for you to enjoy. These rivers have no equal. No one can stop them because they do not originate from you. They are there because I placed them there at your second birth. They are the sources of life that connect you to Me. They flow out of Me to you. When you thirst, you open the gates of these rivers. Intimacy purifies the rivers and cleanses the contaminative elements out of your life. The rivers are yours. Release them in others. I have already released them to you.

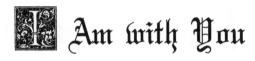 I Am with You

Matthew 28:20
...I am with you always, even unto
the end of the world. Amen.
KJV

You're not alone today. I will stay with you all day and through every detail of your day. I will talk for you. I will carry today's weights for you. I will carry you when you feel unable to walk. I am yours all day till the setting of the sun and into infinity. I will never ever leave you. You will look around and there I will be standing near you, holding your future in My hands, reuniting your life, reinventing you, changing the effects of your past, preplanning your today, and directing your future. I am with you, and that gives you total access to Me all day. Ask Me anything; I will answer. Ask Me to move mountains; I will do it. Ask for Me to destroy your debts, and they will disappear. Stay where I can see you, near Me, close by. Don't wander off; I am staying right here. I am stuck to you for life, and life is stuck to you. Live closely, stay close, sleep closely, walk closely, and be close, for I am always close.

 hen Heaven Smiles

Numbers 6:24-26
The Lord bless you and keep you; the Lord make His
face shine upon you, And be gracious to you; the Lord lift
up His countenance upon you, and give you peace.
NKJV

It is My will for you to live under heaven's smile. When heaven smiles
on you, the whole world must smile, too. No one can control you
with their agendas for you. They cannot hinder My purposes for you
through their manipulations or schemes. When heaven smiles, you are
free from the laws of man, and the laws of heaven take over. Heaven's
smile is life in divine control. No demons, devils, or predators in your
backyard or kitchen. No leeches, troublemakers, or Judases at supper.
No snakes, scorpions, or vultures in your living room. No Egyptians
chasing you through the desert. Heaven's smile is Satan's gallows. I
smile, and he is hanged. Take My smile into your heart. Embrace it
with your obedience. Receive it with integrity, eat it with unity and
love, and wrap it around your neck with faithfulness and resolve.
When heaven smiles, even the frowns become joyful around. My smile
is contagious; it tends to infect everybody, so smile and infect the
world with love.

ntolerable

Exodus 2:23
And it came to pass in process of time, that
the king of Egypt died: and the children of Israel
sighed by reason of the bondage, and they cried, and their
cry came up unto God by reason of the bondage.
KJV

You never change what you're willing to tolerate. Remember that! Life is full of the unexplainable. Don't let the unexplainable circumstances of life mold and frame your world. Let your faith and trust in Me canvas your heart. My faith abiding in your heart will unleash a torrent of victories, a deluge of turnarounds, and a landslide of miracles. Stretch yourself toward Me. Keep your heart safe from foreign and depleting invaders. Reject doubt, fear, and insecurity in every area of your life. Develop intolerance for failure. Claim your inheritance with tenacity and a refusal to be denied what I have bought for you with My life. You show your love for Me by clinging to My victories and displaying them before the world. Now is the time to put your foot down and draw the line in the sand. Remember, what you refuse to tolerate must leave.

aily Bread

1 John 5:14
And this is the confidence which we have in Him: that if
we ask anything according to His will (in agreement with
His own plan), He listens to and hears us.
AMP

I practice answering prayer. It is My daily food, My bread—knowing that you need Me and are trusting in Me, while knowing I will fix the broken, restore the lost, heal the sick, and deliver those in bondage. All of these attitudes bring Me great joy. I love to surprise you, shock you, and strengthen your convictions. I love seeing the look on your face when I say "yes" to your requests. I want you to be at peace, and to know how much I want to give you in order for you to fulfill your destiny. I know that without answered prayer, you can't change, be healed, or have your needs met. I am going to retire your debts, abolish your needs, and destroy your lack. It's time for abundance—cups overflowing, tables full of blessing, and your family celebrating My victories. The scenery is about to change. Your confidence is about to triple, and your adventures are about to begin. Run toward My throne and stay there until every need is met.

It Is Spoken. It Is Written. It Is Done.

James 1:17
Every good gift and every perfect gift is from above,
and cometh down from the Father of lights, with whom is no
variableness, neither shadow of turning.
KJV

Do you believe I am as good as your heart can imagine? Well, believe it! I am trillions of billions of times better than that. I am perfect and good enough to fill all of infinity with shouts of praise. I only have good gifts coming for you. The snakes are out of your grass, the wolves have stopped their stalking, and the cannibals are now toothless, gumming their way through life. Now that we are partners, your life callings are ready to prosper. Your possessions will increase; give them away periodically. Your prayer life will intensify, and your prospects will become limitless because in Me there is no shadow of turning. When I make a promise to you, your troubles are over in that area. Once I speak, the universe stops, listens, and obeys. Every living thing is programmed to obey Me. I am their God and Lord. They don't question, doubt, or hesitate; they simply obey. I don't change My mind. I am not limited to near-sightedness. I see everything at once. I know everything at once. I am everything at once. Therefore, be at peace. It is spoken. It is written. It is done.

You're Worth It

1 Thessalonians 5:24
Faithful is He that calleth you, who also will do it.
KJV

I will not leave you as an unfinished project. Every part of you that is lacking or missing I will replace. Every promise I have made to you I will bring to pass. Those who are weak in faith shall be strengthened by your undaunted faith. Those who are seeking revenge will be delivered from their rage. Those whose pillow is unbelief will wake up to the truth. All those in love with the world will see My world and switch sides. This is My promise; I will bring it to pass. You were not an accident. You are not just one little speck in the midst of billions. No, you are a special gift to the world. You are fearfully and wonderfully made. Let Me draw out of you gifts, talents, and potential that have been buried under a mountain of fear and doubt. Let Me open the gates of faith and turn you loose on the world. You are amazing, and you don't know it yet. You are powerful, smart, wise, and gifted. You are good, patient, and faithful. You are worth saving. I am faithful. I don't falter or cave in. I don't wear out or grow tired or weak. My strength is eternal. My willpower cannot be stopped or resisted. I have no equal, and no one can challenge Me. Remember, there is one Throne and one God on that Throne. You are related to Me, and you are worth the chase.

our Things

Proverbs 22:29
Do you see a man diligent and skillful in his business?
He will stand before kings; he will not stand before obscure men.
AMP

I will grant you four things that will heal your world. First, I will give you wisdom. With this, many doors will open to you that have previously been closed. Second, I will anoint your words with righteousness. Those who hear you will love the sound of your words and grant you favors. Third, I will give you a pure heart, and with it you will never be overcome, seduced, or deceived. This will grant you unlimited access to Me. And finally, I will grant you diligence that will give you power to achieve great works of love for My Kingdom. Never doubt what you can be in and through Me. Doubt everything without Me but stay close by My side. Never leave the sound of My whispering voice. Never walk away from the touch of My hand. Embrace Me like a small child embraces his or her father. Love Me tenderly and totally. Don't hold any part of yourself back from Me. Let your guard down and speak honestly. I have a lot of plans for you today. There are some surprises headed your way, some lost dreams to reawaken, and some faith to exercise. At the end of today, you will be shouting for joy.

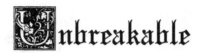nbreakable

Psalm 89:34
My covenant will I not break, nor alter the
thing that is gone out of my lips.
KJV

Once I say it, then it comes to pass. I do not tempt or tease My
children with false hopes or false promises. My Word has no equals
in speed, accuracy, or power. There is no greater force in the universe
than the words that come out of My mouth. My Word is the life
of all mankind's true existence. It destroys the vain life, it creates
permanence for the transient, wandering soul. It calms the restless,
satisfies the empty, and eliminates the recurring contentions of life. If
I say it, I will do it. I cannot tell a lie, just like water cannot be dirt.
I cannot be false or untrue. I am unbreakable. I cannot be defeated,
deceived, tempted, or diminished. No one has My wisdom, strength, or
power. All those who claim to, disappear. I have formed a partnership
with you, and it will never be broken. We are one. What I have is
yours. Use it to do good. Bless someone as I have blessed you.

nchangeable

Malachi 3:6
For I am the Lord, I change not; therefore
ye sons of Jacob are not consumed.
KJV

I am bringing about an unchangeable permanence in you. Not only will you be reliable in your own eyes, but others will trust you as well. I don't change, waver, or alter My opinions. I am constantly dependable. This is My plan for you. I will teach you the skill of preparation, which will guarantee your success. I will give you the gift of wisdom and precaution, and you will only have to do things once, which will bring you favor. I will endow you with power so that My glory is spread. I will protect you from corruption, liars, and thieves. They will never knock on your door without you being prepared to scatter their lies. I made you a promise that I would change you and make you a vessel of honor. With your cooperation, that is exactly what I will do. I will make a weapon out of a worm. You came from nothing, but you will inherit everything. You brought nothing, but you will leave with everything. You knew nothing but will shock the world with My wisdom. You felt nothing, but you will display My heart. Do you see, even as you are reading this, the miracle of transformation has already begun?

When the Clouds Roll Away

2 Timothy 2:21
If a man therefore purge himself from these,
he shall be a vessel unto honour, sanctified, and meet for the
master's use, and prepared unto every good work.
KJV

Clean out the house; purge the questionable, and the clouds will disappear. Rain will start falling, wells will open, and springs of health will run through you. Hear Me, and I will consecrate your day and overwhelm you with waves of encouragement. There can be no doubts in your heart, no questions about other lives you could live. You must leave your whole heart at My altar. Every vine is purged in order that what is left might grow stronger. Two strong limbs are better than a thousand weak ones. Don't grieve over the lost limbs, for they are useless branches only there to weaken the real you. When you are at peace with the way I do things, you will notice that the clouds will roll away. All discouragement, disappointment, and confusion will suddenly and forever be gone. A clean house is an invitation for Me to move in. I would like to build a library inside of your heart. This library is full of My knowledge and has answers to all of life's problems. Let your heart open the books and turn the pages. Let Me teach you what I know about people and life. Be My book. Hold My sacred truth securely in the palm of your hand. Quietly open the pages of your heart to My waiting pen.

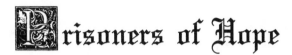

Prisoners of Hope

Zechariah 9:12
Turn you to the strong hold, ye prisoners of hope: even
to day do I declare that I will render double unto thee.
KJV

I will make you a different kind of prisoner, not one addicted, tormented, or abused by your prison. No, you will be a prisoner of hope—one who has a joyful expectancy that something good is about to happen. Your heart will live in expectation, satisfaction, and fulfillment. True love will be your badge. Wear it, use it, love it, and test it. Once you stood inside your self-made cell, looking out through the iron bars, hoping you could be free some day. That day has come. No more jail, no more jailers, and no more bars. Hope is like medicine to the heart. It heals, it repairs memories, it seeks out pockets of pain, and it pushes the puss out of the infected areas of the heart. Because you have been a prisoner, tortured by life, your compassion will go before you, moving your heart to show kindness to the victims of the ravages of life. Don't just open people's cells, wreck them, and burn them to ashes. Leave nothing of the enemy's handiwork. Destroy it all. This is your assignment.

Keep Your Eyes Open

Numbers 13:30
And Caleb stilled the people before Moses,
and said, Let us go up at once, and possess it;
for we are well able to overcome it.
KJV

You are not what they say you are. You can defy their predictions and prosper. People have always laughed at you and underestimated you, but I never will stop believing in you. When others think you are done, that's when I really start showing the world how awesome you really are. No matter what you are facing, it is already defeated. I am putting a new spirit within you. There will be no fear, cowardliness, or timidity in you. You will be like a predator, ready to devour your prey. Have no mercy on evil; overcome it with goodness. Do the opposite of your impulses and urges. Still the people; speak to them about their abilities and talents. Tell them I am coming back for a victorious church. Overcoming will be your motivation. I will reveal to you the location of My shelter, the house where I take people to restore and repair them, where you are totally restored. Feed My sheep. Show them the way to My hiding place. They are looking for the directions. Keep your eyes open.

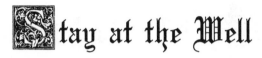

Stay at the Well

Psalm 139:17-18
How precious also are thy thoughts unto me, O God! How great
is the sum of them! If I should count them, they are more in number
than the sand: when I awake, I am still with thee.
KJV

I think of you more times in one day than all the sands of the seas. I
alone can love that much. Never is there a moment in time when I am
not thinking of ways to love you and bless you. It is My occupation.
This is how valuable you are to Me. Never again feel alone, unwanted,
or invisible. Don't feel sorry for yourself. This world is not your home.
You are only visiting. Let My love wrap itself around your thoughts
and deliver you from the bitter traps of life. Yesterday's ghosts and
demons received their eviction notices. Your life has been declared
private property. The "No Trespassing" sign has been posted. You
are now Holy Ground. I have sanctified you as My own. All of My
wealth is yours. All of My titles, names, authority, and power are now
available to you. Live your life as a child of Mine. Walk with valor.
Live with compassion. Don't consider your weaknesses. Look to Me
when you're unsure of what to do. I am on 24-hour call for you. This is
My commitment to you. Live free from emotional entanglements. Stay
at the well. Build your house there, and grow.

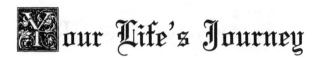our Life's Journey

Genesis 22:8
And Abraham said, My son, God
will provide himself a lamb for a burnt offering:
so they went both of them together.
KJV

I have everything you need for your life journey. I own all the silver and gold; I own every bank, every store, and all sources of life. I own every kind of valuable commodity, so don't strive after the perishable, false wealth that people die for. It will rust and decay. Instead, surround yourself with all things immortal, all things holy and sacred. Live above the base, worthless, temporal desires of the flesh. Cling to the true wealth, that which money cannot buy nor ambition can ever reach. Then every door will open, every promotion will be granted, and all dreams will be realized. This is a glimpse of your future under My care and supervision. Trust these words I speak. Lean your entire self on them, rely on their trustworthiness, and be at peace. Look ahead and see the ladder of success. It is yours to climb and yours to share. Be openhanded, openhearted, and generous.

The Unstoppable Hand

Daniel 4:35
And all the inhabitants of the earth are reputed as nothing:
and he doeth according to his will in the army of heaven, and
among the inhabitants of the earth: and none can stay his
hand, or say unto him, What doest thou?
KJV

When My intervening hand begins to move, the earth stops and listens.
For who can stop My momentum in your life? Can anyone say to Me,
"No," "Stop now," or "You can't do that"? Once I have decided to
bless you, the heavens open, promotions step forward, and life takes
its place in your heart. Thieves run for these lives. Heartaches cease
and war calls a truce. When you remain in a state of unconditional
surrender, My hand will always move the earth for you. Mountains
will melt at the sound of your faith speaking. Valleys will be exalted,
and the dangerous places in life will cease to be a threat. My hand will
rest upon your head. My "Yes" shall be stamped on your forehead.
Let the universe try and hurt you; it will not and cannot. You are safe.
Dwell in this safe place. Take time to soak in these truths. Let them
minister strength to you. Drink barrels of faith and oceans of love. Be
an ocean to the drowning world around you, and I will carry you safely
to life's paradise.

roken Curses

Luke 10:19
Behold, I give unto you power to tread on serpents
and scorpions, and over all the power of the enemy:
and nothing shall by any means hurt you.
KJV

It's time to clear out the enemy from your family. All those devils
that have oppressed your family for generations must leave. The
curses will break, the iniquities will be healed, and the infirmities
will be destroyed. Claim what I have already paid for, and change
your world. You are called to be a curse-breaker. Everywhere you go,
deliver people from their curses — generational, personal, and those
of the world. You are not like other people. You are special. You have
been given a special life assignment. Deliver those who are bound by
the devil. Break them out of jail. Set them on the true path and never
cease doing good. Keep yourself in the hollow of My hand by being
My hand. Bring the torch of truth. Lift it high like an army waving
their colored banners in the wind. Let the wind of the Holy Spirit carry
your torch into eternity. Let your banner be your voice. I guarantee the
world will listen.

When Heaven Shouts

Isaiah 1:17
Learn to do well; seek
judgment, relieve the oppressed, judge the
fatherless, plead for the widow.
KJV

I need you to help the orphans, feed the poor, and rescue the widows.
Take your influence that I will give you and do good to those who have
nothing. This is your true destiny and calling. There are undiscovered
treasures waiting for you inside the orphans and widows. Your life's
wealth is hidden in the lives of the forsaken; their pain is your mission
field. Relieve it; pour healing words into their broken spirits. Fill their
empty hearts with hope. Paint a picture with your words for them to
dream about. Draw a map for them to follow. Show them what kind of
life they can have if they follow Me. This is your assignment. Follow
it, be absorbed by it, and listen for the sound of heaven clapping.
Every time one lost soul is rescued, heaven shouts!

he Warehouse

Nehemiah 9:21
Forty years You sustained them in the
wilderness; they lacked nothing, their clothes did
not wear out, and their feet did not swell.
AMP

If I did it in the past, don't doubt that I can do it in your future. There are warehouses of provision waiting for you. These are not secondhand blessings, not used-up blessings with holes in them, not fake pretensions; these are blessings that increase and multiply the more you use them. Test Me, try Me, and see if I won't increase you as you let go of what is in your hand. I have a history of providing for My children. I am the Warehouse, I am the Source of the Warehouse, I am the Food in the Warehouse, and I have the keys to the Warehouse. I want to give them to you. I can sustain you in the desert or the open seas. Wherever you are, I will take care of you. Don't cast away your trust and confidence in My Word; take it like vitamins. When I assume the responsibility as your Provider, I am never late, and you will never lack. I give you life, health, and wealth. Now use it for the good of mankind.

Twenty-four Hours a Day

1 Peter 1:5
Who are kept by the power of God through faith
unto salvation ready to be revealed in the last time.
KJV

My eye is fixed on you 24 hours a day. I see every step you take. Even
before you take it, I go ahead clearing the way of evil. I exterminate
destruction before you, I eliminate cruelty, I remove disease and
destruction. I make the sun shine for you even when it's rainy. You
never have gloomy, depressed days when you stay on My path. Your
future has already been written, and there's no bad news in it. If you
stay where I tell you, life will smile at you. My power will be like a
shield around you. It is time to depart to a solitary place and seek My
will. Do this; take advantage of our time alone, and don't squander any
opportunity I give you to be with Me. Cling to My presence, embrace
My faith, and it will be like impenetrable armor to you—remember
that. Love is your weapon. Truth is your banner. Use them skillfully
to set people free. Be endowed with power from on high. Smash the
devil's servants and proclaim freedom! I will never look away
from you.

he Prize

Philippians 3:14
I press on toward the goal to win the prize
to which God in Christ Jesus has called me to.
Author's Paraphrase

The treasure of life cannot be found casually. It must be searched for
with passion and determination. It must be pursued with a holy fury.
Counting the pleasures and false treasures of the world as worthless
is the only acceptable mindset for you. There is a prize more priceless
than all others, so valuable that thousands of seekers have given their
lives for it. The prize I am speaking of is already seeking you. It is
waiting for you, and it will complete you. Press hard toward this prize.
Value it more than you value your own life, and you will find it. If
you search for it with every fiber of your being, it will present itself
to you. Take the restraints off your seeking. Throw yourself into it
completely, for it is worth the effort. No amount of sacrifice or loss of
other things can be considered. This is what you have been searching
for your whole life. The prize of life—Me, only Me. Remember how
this works: You run to Me, and I run to you. It shortens the distance
between us quickly. Love Me. I love you. It is in your hands to decide
the life you live. Take action and live.

verwhelmed

Joshua 3:15
Dip your feet in the garden, and the
waters will overflow its banks.
Author's Paraphrase

This day is your day to overflow with My rivers. Your banks and
the restrained areas of your life will be overwhelmed with joyous
expectations because you carry in your heart My ark that holds My
Shekinah glory. Your steps will be guided by divine revelation. Your
personal anointing will be released, and snakes will be cursed. As you
walk your eyes will see hidden truth, and your heart will meditate on
peaceable results. Dip your feet into My river. Notice how the water
rises when you do. The deeper you go in your relationship with Me,
the higher the waters of My river will rise. I want you to know that
you are never to live without the overflowing blessing. I want your
river banks to overflow with blessing. I want your cup of wisdom to
run over. I want your barrel of meat to never run out, and I want you to
have strength for the journey.

onquering Warrior

Isaiah 14:3
I will lift your heavy load and give you rest from sorrow and fear.
You will know that all the mighty tyrants have been destroyed.
Author's Paraphrase

Don't look for your lost chains. Don't long for the melons and leaks of Egypt; crucify all of them. For every temptation you overcome, I will give you a spiritual promotion. For every chain you reject, I will double your strength. For every tempting melon you smash, another piece of armor will grow on you. When the day is done and you have won, I will call you Conquering Warrior. I will not stop working on your behalf until every dream you have is a reality. I don't tease people with hope. I don't dangle the carrot in front of their nose and not let them eat it. Generational curses have been broken off of you. Your tree is firmly planted, deeply rooted, and permanently flourishing. You are a conquering warrior, and all of life's possibilities are yours. You are a destiny child. You are born to be great—great in love, great in passion, great in mercy. Your past is being erased daily. My eraser also replaces the past. It rewrites your future. It redefines your value. It sends your mercies ahead of you. Love is your banner. Wave it in front of every battle, and you will always conquer.

Double Your Strength

Numbers 11:17
And I will come down and talk with thee there: and
I will take of the spirit which is upon thee...
KJV

Your load is about to get lighter. The burden on your shoulders is about to break. Swing your arms in freedom. Notice that your heart is no longer burdened. You have new air to breathe and new room to run around in. The slippery places are gone, and you are standing on solid ground. I empower you to do what you are responsible for. Every part of your life will be working like a finely tuned watch. Every time you kneel to pray, know that I will pour another gallon of anointing oil on you. Double your strength by being transparent. Triple your strength by living the second-mile life. Quadruple your strength by putting others first. Finally, totally transform your strength by living dead to yourself and alive to others. These secrets are your pearls. Keep them in a safe place because they are very valuable. They will give you unnatural strength. They will enable you to do amazing feats of strength for Me. I need you to know that your job is to be a conduit. Pass it on; give it away in gifts. Find the weak, helpless, and defeated and give it to them. Don't keep it. Give it, and it will always multiply.

My Waiting Arms

Isaiah 52:7
*How beautiful upon the mountains are the feet of him that bringeth
good tidings, that publisheth peace; that bringeth good tidings of good,
that publisheth salvation; that saith unto Zion, Thy God reigneth!*
KJV

Your calling is to be an encourager, to lift people out of the dungeons
of despair, to pull them out of their self-made pits. I empower you
to drag them out of the quicksand of temptation. Rescue them from
worldly distractions. Grab their hearts in your hands and point them
toward Calvary. At the feet of Calvary their sagging heads and
limping hands will be lifted up. Then they will run into My waiting
arms. Because you pursue those who have no helper, your feet
will be famous in heaven. Now get busy liberating, emancipating,
and delivering the world around you. Declare hope to the dying
generations around you. Call them back home. Many are ready to
listen. They are tired of their lonely pits and empty pursuits. You are
what you do when no one is watching. I reward you in public for what
you do in secret. Your job is to publish My Word any way you can. Put
that Word in people's hands. It will lead them to Me and save them.
It will be a light for their life's path and a fire to warm them on their
journey. I reign forever. No one can challenge Me. Proclaim this to the
whole world and live safely in My arms.

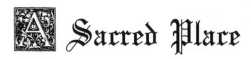 **Sacred Place**

Exodus 25:22
I will meet with you and commune with you from
between the wings of the cherubim from above the mercy seat and
reveal to you everything you need to know.
Author's Paraphrase

There is a place I want to take you, a sacred place that I don't show to everyone—only the chosen. In this place of mercy and truth, all of My secrets are kept. It is here where I reveal My truth to those who know Me. These are not old secrets known by everyone but special, love secrets. Here you will see and know what I am really like, what I think and feel and want from you. Your life will be permanently reshaped by My abiding presence on you. My presence has healing life and transforming power. No human can stand in My presence and remain the same. Communion with Me is your personal life goal. Here is the sacred place of fellowship. All the holy exchanges take place here, and here is where you see Me, hear Me, feel Me, and know Me. Here is where I become tangibly real to your natural and spiritual senses. Here is where My thoughts become your thoughts. Here is where I stamp My image into your soul, and your course is altered forever. When you take this path, your feet become blessed. Take it and stay on it for the rest of your life.

If I Speak

Isaiah 46:11
Yes, I have spoken, and I will bring it
to pass; I have purposed it, and I will do it.
AMP

If I say it, it is done. If I declare it, it is accomplished. My word is unalterable, unchangeable, and unstoppable. I say that you will prosper and succeed in life. You will live without offense. You will walk with no limp. Your eyes will see what is hidden. Your arms will never tire of carrying My will. Your legs will grow stronger the further you walk. No man or woman will be able to stand before you all the days of your life. If I speak, the rocks pay attention, the mountains skip, the hills clap their hands, the islands dance, and the seas cheer with shouts of victory. If I speak, the earth ceases to move, the stars sing their song, the universe bows its head, and the angels fall on their faces. The cherubim ceases to breathe, dead rise from their graves, and the earth trembles. If I speak, all is Mine to command. Don't doubt what I say, when I say it, or how I say it. Do it, say it, and be it. If I speak, you are born, and your life is hidden with Me. Now, do what I say and change the world.

The Unveiled Heart

Isaiah 33:16
[Such a man] will dwell on the heights;
his place of defense will be the fortresses of rocks; his bread will be
given him; water for him will be sure.
AMP

Who are you, and what kind of person do you want to be? I need your cooperation to make you a person I cannot resist. If you allow Me, I will reshape your heart. I will change the elements of your personality. Everything you ever disliked about yourself will disappear. You will become a blessing to yourself. Don't listen to the voice of your past experiences. Don't incline your ear to your enemy's voice. Don't stop and give the devil any airtime. Listen to Me. I have a refuge all reserved for you. Room service is provided and all bills are paid. Everything you need to live like a child of the King is yours. Any place you go, My bodyguards go with you protecting you from landmines, assassins, and hidden traps. Don't worry; the special forces I have assigned to you can see through walls. They have never lost anyone I have assigned to them. Stay where I tell you. Do what I tell you. Everything you love will be safe. I am looking for an unveiled heart— transparent, vulnerable, and unprotected. I want to have unlimited access to your heart. If you can do this, I will give you the keys of life, and anything will be possible. You choose; I already have.

he Naked Heart

Joshua 3:5
...Sanctify yourselves: for tomorrow the Lord will do
wonders among you.
KJV

Outrageous miracles are My specialty. I love to surprise you. I long to shock you into greatness. The greater your calling, the greater the miracles. Do you believe you were born to be obscure, or do you feel greatness beating in your heart? Live expecting the impossible, and the impossible will happen. Wallow in My supernatural surprises for you. Let Me alter the worlds of your friends and enemies. Let Me surprise your family with greatness. Let Me draw the genius out of you. I know where you are gifted, and I know exactly how to bring it out of you. Let Me fulfill your dormant dreams and rearrange your life schedule. Let Me take you by the hand and reveal to you the secret place of the naked heart. I will establish your life plan, each section of your life perfectly organized and ordered with some awesome surprises along the way. There is a time in all believers' lives in which they must separate themselves and find My face. They must turn aside from all other distractions and find the well of life. They must cast off all their burdens and heavy loads. They must strip off the dust, dirt, and mud of life and come naked and clean before Me. They must choose between the love of the world and making Me the Lord of their hearts. They must throw away the false masks they depend on to survive among the wolves. They must pull down the fences that protect them from the cannibals without. Find the secret place where I live. If you will do this today, I will release the waiting miracles. The naked heart is the trumpet that summons Me.

nwind

Psalm 37:7
Rest in the Lord, and wait patiently for
Him: fret not thyself because of him who prospereth
in his way, because of the man who bringeth
wicked devices to pass.
KJV

Today I want you to unwind—no stressing over finances, relationships, or health. Relax, sit down, and read. Give yourself a holiday from anxiety and pressure. You need your spiritual battery recharged. You need time alone with Me. Take time right now to refocus your attention on the miracles and breakthroughs of the past. Remind yourself of My faithfulness. This will produce a wave of healing outbreaks that will run through the heart of your entire family. One blessing received equals one hundred blessings released. You are a fountain of blessings. A rested land produces seven times the harvest of a used and exhausted land. Refuel slowly and intentionally. Every part of your life will improve. Your heart will beat in rhythm with Mine. Your body will not betray you. Your mind will not rebel against My Word. Your spirit will draw in My manna like a magnet. Unwind, rewind, and live freely and refreshed. Do it.

My Divine Yes

Exodus 3:21
I will grant you favor in the sight of the Egyptians,
and it shall come to pass that when you go out,
you will not go out empty-handed.
Author's Paraphrase

Favor is your destiny. I am removing the blockades and the "nos" from your life. The best is yet to come for you. You have not seen what My favor can produce in your life. My favor is My divine "yes." I love to say "yes" to your prayers. My goal for you is that you receive answers for all your prayers. I want your desires and dreams to be fulfilled; even lost and forgotten dreams will be resurrected. You will stand in front of doors that have always been closed to you before. Suddenly they will swing open. Doors that you never thought of praying about will open, and your life will become a door for others to walk through. Never accept a closed door until I tell you that I have closed it for a divine purpose. I say, "Yes!" Believe it. Speak it. Receive it. Stand on it. Proclaim it to everyone. Live a "yes" life. Receive the spirit of favor. Take it and wear it like a coat. Give it to those I tell you to and enjoy the unlimited benefits of My favor and My divine smile.

estroying Yokes

Isaiah 10:27
The burdens shall depart from off
your shoulders and the yokes from your neck.
Author's Paraphrase

I am a Yoke Destroyer of all that wishes to cling to you like a dead corpse and weigh you down in order to hinder you from finishing your race. The yokes of heritage are those passed down from generation to generation, leaving you crippled by unwanted deformities. The yokes of damaging, abusive words shall all dissolve off of you. Your yokes of personality and insecurities that have plagued and hindered your freedom will be destroyed. I finish what I start. I will not tolerate bondage or failing of any kind in your life. No one will stand in your face declaring their victory over you. No one's behavior will ensnare your emotions anymore. Peace is your umpire from now on. Your unresolved conflicts will be put in order. You are a yoke-breaking child of God. Your words are hammers, wrecking yokes and destroying hopelessness and despair. Speak your life-giving words and set the world around you free.

nees

Leviticus 10:7
Stay in the tent of meeting, lest you die:
for the Lord's anointing oil is upon you.
Author's Paraphrase

The door to My anointing is a life of prayer. Your knees unlock My power. Stay on your knees by submitting your attitudes to Me. Let Me train your soul to be Christlike. Your will is My treasure. I cannot and will never override your will, but I long to have it. For only then can I truly lead you in the path of righteousness or make you lie down in green pastures. Without your kneeling will, I cannot use you, anoint you, or truly send you My blessings. Your will needs to cry out to Me every day in every situation. When you violently surrender your will, My hands open and My blessing flows forth like an unhindered spring throughout your journey. My Spirit will be searching for your will. Your bended knees present your will to Me on the sacred altar of free will. You choose Me. I have already chosen you. I see your kneeling will. It moves My sovereign hand and grants you access to My best blessings.

he -Ites

Joshua 3:10
I will drive out from your midst the Canaanites,
Hittites, Perizzites, Girgashites, Amorites, and the Jebusites.
Author's Paraphrase

The cannibals within and without are My targets. They are the unseen destroyers, the hidden plagues of deadly -ites slithering around in the dark. They are shadows of disease, grave-dwelling attitudes, devouring parasites, and invisible destroyers that come in the spiritual food you eat—My word slightly altered by well-meaning speakers, books, and programs. I am intolerant of these invaders. The army of Satan is defeated. Your dwelling in Me is not susceptible to them. I have placed you in a sheltered hiding place. Stay there. Don't ever move from this place of safety, and you will never be invaded. You will live a life with unhindered wings, driving out these intruders from families and people who long for a new start. You are in the destiny of the preserved. Your place of honor, freedom, and influence is already paid for. You will never be bitten by these dark forces again. Now you are My exterminator. Wipe them off the face of the earth and let freedom reign.

Live in Reverse

Exodus 1:12
But the more they afflicted them, the
more they multiplied and grew...
NKJV

I reverse all of the effects and consequences of your bad choices, mistakes, and presumptions. The more people who persecute you, the more you will grow and increase. I have condemned you to victory and success. I will increase your spiritual senses; they will be sharp and undiminished. I will sharpen your mental faculties so they are clear and unimpaired. I will double your physical strength and fortify your bones. In response to the enemy's intrusions into your life, I am activating reversals for every area where you have lost anything. Don't worry; when I am done, you will be wealthy, wise, and compassionate—wealthy with Me, wise with insights, and compassionate toward the victims of Satan's army. Live in reverse now.

ut of Egypt

Deuteronomy 26:8
I brought you out of the house of bondage
with a mighty hand and with signs and wonders.
Author's Paraphrase

I am your true King. I will do whatever it takes to bring you out of every hard and difficult place. If I need to move a mountain, I will do it. If I need to change someone's heart, I will do it. If I need to send signs, wonders, and miracles, I will do it. There is no length that I will not go to set things in order for you. All things that have not been organized or flowing smoothly will start to run like a watch. I bring you into the house of destiny, your true dwelling place. You have a destiny bigger than anything you are doing now. I took you out of a horrible pit to a place of goodness. I am bringing you into a wealthy place, a paradise. I am bringing you to a resting place in Me, a treasure house of fulfillment, a glory house to gaze at My creation, and a house where you can put everything you like in it. Out of Egypt; into life.

Fruit that Never Wastes

John 15:16
You did not choose Me, but I chose you and
appointed you that you should go and bear fruit,
and that your fruit should remain, that whatever you
ask the Father in My name He may give you.
NKJV

I will give you perseverance as a gift, the ability to endure without side effects, hardships, negative people, and intimidation. Long-suffering will enter your bloodstream and help you enjoy difficult people. Great patience brings great honor, and great honor brings great, unreachable opportunities. You are called to greatness—great love, great power, and great humility. Your life is the life of a child of blessing whose fruit never wastes. With each fruit you bear, your harvest will double. Your spiritual fruit will be picked, packed, and shipped around the world. Fruit is life-giving and enjoyable. People love the taste of ripe, sweet fruit—ripe love, joy, peace, sweet goodness, gentleness, meekness, long-lasting faithfulness, self-control, and longsuffering. These will appear on your tree each morning. Water it with prayer and praise and eat as much as you need, for your life is now indestructible.

Tied to Me

Hosea 11:4
I drew you with cords of love and I removed
your yokes and bent down and laid food before you.
Author's Paraphrase

I am taking you on a spiritual quest to discover all of Me and all of My mysteries. We can never be strangers; we must be best friends. These cords of love are the music of your restored soul. I will tie you to Me with these cords. They will keep us together forever. They will remain between us as a reminder of our mutual commitment and lifelong dedication. These cords will lead you through the garden of grace and to the cross. Here, at this most sacred place, you are accepted just the way you are. Here, My grace and its life-giving power take over. This grace will appear outwardly to reveal itself inwardly by revealing My attributes and virtues to the world. You cannot be ripped away from Me. Not even wild beasts could tear you from Me. Live tied;
walk freed.

The Inner Chamber

1 Samuel 19:2
…Abide in a secret place, and hide thyself.
KJV

There is a place where your soul is freed from all earthly pressures, where the elemental desires no longer captivate your attentions. It is the inner chamber, the most secret, sacred place I can take you to. There is only one place like this in the universe—a place of openness where no fear of revealing secrets exists, a place of total satisfaction, a place of being born into the eternal, a place of dismantling where you are remade, reconstructed, and reconnected. This place I made and built with My own hands just for you. Give Me yourself and be freed from the fear of intimacy. I am incapable of failing you. I cannot hurt you, betray you, or forget you. In the inner chamber, you are My total focus. My eyes are only on you. My ears are open to your heart's thoughts. In this sacred place of exchange where you give yourself to Me, I give Myself to you. Dare to walk in. I am already here waiting.

The Kisses of Surrender

Song of Solomon 1:2
Let him kiss me with the kisses of his mouth:
for thy love is better than wine.
KJV

Kiss Me with your soul. Draw Me with your longing. Tell Me I am all you need. Need Me more than life itself. Long for My company more than any other. Stretch your soul up into eternity where I dwell. Let Me feel your dependency, and freedom will come on the wings of your holy desires—boundless, liberating, intoxicating freedom with songs, joys, and raptures of happiness. Cling to Me in love and holiness; these are your spiritual hands. Loving-kindness will follow you. Affection will surround your heart. Attraction will clothe you. Instruction will captivate you. New expressions of faith will follow you. Your new address is now the secret place. Every act of obedience is a kiss of honor where love and truth meet. Live near Me. Stay near Me and find all you have ever wanted.

That Love Divine

Romans 5:8
But God commendeth His love toward us, in that,
while we were yet sinners, Christ died for us.
KJV

Jump into My river of love. This river cost Me every treasure I have. I gave it all for you. I surrendered Myself for your salvation. Perfect Me for imperfect you. This was the trade. I gave everything for nothing, to gain everything. I did it because of My unconditional love for you. You are the object of all My love—unrestrained, unlimited, inexhaustible love. It flows toward you every day. This love is bigger than your mistakes and imperfections. Love that scales a thousand mountains across a million rivers to rescue you from you. Love unparalleled and immeasurable. Love that blindly loves you for who you are—good, bad, ugly, beautiful, amazing, poor, rich, young, and old. I always have, and I always will. This is who I am. I am your #1 Friend and Helper. Take the hand of My love and never let Me go. Turn the dark days into crowns of victory for Me. My love can change any life that is willing. Anyone who comes to Me and lives in My house of love will be completely healed and restored. It is impossible to remain unchanged once the hands of love have touched you. Make your covenant with this love divine. Now thrive.

When I Come to Stay

Song of Solomon 2:16
My beloved is mine, and I am his...
NKJV

I am no longer looking for someone to visit. I have come to stay. Some people want Me to visit them at their convenience. They don't realize that I don't want to be a visitor. I want to move into the house and be a dweller. A dweller owns the house and everything in it. I don't need a tour of your house; I need a room in your house. Give Me ownership, and we will be partners in all of life. I want to be near you 24 hours a day, to be there when you wake, eat, and walk, when you read, sleep, and work, when you think, feel, move, rest, when you struggle. I want to own your soul and give it color. I want to fill your soul with true happiness. I want to hear your prayers and silent thoughts. I want to live, move, and have My being in you. I long to be a permanent resident in your life, not a visitor who must leave when their stay is over. I come to stay. I come to be welcomed home. Do this and see that I will do for you what no one else can do: eternal restorations, renovations, and transformations.

 Garden Called Loved

Song of Solomon 4:12
A garden enclosed is my sister...
NKJV

I take great care over My garden. I am the perfect Gardener. I leave no rock out of place. I know where each rock belongs. I till the soil of your heart, searching carefully for all types of choking weeds. I know them all. I know where they hide. I can spot the flowers and fruits of My garden coming. I know exactly what to put into the soil to make it fertile and capable of producing the best harvest. I tenderly pull all destructive thorns and thistles out of My garden. I spade, hoe, and dig until My garden is perfect. Nothing escapes My watchful eye. I see the end result. I have done this many times and never had a failure. I have a gift for spotting worms—fruit worms, root worms, leaf worms, and heart worms. Each one is a deadly devourer of My growth. So relax and don't fear infestations or invasions by locusts or pests. I dream of My garden being finished. So I spend hours preparing the soil making it soft, pliable, and broken up with no hardness that could resist My seeds. I remove all poisonous elements and clear the soil so that every inch can produce when I am done. The world will see that I am the perfect Gardener with the perfect garden called Loved.

rink Deeply

Song of Solomon 5:1
Drink deeply my milk and wine and the honeycomb.
Author's Paraphrase

I am coming for you. I am gathering My vineyards. I am claiming My harvests. I eat your prayers like precious fruit early in the morning.
I drink your freely given love like nectar from the tree of your surrendered will. Drink deeply of the fruits of love. They produce a beautiful aroma in your personality. They heal sores, aching muscles, and eye and heart diseases. They rebuild torn ligaments and replace blood cells to the heart. This heavenly milk is from My heavenly dairy. It carries vitamins that cannot be found on earth. It will make your bones fat with life, with cancer-healing properties. Drink deeply My wine, the fresh revelations about Me, you, and everyone around you—revelations about living, love, death, and all things divine. Drink like you are in a parched desert, thirsting, longing for life-giving water. Become a wine addict, not of old wine but new wine. Drink from heaven's honeycombs. Heavenly honey produces immune-building enzymes. They work to protect you from all other diseases of life! They create a divine immune system. Drink deeply from My open, unlocked fountains and live in divine health.

The Fabric of Eternity

Ecclesiastes 3:14
I know that, whatsoever God doeth, it shall be for ever:
nothing can be put to it, nor anything taken from it: and God
doeth it, that men should fear before him.
KJV

I have placed inside of you the fabric of eternity. Every word of Mine
carries eternity with it. If you dwell in My Word, you dwell in the very
fabric of eternity. What I am doing in your life is not temporary. It is
not shallow or plastic, and it will not collapse under the microscope
of time. It will not change with trial, test, wear, or tear. My work in
you is eternal. I will place eternity in your heart. You will not live
for the temporal, passing pleasures of your flesh. You will wake with
a sense of the eternal. Eternal living focuses on heaven. Temporal
living focuses on immediate gratification and self-indulgence. Live
for eternity, and eternity will come to your aid. I am placing eternal
principals in you for your life. These will guarantee you prosperity.
Those who walk with eternity build for eternity. Those who walk with
eternity leave the footprints of the eternal in every heart they meet.
Choose eternity. Eternity has already chosen you.

ully Persuaded

Romans 4:21
And being fully persuaded that, what he had
promised, he was able also to perform.
KJV

Your power lies in your convictions, and your convictions are the result of your persuasion. I am on a quest to persuade you toward My ways and thoughts and My way of doing things. There will be no doubt left. We shall be one mind, one life, and one breath. No unbelief. No scandal in your heart toward yourself or others. No double-mindedness in your actions. This is because My promises have won your heart. The lost and unsatisfied man will turn to Me. The affluent will be humbled. The bookworm will be convinced. The selfish bachelor will commit to Me. The sick soul will rise from the emotional pallet. The mental invalid will be released. The poor and broken soul will be mended. All these blessings are ready, standing on the starting line, waiting for the sound of the gun in order to race to your door and present you with the prize. Be persuaded, convinced, and convicted. Live without doubt and walk without fear.

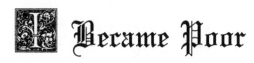 Became Poor

2 Corinthians 8:9
For ye know the grace of our Lord
Jesus Christ, that, though he was rich,
yet for your sakes he became poor, that
ye through his poverty might be rich.
KJV

I emptied Myself of all of My Godlike privileges, all of My undeniable characteristics, all of My irresistible powers. I became poor so you would never lack any of your inheritance. I bought your wholeness with My poverty, your life with the emptying of Myself. I became sin so you would receive My righteousness. I became sickness so you could be healed. I became despised so you would be valued. I became a curse so you would receive My blessing. I was rejected so you could never be rejected by Me. I took your pains so you would be comforted. I took the hate and wrath that all sinners deserve so you could receive all the love that you deserve. Never embrace the curse of poverty, sin, and death. They are My enemies and your enemies. Destroy them by walking in faith and dwelling in love. You will never possess a poor soul, spirit, or life. Never.

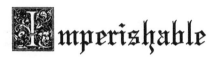mperishable

1 Peter 1:23
You have been born again not of perishable seed,
but of imperishable seed through the living and enduring Word of God.
Author's Paraphrase

You were once dead to Me. Your spirit was disconnected from Me, unable to fellowship with Me. Your soul was out of tune with Mine. But now having come to life, you have been born from My incorruptible seed of life. You have My life living in you, birthing Me in you, and causing your dead, Adamic cells to die and your life-giving, Christ cells to live. Immortality lives in you. Eternal life is your gift from Me. Every seed of truth you receive from My Word will awaken another piece of eternity in you. Nothing about you is worthless now. You are indispensable. Nothing in you is connected to death. You are life flowing from life. The useless parts of your life are slowly falling off. Your value is coming to the forefront. The needless introspections are ending. Confidence, security, and identity are pacing to the front. The value you see in Me is the value you have in Me. I am a universe of depths and heights, a galaxy of wonder and discovery, and a lifetime of infinite peace. We are imperishable truth.

The Tailored Life

Colossians 2:2
That their hearts might be comforted, being knit
together in love, and unto all riches of the full assurance of
understanding, to the acknowledgement of the mystery of God,
and of the Father, and of Christ.
KJV

I am sewing your heart to Mine like a tailor who carefully chooses his material and with each stitch sees the finished product. I know what fiber you are made of. I know which colors fit you best. I am making you a garment that the world can wear. You will be attractive to truth seekers. They will stop and ask for your tailor. Tell them where My shop is to be found. I am the Tailor of heaven. I fit and measure each child individually. I pick your favorite cloth for each important occasion of your life. Heaven dresses a certain way. Our clothing bears the marks of the Savior's death and resurrection. In heaven, the colors are white for purity, gold for divinity, blue for heaven, red for redemption, and purple for royalty. All of these are yours because the Tailor of heaven has chosen you for a new set of clothes. Wear them and give them away. Use your cloth and scare the devil, for his colors are only black. Your heavenly cloth contains special powers of healing, wholeness, and love. Tell them all Who the Tailor of heaven is.

My Name Is Beauty

Ecclesiastes 3:11
He has made everything beautiful in its
time. Also He has put eternity in their hearts…
NKJV

My Name is Beauty. All of the ugly memories of your life will begin to change within you. There will be no more fear or anxiety attacks because of the footsteps of your troubled memories running around in your head like ghosts on a crusade of torment. All of the ugly people who have walked in and out of your heart leaving their trash piles behind shall be erased, their faces will fade, and their words lose their sting. Their hurtful actions will become dust blown away by love's wind. All of the ugly places you were forced to live in, the places of loss of control, grief, sorrow, despair, and hopelessness will melt out of your mind's heart. All of the ugly actions you have beheld that gripped and paralyzed your heart, that stole your joy of living shall walk out of your life, and you will see them no more. I make all things beautiful in their time. I will beautify your life with truth, sincerity, love, and family. Beauty is My name. Beauty shall be your banner. Raise it high.

Live with Your Wings Spread

Psalm 37:5
Commit your way to the Lord [roll and
repose each care of your load on Him]; trust
also in Him and he will bring it to pass.
AMP

I want to teach you the art of carefree living: no racing heart or sweaty palms. No feelings of disaster or fearful expectations. No sleep deprivation or moral conflicts. No more mountain carrying. No more corpses on your back or tormentors on your shoulder. No more tied up emotions or overpowering people running your emotional world. Roll and cast each care on Me. My shoulders are as wide as the universe, and your problems are as tiny as a proton compared to My life-saving abilities. I can solve the problems of all existing things at once. This is who I am. Choose a life of carefree living; you can serve Me best this way, free and unencumbered. Live with your wings spread. Soar, fly, and glide in security and peace. Above all, don't worry about the threats of your mind. They are only untrained, old life thoughts. Take them and force them to submit to My way of thinking. Make your mind a peace factory, make your emotions a healing hospital, and make faith your wings.

The Pleasing Heart

Colossians 1:10
That you may walk worthy of the Lord,
fully pleasing Him, being fruitful in every good
work and increasing in the knowledge of God.
NKJV

All that I do in you, for you, and through you is to develop a pleasing heart in you. A pleasing heart is My playground; it is the place where I delight to dwell. There is no delight that I cannot experience within a pleasing heart. All of My dreams come true within a pleasing heart. There is no request that I would deny to a pleasing heart. A pleasing heart knows who I am, what I like, and what I desire. It understands Me and is able to perceive My unspoken aspirations. When I desire to accomplish something great on earth that requires a great sacrifice, the pleasing heart is there saying, "Take me, use me, and let me please you, My God." All you need to be truly happy is a pleasing heart. It will never deny Me, betray Me, or walk away from Me. When I call, it answers. When the alarm of battle sounds, it is there. Pleasing Me is all it wants, needs, and craves. A pleasing heart unlocks the doors of wisdom, power, and strength. Rest yourself on your pleasing heart. I am already resting there.

lowing

Romans 12:11
Never lag in zeal and in earnest endeavor; be aglow
and burning with the Spirit, serving the Lord.
AMP

My Spirit is like a lightbulb inside your heart and soul. It dispels
all darkness within you. No darkness is allowed in. When it is on,
everybody can see it. I will make you glow and burn with holy zeal.
Light will emanate from your spirit. Illumination will come easily to
you in the morning. Powerful, overpowering passion to see My will
accomplished will flood your life. All slothful spirits will be destroyed
from all members of your family. Spiritual apathy will never touch
your doorstep. Love will be your banner, the signpost on every action
and family deed. Spend your life glowing with radiant, inner light.
My light is the door to My glory, and glory is where I live. Stand in
the light and there will be no stumbling in your life. Your success will
follow you all the days of your life. Serve Me in the light. Destroy
My enemies with light. Light the paths of the blind. Open the sealed
eyelids of the rebels and show the world the path to Me.

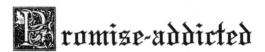romise-addicted

2 Peter 1:4
Whereby are given unto us exceeding
great and precious promises: that by these ye
might be partakers of the divine nature...
KJV

Every promise received is a doorway to a part of Me. Every promise digested is a light aglow within you. Every promise memorized is My footprint in your mind. Every promise proclaimed is an arrow released to its target. All of My promises are pieces of Me. Eat My promises, and you will add a new part of Me to your life. Eat all of them, and you will have all of Me. My promises are My bond. They reveal Me to you. They draw the lost out of their dungeons and caves. They bring hope to the lost and joy to the rejected. My promises answer all of the questions of the searching heart. My promises are medicine to the sick, resurrection to the dead, peace in the storms, and a rudder for your ship. Tie My promises to your soul, and you will escape every corrupting influence of this world. You will be preserved from the Adamic nature and all of its evil impulses. Become promise-addicted. I have already sent you your next promise.

esigned

Ephesians 2:10
For we are God's handiwork, created in Christ Jesus
that we may do good works, that we should walk in them.
Author's Paraphrase

Do you think that I leave people as I find them? Never! I designed you
to win, to love the broken, and to strengthen the weak. I designed you
to see the invisible and touch the untouchable. I designed you to live in
undisturbed peace, constantly growing in My grace. I designed you to
walk in harmony with My plan for your life. You have a fail-safe built
in you that will override any incident, failure, or invasion. I designed
you with powerful, unbreakable spiritual components for lifelong
service. I have invested within you My own Spirit that runs through
your God-designed veins. My blood is your oil; it guarantees your
longevity. You cannot break down, burn out, or run out of gas. You
are My personal design, built on My mind's design. Live free from all
other designs. Cling to your Designer. I guarantee what I have made
is very good.

The Irresistible Blessing

Genesis 39:5
And it came to pass from the time that he had made him
overseer in his house, and over all that he had, that the Lord blessed
the Egyptian's house for Joseph's sake; and the blessing of the Lord
was upon all that he had in the house, and in the field.
KJV

I am always with you, and I am interested in your business and your family endeavors. I will make you successful even where you lack skill or knowledge. When you put your trust in Me, promotions will come. I will take up the slack, and I will never let you fail or be in bondage. Your time has come; prepare yourself for the weighty power of the Spirit to promote you to places you could never reach. I give you unreasonable favor with everyone you have to deal with. They cannot deny you because you are empowered to be a success. I give you heart purity; with it you cannot be swallowed up. I give you spiritual hunger; with it you will never grow cold. I give you faith that moves obstacles; with it you will never be defeated. I will blot out the memory of your life in Egypt. I wash you in clear water. Now your conscience will be at peace, and I create in you a good heart to always bless others. Drink My irresistible blessings and thrive.

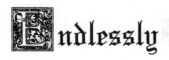ndlessly

2 Chronicles 26:5
...And as long as he sought the Lord,
God made him to prosper.
KJV

I will love you endlessly. I will provide for you endlessly. Seeking Me cannot be like work. You must find the hidden, holy pleasures of time with Me. There is a place of great satisfaction where your soul finds its rest and peace. True prosperity flows from this holy place of prayer, endlessly receiving My blessing and endlessly distributing My love. This place cannot be found by the indifferent or the distracted. Only the truly sincere can find this spiritual fountain of youth. True happiness, true peace, and true health are there waiting for you. Seek Me as if I were hidden treasure. Search for Me as if it were your last day on earth. Use all your strength, all your passion, and every ounce of your hunger. Then your light will appear. Your hindrances will vanish, your strength will double, and your destination will be secure. Remember, I love you endlessly.

n the Hollow of My Hand

Psalm 128:1-2
Blessed is every one that feareth the Lord; that walketh in
his ways. For thou shalt eat the labour of thine hands:
happy shalt thou be, and it shall be well with thee.
KJV

Absorb this promise and this word. If you walk in My ways as a good son or daughter and mimic My ways in every area of your life, you will eat the good fruit of your labor. You will live your life in happiness, peace, divine favor, and good fortune of every kind. Your family will be fruitful and productive within your house. Your children will be blessed at your table. Your life will be a pleasure to live. You are not like those who shrink back in shame or doubt. You are as a bold warrior who already knows the battle is won. You go into a battle with My battle cry knowing that I am much stronger, I am much more skilled, and I have a greater history of victory over all My enemies. Because you fear My name, I will show Myself strong on your behalf.

You should prepare yourself and stand at the door of expectation waiting for the things that I am going to do for you today. I will stretch down My hand from heaven and rescue you. I will set your feet upon a rock and establish your steps before you because you fear My name and tremble at My Word.

 My Eyes

Luke 15:20
And he arose, and came to his father. But
when he was yet a great way off, his father
saw him, and had compassion, and ran, and fell
on his neck, and kissed him.
KJV

Look into My eyes. You will see yourself being loved, cared for, and restored. My eyes are for you; never against you. My eyes dissolve fear, doubt, and terror. My eyes break emotional chains and mental strongholds. My eyes are pools of love; come and take a swim in My love. The waters have healing powers. My eyes birth truth in you. They lead you away from danger and into a secure, hiding place, an impregnable fortress of peace. My eyes heal the memories of hate and prejudices. They unlock the secrets of love and intimacy. My eyes are never off of you. I am always watching over you, making sure the road you are on is safe. I go ahead of you, removing the dangers from your road. I take care of those I love. I keep My eyes fixed on your destiny. I know how to get you to your destination. My eyes see everything at once, the past, present, and future. Look into My eyes and find yourself.

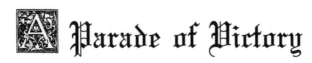 Parade of Victory

2 Corinthians 2:14
Now thanks be unto God, which always causeth us
to triumph in Christ, and maketh manifest the
savour of his knowledge by us in every place.
KJV

Let the parade of victory begin. Climb aboard and let Me take you on a tour of victory where no torment can play its devilish song in your head, where no weaknesses passed down to you through generations and relatives can change your destiny. A parade of victory is your inheritance. Stand and behold Me, your Victor. Let Me play the songs of victory for you. I have written every victory melody, and each song has your name written into it. No defeat for you. No sounds of being rejected or abandoned. No screeching hearts and no mocking laughter around you. Only the liberating sounds of a victory parade. There is no discouragement in a life of victory. No witches, manipulators, or distorters allowed. Take a trip with Me. Let Me be your victory guide. Spend your life smiling, laughing, and helping others into the victory parade.

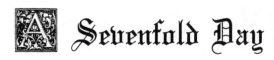 A Sevenfold Day

Luke 7:50
And he said to the woman, Thy faith
hath saved thee; go in peace.
KJV

Today your faith will actually save you from circumstances and situations that you are going to face. The only thing that you are going to have when it is all over, when the dust settles, is peace. You are going to go out in peace and stand in peace because your faith will carry you and rescue you from every destruction and calamity. Now you will have the peace and freedom that comes from My own hand—the peace of being delivered from every snare. No matter what you face today, the enemy's plans will blow up in his face and you will stand there with all his spoil. Today is a sevenfold return day. Be prepared and get ready; great things are going to happen! Drink in the knowledge of My forgiveness and heal the bitter pools in people's hearts. Enjoy My abiding presence upon you and walk in the realization of My power. Revel in the sweetness of communion with Me. Celebrate each soul that you introduce to Me and practice surrendering your will to Me when you don't want to. Let your life be a living sacrifice all day long, for this is the highest form of worship you can offer.

Before You Call, I Will Answer

Isaiah 65:24
Before you call, I will answer
and while you are yet speaking, I will hear.
Author's Paraphrase

No more waiting. No more delays. No more being put on hold. The time has come to hear the sound of "Hello" and "Yes." I am anxious to answer your prayers, even what you think and feel. I want your prayers to be like trophies sitting on My mantle, like stars shining in My universe. Your prayers are My pearls; they light up heaven. When you pray, you tell the universe you trust Me. You sound the trumpet heard around the world. Righteous prayers are like bells played around the clock. Those who ring the bells are highly respected and honored in heaven. The sound of your prayer bells scatters your enemies. When they hear you pray, their weapons explode in their hands. Their schemes dissolve, and their curses evaporate. They are left naked, unprotected, and exposed. Your holy prayers are the bullets of your gun, made by God. They are lethal to the enemies of the cross, and they open the treasure cities of heaven. Sound the call and alert the people that the storehouses of heaven are open! Gather the people together and raid My storehouses. The doors are open and everything belongs to you.

ntil You Look Like Me

2 Corinthians 3:18
But we all, with open face beholding as in a
glass the glory of the Lord, are changed into the
same image from glory to glory, even as by
the Spirit of the Lord.
KJV

I will never stop changing you. Until you look like Me, I will never stop helping you understand who I am. I will never forsake you or abandon you in the middle of a trial, test, or crisis. I am not capable of betrayal. I will never walk away from you. Know this, repeat this, and write this down: I will never stop blessing you until you look like Me. I will never stop removing your flaws and healing your wounds until you look like Me. I will never grow tired of listening to you or grow weary of your requests and petitions until you look like Me. I will never stop answering your prayers and showing Myself strong on your behalf until you look like Me. I will never stop increasing your God-wealth and multiplying the resources of your righteousness until you look like Me. I will never stop blessing your daily life with love, joy, and peace. I will never, ever stop being all you need until you look like Me.

Failure's Farewell

Psalm 25:9-10
The meek will he guide in judgment: and the meek
will he teach his way. All the paths of the Lord are mercy and truth
unto such as keep his covenant and his testimonies.
KJV

Do not fear failure. Do not allow failure's undermining thoughts to lodge in your mind. Use failure as a step to come closer to Me. Use failure as a ladder to climb into My will for your life. Failure's farewell is here. Get up every time. Never quit. Only in quitting can Satan rule your life. If you say no to failure, it will walk away from your life one day soon. You will see failure no more. Each area of your life deserves a chance at grace, mercy, and empowerment. Don't build your house on yesterday's mistakes. Don't lay the foundations of your life with the sand of your failures' memories. Use them to motivate you to succeed. Remember, with Me you are a majority. With Me, you hold the keys of power and success. Remind yourself that He who dwells in Me cannot fail permanently, cannot be overcome, defeated, or wiped out. I am eternal, everlasting, and unconquerable. I am your victory. Hold this banner of truth high. Wave it for the whole world to see. Say farewell to failure's songs.

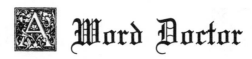 Word Doctor

Luke 21:15
For I will give you a mouth and wisdom, which
all your adversaries shall not be able to gainsay nor resist.
KJV

A word doctor is one whose lips have been touched by My hand. They speak words that heal broken hearts. They repair the shattered lives and refresh the thirsty and dry. A word doctor has special powers of repairing what could not be repaired. Word doctors carry disease-killing medicine in their words. Their tongue is a sword of deliverance for the oppressed and enslaved. One word from a word doctor and the sick are made well. Use your words as arrows of medicine. I have empowered you with holy and sacred words. Speak life; say what the lonely heart needs to hear. Never say what you feel. Say what I say. You are a word doctor. Repair the breaches of the soul. Rebuild the broken walls of the personality. Comfort those who have lost their hearts. Speak words that contain life, power, and health. Use your tongue as a weapon to destroy the mental strongholds in people's lives. I created everything with My words. Now speak life into the voids of death and change the destiny of people forever. Practice what you are.

Till the Very End

John 13:1
Jesus knew his time had come and he
loved his own till the very end.
Author's Paraphrase

You are skilled in what I have called you to do. I have anointed you
with great expertise in your job, at home, and in the work of the
kingdom. In all matters that you are faced with, you are competent and
well able to perform extraordinarily. I will begin to give you songs
in the night that will delight your soul and rid you of all anxiety and
tormenting fears. Don't wait to do what I have put in your heart. If it
is good, then do it, say it, and live it. Don't hesitate. Break all the false
allegiances of your life. Sever the chains that bind you to the past. You
have a lot of work to do for Me. The healing balm is in your hand; use
it! Stop those who prey upon the weak. Strengthen the helpless. Use
the wealth and power that I will give you to help the orphan, support
the widow, and feed the poor. Chase down the lost to the very gates of
hell if necessary. Never give up on anyone. I never do. Remember you
have My love living inside of you, the same love that keeps loving till
the very end.

#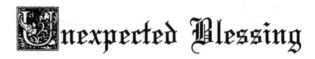

Psalm 119:9
Wherewithal shall a young man cleanse his way?
by taking heed thereto according to thy word.
KJV

Because you keep your way pure and do those things that the Word commands and you refuse to stray from the Word, your unexpected blessings will manifest themselves shortly. Because you recount My words with your lips and the relevancy of My Word, you will rejoice in your heart as one who finds great treasure. Because you daily give time to the Word and are careful not to neglect it, I will give you revelation knowledge to change your world and expand your horizons. Only good things are prepared for you, things that you cannot imagine. Long life and years of pleasure, peace, and rewards will come to you. You will be consumed with a desire for My Word; it will go before you, breaking curses. All scorn and contempt are removed from you. Mockers and slanderers lose their voice, and you stand untouched by evil. This will be your portion: to live in unexpected blessings.

The Trusting Soul

Psalm 37:39
But the salvation of the righteous is of the Lord:
he is their strength in the time of trouble.
KJV

Your salvation and deliverance come directly from Me. Because you have chosen to trust and rely on Me, I will deliver you from every trap of man, every scheme of Satan, and make sure you come forth smelling like a rose. No trouble shall stick to you. You will be covered in oil, which will make it impossible for your enemies to lay their hands on you. Health, wealth, and well-being shall surround you. Every devious, diabolical scheme will be exposed and destroyed. Your path is the path of life where there are no rocks, ditches, or traps. Your road shall be easy to travel on. Remember that a trusting soul always takes refuge in Me, but a tortured soul hides from Me. You are a triumphant soul, ready to sing the songs of life. You and death have nothing in common now. Trust Me and put your hand in Mine. Lay your heart at My feet. Surrender your thoughts to Me. Trust what you do not see; trust and jump off the cliff of faith. Live like a hero. Act like a champion. Think like a saint. Love like the redeemed. This is the food of a trusting soul.

When Your Barns Are Full

Proverbs 3:10
So shall thy barns be filled with plenty, and
thy presses shall burst out with new wine.
KJV

No more empty pockets or delayed breakthroughs. The day of abundance is upon you. Your barns of love will be full. The love you have needed will appear. The financial miracles will no longer be out of reach. The life of true fulfillment will embrace you. The walls of resistance in every area of your life will start to crumble. I will show you My loving-kindness and tender mercies. You will not look to the right or left for the sound of destruction because it will not come near you. Instead, you will hear the sound of good news and release. The result of your new inherited blessings is a larger heart for the hurting and the poor. You are called to be an emancipator, a conqueror of evil, a provider for the hungry soul, and a witness for Me. Take your mantle and provide for others. Part the seas and lead people across to their places of provision. You will never need to worry about paying your bills or lacking any natural provision. I will take care of you more than you could take care of yourself. I will fill the barns of your heart with wisdom, understanding, and the fear of the Lord.

Living in Full View

Ephesians 1:18
The eyes of your understanding being enlightened;
that ye may know what is the hope of his calling...
KJV

I see you completely. I observe the ticking of your heart. I hold you in My hand. The light is about to be turned on. Every mystery in your life will be explained because of this new insight. Your path will reveal itself, and your choices will stand up and reveal themselves to you. You will know the hope of your calling and the power that has been invested in you. Your full inheritance will be revealed. Therefore, stand up and fight! Claim what belongs to you! Submit to the searching power of My Word. Let it adjust you. Let it save you from all the leeches of this life. Let it keep you from the power of the world. Let Me energize you with wonderworking faith and baptize you in the resurrection power of My Spirit. Can anyone prevent Me from doing for you what I have promised? Not now. Not ever. Riches beyond your imagination await you. Inside My Holy place are unfathomable secrets that men have searched for their whole lives. Open eyes lead to open hearts, and open hearts lead to Me. I am your Reward and Portion.

 piritual Immunity

Isaiah 54:17
No weapon that is formed against thee shall
prosper; and every tongue that shall rise against
thee in judgment thou shalt condemn…
KJV

All of this week you shall have victory in your life. You shall not be offended, nor stumble over people's behavior. Your finances shall increase, and you will come out of debt. Your mind shall be at peace—undisturbed peace. Every circumstance shall conform to My plan. Your body shall be healed through the Holy Name of Jesus, and waves of encouragement shall show up at your door. I place a gift of impassioned intercession upon you. Now you will see the curses, plagues, iniquities, and infirmities stop, and like Phineas who drove his spear through the devil's advocates, you will wave My spear in the face of the enemy and kick him out of your family. I will give you great and divine interventions. Spiritual immunity from the enemies' weapons is yours. Curses cannot descend on your house. Disease cannot find a home in your body. Torment cannot get past the door of your mind. Fear cannot live hidden within your emotions. Charge at your enemy. He cannot withstand My power in you.

othing Is Too Difficult

Jeremiah 32:17
Ah Lord God! ...there is nothing too hard for thee.
KJV

This is your breakthrough day. Your enemies who come against you will scatter before you, and your impossible problems I will turn into miracles. Nothing is too difficult for Me. No matter what you are going through, whether in body, soul, spirit, relationships, finances, or circumstances, all of it bows to Me because I specialize in things thought impossible. Expect a lifetime of grace, a future full of guidance, and an eternity of glory. Expect all this with no weeping.
Let mercy and truth be your daily song, wisdom your companion, peace and justice your holy banners, and My Word your prosperity and your gift to the world. From now on, everywhere you look there will be amazing breakthroughs. I will take you to places that you thought were unreachable. I will use you in ways you thought were impossible. And I will change you in ways you thought you were unchangeable. Nothing is impossible for Me.

Even Deserts Are My Opportunities

Isaiah 51:3
For the Lord comforts Zion; he comforts all her
waste places and makes her wilderness like Eden, her desert
like the garden of the Lord; joy and gladness will be found in her,
thanksgiving and the voice of song.
ESV

The desert shall be like a garden to you, not a place of heat, stress, and torment. Even deserts are My opportunities. Your doubts will vanish today; your self-doubt will be a laughing matter. You will see what I can do to your desert. Even your friends will notice the difference. Come to Me, spend time alone with Me, pour out your heart to Me — the good, the bad, and the ugly. I already know it all anyway. It is not for My benefit but for yours. You see, I can only change what you reveal, not what you conceal. I am fortifying you like a stone wall. I speak life, wealth, and health to you. I break all forms of poverty over you now. You will be known as My object of compassion. Your true identity has been hidden beneath a mountain of uncertainties. Now the negatives of life will become stepping-stones into your destiny. Day by day, the spiritual you will emerge like a butterfly from its cocoon. And with each struggle you go through, your strength will double and a new color in your wing will appear. Fight and take flight.

The Journey of Life

Exodus 33:14-15
And he said, My presence shall go with thee, and
I will give thee rest. And he said unto him, If thy presence go not with
me, carry us not up hence.
KJV

Rest. How long have you needed it? The rest of My Spirit cannot be disturbed or stolen; it is immovable. Your body, soul, and spirit need My rest like the soil from the plow. In your daily grind and stressful routines, My presence will be with you relaxing and massaging your spiritual muscles, relieving your stress, and removing the toxins from your soul. This renewal is to ensure your future victories. I am purging iniquity from your family to set them on a sure foundation to build their future on the unmovable Rock of Ages. I am preparing you to be a weapon for Me. I am developing your character day by day so you will last and survive throughout your life. Your new address will be My house, and your provisions are already waiting for you. Take what you need for your journey. The journey of life requires that I go with you, in the form of My presence. I will be there through every battle. I will stand on the mountain giving you direction, telling you where to turn and what to say. You will never be alone; not now, not here, not ever. This I promise you.

he Healing Spring

Psalm 52:8
But I am like a green olive tree in the house of God:
I trust in the mercy of God for ever and ever.
KJV

There is a Treasure City for those who hunger and thirst for it. For those who are not content with what they already have, hunger is the key that unlocks the door to heaven's oil. Oil is a natural healer. Olive oil restores the heart and digestive system. You will now be able to walk in My heart, and you will not miss My will nor have problems digesting My Word. Like an olive tree, you will stand tall and ready for anybody who comes to receive from your healing branches. Healing will break out in every area of your life. You are just passing through the situation you are in. You are not permanently stationed there. Pack your bags for a glorious journey with Me. I will be your tour guide. First, we go to the Healing Spring to restore you. Then, to the Fountain of Life to fill you. Next, to the Cleaning Streams to wash you. Then, to My House so we can get to know each other. And finally, to the Treasure City where all your dreams come true. No rejection can live here. No darkness, pain, sorrow, or failure is allowed within its walls. Trust is the soul of the city; therefore, trust. Always trust.

The Tattered Coat

Genesis 37:3
Now Israel loved Joseph more than all
his children,because he was the son of his old age:
and he made him a coat of many colours.
KJV

Each person on earth is wearing some kind of coat that defines them. For most, the coat is tattered and torn. It has seen a lot of hard times and long, emotional journeys. The coat tells the world where they have been and who they are. Each tear reveals something about the person, and it gives insight into their true character. It tells whether the person can be trusted or if they should be watched. No two coats are the same; each person has his or her own coat. I am the Tailor of heaven, and I replace tattered coats. I do not repair the tears in the old coat, but I replace them completely. When I am done with people's coats, they are unrecognizable. You see, I bought these new coats with a very costly price. No one else could have bought them, for only I had the price that was needed. Now, anyone who comes to Me as their Tailor can receive their new coat that never wears out, never tears, and fits all sizes. Wear My coat, and you will look brand new with no memories of the old, lonely, dirt roads you have walked. Now, put on My coat, and let's go somewhere you have never been before.

ever Doubt

Psalm 23:5
Thou preparest a table before me in the presence of mine
enemies: thou anointest my head with oil; my cup runneth over.
KJV

Never, ever doubt Me! I will feed you from the ovens of heaven. Your food will have such power and spiritual energy that one crumb from My table will last you forty days. Never doubt that I will help you out of every trouble that comes upon you unexpectedly. Never doubt that I will save you from yourself and your enemies. I will never let them touch you or hurt you in any way. Never doubt that I will love you in spite of your failures and mistakes. Never doubt that I will get you out of all debt and tight places. I am very, very, very rich. I have enough gold and silver to pay off the debt of every person, nation, and country. I own the printing press. So now it's time to relax and pass on this knowledge. Give it away to others as easily as I have given it to you. Your giving reveals your Source. Your giving tells the world Who you trust.

ron Cages

Isaiah 45:2
I will go before thee, and make the crooked
places straight: I will break in pieces the gates of brass,
and cut in sunder the bars of iron.
KJV

With each day you spend in My embrace, the iron cages that life has
built around you begin to crumble. No cage can hold Me. No iron bars
can keep Me from reaching you. I am not limited by matter, space,
time, or emotional walls. The reach of My embrace encompasses the
universe. I hold every created thing in the hollow of My hand. My grip
is sure, My reach eternal, and My power unlimited. It's time to relax
and stop your business. Let Me refresh you from the wars you have
fought. Let Me replenish your natural and spiritual resources. Let Me
carry you to the mountaintop and show you your future with Me. You
will see no cages, prisons, or jailers, no slippery slopes, invisible traps,
and no dangerous predators waiting in the shadows. You will not see
ominous clouds hanging over you. What cages they built to hold you
in are now broken. What limitations you had around you are gone.
Mount upon My words. Use My promises like wings and fly out of the
valleys and shadows. Go discovering.

ith Every Cell

Romans 5:8
But God commendeth his love toward us, in that,
while we were yet sinners, Christ died for us.
KJV

Each moment of loneliness has been the voice of your heart crying out for Me. I placed a longing and yearning in every heart. It will cry out with needs and longings. All the efforts that people make to satisfy their longings apart from Me only make longings more intense and acute. How much do I love you? More than all the friends you could ever have, more than a million mothers and fathers, more than all the husbands and wives, more than anything good you can imagine. I love you with perfect singularity. I love individually. I love you just for you, just the way you are, unrefined and unfinished. I love you before time began, before you took your first breath, and after you take your last. I love you perfectly and forever. No one else will ever love you with every cell, fiber, and breath like I do.

The Thieves' Den

Proverbs 6:30
Men do not despise a thief, if he steal to
satisfy his soul when he is hungry.
KJV

I will catch every thief of your past, present, and future. They will never be able to steal from you again. They have taken enough from you, and now I take My revenge on them. They will repay you sevenfold. I will return every second of love, peace, and joy. I will restore every memory, every redeemable relationship, and every piece of your heart. All the damage to your soul will be restored. The genuine, real, unaffected you will be revealed, healed, and sealed with love's songs. I will repair the breaches in your mind and personality. The defects and deformities in your character will disappear; your words will be arrows of healing, your deeds discoveries of gold for Me. Your acts of love will fill your family tree. Everyone related to you will be enriched by your life and your love. The thieves' den will be exposed and emptied; your thieves handcuffed and put in prison for the length of your life. Live freely and unhindered. Rule and reign in this life I have given you.

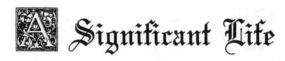 A Significant Life

Psalm 37:23
The steps of a good man are ordered by the Lord:
and he delighteth in his way.
KJV

The birth of a significant life—what value I have placed on each life. To see the birth of a truly great person is My daily joy. You are that person. Yes, you. All the days of your life are numbered and ordered for greatness. I created you for great things—exploits, mighty deeds, the taking of cities, the conquering of giants, the destroying of strongholds, the releasing of the captives, and the healing of the broken hearts you meet along the road of your journey. Your destiny does not lie with the obscure and insignificant procrastinators. Your road is not the road of smallness and obscurity. There are no invisible wrecks ahead for you, no calamities or tragedies approaching you. Your best days are ahead of you, and your influence will glow like the brightness of the sun. Give Me your every moment, and I will conduct your life into perfect harmony.

The Green Light

Isaiah 56:5
...I will give them an everlasting name,
that shall not be cut off.
KJV

All of your life people have been mocking and resisting you, trying to cage you in and put you in limited boxes, categorizing you in some negative place, saying you can't do this or that, and telling you to stop trying because you are not gifted or talented enough. Rebel against their nos and embrace My yes. My big, giant green light is in front of you. I want you to try everything you can dream of. Try it now; jump off that Faith Cliff. Take risks; go where no one else has ever gone. Invent new things; make a million dollars a day. Live big—as big as you believe I am. Remember, I created the universe with My words. Now take My word of "yes" for you and create the "yes" life you want. Throw out the doubts, fears, and limitations and grow your wings. Fly, fly, fly into the uncharted universe of life before you. Show everybody what I can do in them and through them.

rotection's Name

Isaiah 41:10
Fear thou not; for I am with thee: be not dismayed;
for I am thy God: I will strengthen thee; yea, I will
help thee; yea, I will uphold thee with the
right hand of my righteousness.
KJV

My names are Safety, Security, Peace, and Protection. There is nothing to fear in your trip through life. Nothing is waiting to devour you. No one is hiding in the shadows. There are no ghosts that will suddenly appear from yesterday's train wrecks. There are no bad events on the horizon. I have hidden you inside of Me. Can anyone harm or damage you with words or deeds? Can any missile accidentally slip through and still hurt you? No. Absolutely not. Be calm and at peace. Stay in peace today. Your family is safe, your body is safe, your relationships are safe, and all circumstances are now under My control. Trust Me with unconditional, emotional commitment. Do not resist Me with fear or doubt. Say this: "I am safe, secure, protected, and guarded. All is well with my soul. I live to rule and reign in this life. I surrender to my God and Maker who loves me perfectly. He will keep me perfect today. I am safe." Say it, believe it, know it, live it.

The Narrow Road

Matthew 7:13-14
Enter ye in at the strait gate: for wide is the gate, and broad is the way,
that leadeth to destruction, and many there be which go in thereat.
KJV

There are only two roads you can take: the narrow and the broad.
One has many games, players, joyous sounds, options and churches,
every kind of experience, every possible pleasure your mind can
imagine. But this seducing, loved, overwhelming road leads to one
place regardless of which path on the road is chosen—destruction.
That is the end. I want you to choose the small and narrow road where
there is only room for two, Me and you. This road is clear, quiet,
simple. All the road signs are easy to read; there are no surprises or
predators on it. With every mile you tread, you become stronger,
wiser, and compassionate. Your possessions become less important,
your priorities change, and love is your daily guide showing you
the way to heaven. No fears are allowed, no wounded souls can stay
wounded, and no sad memories of failure or disaster are allowed. No
pits, ditches, or landslides. No dark clouds, tornadoes, or spiritual
hurricanes. I will never leave your side on this narrow road. I will be
with you day and night, always with you—everywhere, every day,
always together.

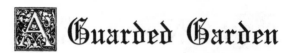 Guarded Garden

Song of Solomon 4:12
A garden inclosed is my sister, my spouse;
a spring shut up, a fountain sealed.
KJV

The worms are crawling around. They think they can reach your garden. How foolish they are. How little they are; how weak and useless they are. They are trying so hard to reach your ripened fruit. You see, they live on what you have already grown and finished, that which is fully developed and ripe in your life. They are the spoilers longing for the taste of forbidden fruit. But they have forgotten that you are My private garden and that I am your Keeper. As your Guardian I stand watch at the door day and night. I guarantee the planting, weeding, and harvest of your garden. Oh, how beautiful your fruit will be this year! Better than all the other years put together—big, juicy, and ripe. How much delight it will bring to those who buy it and eat it. It will refresh them and restart the weary hearts. Your fruit will satisfy the hungry soul and restore strength to the weak. Those on long journeys will sit under the shade of your trees, rest, and revive themselves. Yes, you are My guarded garden—untouched, undamaged, and flourishing with buds, blossoms, and fruit.

ime for a Jailbreak

Acts 16:26
And suddenly there was a great earthquake,
so that the foundations of the prison were shaken:
and immediately all the doors were opened, and
every one's bands were loosed.
KJV

Get your gear ready. Find all of your belongings. Find every precious thing to you and pack it because it's time for a jailbreak! You are being completely freed from all imprisoning thoughts, passions, and desires. Even your dreams will go free. Your life is about to soar into its greatness. The foundation of the prison house will crumble today. The bars will melt, the jailor will disappear, and the liberator's trumpet will sound for you. Notice that your freedom becomes your ministry. Where you are freed, you free. Where you are healed, you heal. And where you are restored, you restore. I never waste a life. I never lose anything precious. I keep and preserve. I improve and replenish. I heal and mend; so will you. Close your eyes and forget the jail of life. Forget the jailor's clanging keys. Let your mind be erased and reprogrammed with life. The captive has become the liberator. That's you, and that's it.

ut Me

Psalm 139:1-2
O Lord, thou hast searched me, and known me. Thou knowest my
downsitting and mine uprising, thou understandest my thought afar off.
KJV

No one but Me knows what makes you work or how to fix you. No one but Me knows the answers to all of your questions and can heal your wounded heart. No one but Me sees the true, finished you, or hears your unspoken prayers. No one but Me remembers your best wishes and secret dreams. No one but Me will rescue you always, everywhere, and every day. No one but Me loves you always, purely, and unconditionally. No one but Me will bless you over and over and over again. No one but Me will stay with you through thick and thin and lift you out of every trouble and pit. No one but Me is preparing a place for you in heaven and writing your name in My Book of Life. No one knows your pain and heartache like I do. No one but Me feels your soul tighten when poisonous words are spoken to you. No one but Me anticipates your heartbeat and calculates your victories. No one but Me stands by your bed watching over you as you sleep. No one but Me holds your heart in their hands while it skips a beat for the sorrows of those you love. No one but Me mends the wounds, heals the brokenness, and restores the lost. No one but Me will stand with you and hold your hand while you cross through the Golden Gates of Eternity.

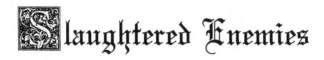laughtered Enemies

Psalm 41:11
By this I know that thou favourest me, because
mine enemy doth not triumph over me.
KJV

Your enemies are stepping stones to Me. They can make or break you depending on how you perceive them. Give them no airtime in your thought life. Ignore their insults and verbal attacks. Use them as motivational fuel and be what they say you are not. Become what they say you cannot become. Everyone who loves Me truly, wholly and completely has enemies. But I will slaughter their weapons and make them powerless against you. I rescue you, and you will rescue them. I deliver you, and you will deliver them. Some of your enemies will become your closest friends after My love reaches them. Their hearts will change, and they will remember how you treated them. In their journey with Me, you will become their mentor. Through your life of Christlikeness, they will be liberated from their demonic chains and follow in My footsteps. They will also set others free, and the unending cycle of love will continue. Waiting at the end are your amazing rewards.

at Catchers

Psalm 141:10
Let the wicked fall into their own nets,
whilst that I withal escape.
KJV

Rats are gutter dwellers. They love cold, dark, dirty places. They love to steal food from others, they can chew through the power connections of your life, and they leave you weak and powerless. They die at high altitudes and cannot take the stress of thin air. Therefore, rise and fly high into Me. Become unreachable to the rats in your life. Rats always abandon the ship; they forsake, and they are betrayers. They look out for themselves. They are self-preservationists before all other things. They spread all types of diseases with their bite. They eat and steal. All good and precious things are their targets. There are speaking rats that will try and poison you with their words, twisting truth to meet their sick desires. You are a rat catcher, and for this blessing you receive a double portion of joy. The double is yours— double love, joy, peace, life, strength, and favor. Double intimacy, knowledge, power, and double portions of Me. Live a rat-free life. Deliver the rat's prisoner, and let your days be filled with freedom and ease of spirit.

 ivine Outbreaks

Mark 2:2
And straightway many were gathered together,
insomuch that there was no room to receive them,
no, not so much as about the door: and he
preached the word unto them.
KJV

You were not born for smallness. You were not created for a limited life. There is no end to your potential, no end to what you can accomplish with your gifts. Dream a little, and I will make you live a lot. I have planned for some divine outbreaks in your life. There will be times when it will seem as if nothing is happening, and then suddenly an outbreak will start in every direction you look. Blessing will begin to break out, and no one will be able to stop these outbreaks. I started them, and I am the only One who can stop them. Be assured I will not do that. Outbreaks of money are coming, outbreaks of family revival, outbreaks of love and restoration, outbreaks of My presence and favor with you. Yours is the life of continual increase. Embrace it and grow strong.

The Anchor Smith

Hebrews 6:18
That by two immutable things, in which it was
impossible for God to lie, we might have a strong
consolation, who have fled for refuge to lay hold
upon the hope set before us.
KJV

The unsteadiness and instability that was in your relatives' lives will never touch you, for I am the Anchor Smith. I make unmovable, unshakeable anchors. My anchors hold any ship, any size, anywhere. Let the winds blow, and let the rains come. Let the floods raise their ugly heads, and your anchor will hold. Let the sand lift and move. Let the world cry out in instability. It doesn't matter; your anchor is divine. Your stability is eternal. Nothing can move you from My place of security and strength. There are no shipwrecks coming for you. No unexpected disasters, no breaking, crushing storms. I have preprogrammed your anchor to hold you safe through it all. Stand still, stand confident, and rescue everyone who is not on your boat, perishing all around you. Do this, and I will be very pleased with you. Love them as much as I have loved you.

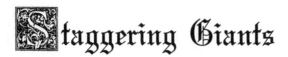 taggering Giants

Psalm 18:17
He delivered me from my strong enemy, and from
them which hated me: for they were too strong for me.
KJV

Your giants are staggering. They are losing their footing and beginning
to stumble and become confused. Their equilibrium is faltering; soon
and very soon they will fall forever. Their voices will disappear from
your head. No more reminders of the powers and strength over you.
No more mockery and laughing at your weakness and compromise.
Those days are over! Those giants are nothing more than midgets
before Me. They quiver at My name. They run and hide in the
shadows when I pass by. Their power over your wants and desires is
disappearing forever. Soon your whole body, soul, and spirit will be
perfectly giant-free. There will only be trophies of My grace and love,
reminders that the bigger they are, the easier they fall. Keep these
promises in your heart. Break all emotional ties and addictions to
these giants, and let Me replace them with visible advancements and
tangible promotions. This is My plan and your future.

Bag of Magic Tricks

2 Corinthians 1:1
Paul, an apostle of Jesus Christ by the will of God, and
Timothy our brother, unto the church of God which is at Corinth, with
all the saints which are in all Achaia.
KJV

People trust in their bag of magic tricks: emotional blackmail, threats, intimidation, verbal abuse, flattery, pressure, pleasure, false promises, slander, pleading. They drink and use guilt like a sword to control and manipulate. They devise scenarios of fear and then feed them to you for breakfast. They use their domineering personalities to overpower others, yet they are never willing to surrender to Me. They are snakes in the grass and black widow spiders ready to devour their prey caught in their web. They cannot and will not be tamed. They are rabid dogs looking only for food. But you are the deliverer of the captives! Your power is in your mercy. Your strength is in your fearlessness. You will face them down like the lion I have made you, and they will see that against Me they are fleas on a dog. You will show them the highway to heaven, My City. They will be restored, delivered, and healed. The waters of Zion's river heal every known and unknown disease. Whoever walks into its waters is transformed forever. All the guilt and shame is cleansed away. They stand anew with no residue of yesterday's mistakes. This is your life's assignment.

An Ever-Present Fixture in My Sight

Daniel 4:35
And all the inhabitants of the earth are reputed as nothing:
and he doeth according to his will in the army of heaven,
and among the inhabitants of the earth: and none can stay his hand,
or say unto him, What doest thou?
KJV

I dwell in the sky that hangs above you. I see all things simultaneously. I behold all of creation. Nothing escapes My eyes. You are an ever-present fixture in My sight. I am going to release the sweet aromas of heaven into your life. Years of waiting for My promises to be fulfilled are at hand. Open up the doors of your heart. Sanctify yourself with prayer and fasting. Turn the clock back. Regain your lost territory; it belongs in your hand. Claim life. I will remove the steel gates. The bars of iron shall melt away. I will send rivers of oil into your veins. I will heal your eyes to see the invisible realities of My kingdom. I will restore your armor and place a destiny sword in your hand. With it you will vanquish My enemies and distribute My blessing all over the world. You will see what I see. You will feel what I feel, and you will love what I love. Live eternally in My view.

Time Is Ticking

Ephesians 5:16
Redeeming the time, because the days are evil.
KJV

I live outside of time. I am Time itself. All things are in harmony with Me. Like a perfect watch, the universe keeps time with Me. I know what you need and when you need it. Keep in step with Me. Do what I do when I do it. Listen before you act. Drink patience; let it fill your veins. It will always serve you well. Quietly go about following My footsteps. Each step brings you closer to My plan for you. Drop the bad habits. Discipline your life, each area and every detail. Curb your appetites and let Me replace them with the best hungers. Time is ticking. Redeem it, use it, discipline it, and let it serve you. Come and live outside of time with Me. Let Me show you the secrets of My kingdom. We have much to do, you and Me. Let's get on with it.
Time is ticking.

arry Your Medicine with You

Isaiah 53:3
He is despised and rejected of men; a man of sorrows,
and acquainted with grief: and we hid as it were our faces from him;
he was despised, and we esteemed him not.
KJV

Never leave your house without your medicine bag. It contains powerful healing medicines. You are one of My doctors. You are a traveling doctor, one who goes from life to life, sharing your knowledge of My healing medicine. Never be ashamed of My healing medicines. They can save the lives of drifting men and women, forsaken hearts, broken hearts, twisted hearts, and deformed souls. These healing medicines were bought with a great price. They are not the fruit of man's thinking or man's fake, plastic inventions. These medicines were made by Me out of a heart of love for all mankind. I hate disease. I hate suffering. I hate broken souls and shipwrecked lives. All of My medicines repair what is unable to be repaired. They replace the health that has been lost. Use your medicine daily; first, on yourself, and second, on everyone else. Your destiny is to be a conduit of My healing power. Love the way I love, and the medicine will flow from your words, dissolving the stone mountains in people's hearts.

Come to My healing fountain and drink from it. Leave your past behind. What you were is not what you are. What you did is not what you will do. You are a doctor working for Me.

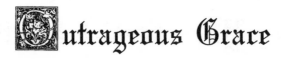utrageous Grace

2 Corinthians 9:8
And God is able to make all grace abound toward you; that ye, always
having all sufficiency in all things, may abound to every good work.
KJV

My grace is outrageous in its supreme power to save, heal, and deliver
people from their weaknesses, failures, and mistakes. Outrageous
grace cries out for mercy for the forsaken, abandoned, and unwanted
souls—those who have thrown away their help over and over again
and have shunned and rejected love and mercy, believing it to be
corrupted by the touch of man and defiled by impure motives and
diabolical intentions. Outrageous grace can reach the unreachable soul.
It can restore hope where there is no hope. It can produce a harvest
from a dead field. It makes water flow from a dead well and makes
the sun shine through a storm. This grace is yours. It is available
for you at every trial, through every burden, and in the moments of
solitude. Spend this grace; use it. Don't waste any more time trusting
the chariots of Egypt. Lift yourself by lowering your heart. I dwell
with the lowly and with those of a broken spirit. I give grace to the
humble and support the servant. I unlock heaven's storehouses to those
whose intention is to give its contents away. Bathe in this outrageous
grace and feel My power and presence surrounding your life, encased
forever in grace.

 nlimited Resources

Philippians 4:19
But my God shall supply all your need
according to his riches in glory by Christ Jesus.
KJV

Resources are the necessary provisions you need to build your indestructible future. When you were in your mother's womb, I appointed you as an ambassador to the world and the nations. Don't limit your potential by obsessing over your limitations. Limitations are the opportunities for My grace. They are the diving board into the supernatural power of My Spirit. Those who limit Me by reducing My power change Me and, therefore, do not have Me. They only see pieces of Me instead of all of Me. Your resources include all of Me, not just a piece. Men insult Me by making Me powerless in their doctrines and beliefs. They forget that some things require supernatural resources in famine and drought. Know this: I measure the heavens with a span. I name the stars, and I know the number of hairs on your head. The nations are like a drop in the bucket, and the oceans are one tear drop. I am your Resource. I am All in All. I am your Source. I am all you need, all you will ever need, and I am all yours.

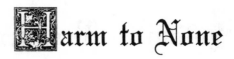arm to None

Matthew 10:6
But go rather to the lost sheep of the house of Israel.
KJV

Harm to none; help to all. This is your motto. Now take it as your own. Harm no one with words, attitudes, or deeds. Love the weak and helpless. Remember the forgotten. Nourish the starving. Feed the hungry. Claim the forsaken. Add these attributes to your spiritual arsenal, and you will be a fully functioning weapon for Me. Harm the works of darkness. Destroy the strongholds of the enemy in people's vanquished lives. Wreck the fortresses of hell and cleanse the dirty temples. Offer your gifts to mankind. Give them your time. Surrender your rights to humanity. Cherish the ugly. Embrace the worthless and carry the lame. Climb the impossible. Dress in the holy and eat the sacred. These are your resources in life. Surround yourself with like-minded people with strong faith and untainted convictions. Run your race with determination. Surrender no territory to your enemies. Never look back. Never hesitate to conquer. Take your giant's head. Wear it as a trophy for the weak to see. Remind them they too can do the same.

The Transformation of a Stone

Ephesians 4:32
And be ye kind one to another, tenderhearted, forgiving
one another, even as God for Christ's sake hath forgiven you.
KJV

The stone-hearted people of the world are your mission field. The transformation of a stone is My masterpiece of grace. I pick the hard, unreachable souls to manifest My loving-kindness. If I can change a stone into a flaming sword for Me, I can change anyone. That is My purpose and goal: Pick the worst and make the best. It is the lukewarm who are unchangeable, unreachable, and unconvertible. They are content in their slipperiness, happy in their pleasures, and satisfied with their possessions and entertainments. They live to be pleased. They live for self-indulgence. Their goal is to rest leisurely with no work, struggle, or responsibility. These are ships without a sail, hearts without a beat, and the lack of a tangible pulse. I empower you to be anointed to change the stone-hearted people around you through prayer, fasting, and a life of love. They will never stand a chance. Rip them from the jaws of death. Tear them from the mouth of hell. Rescue them from themselves. The goal is a transformed heart. Every stone is a potential soldier for Me. Remember, you were once a stone, too. Now you are a tenderhearted hero of the lost.

he Hungry Heart

Matthew 5:8
Blessed are the pure in heart: for they shall see God.
KJV

Beware of hunger thieves. These are thieves designed to steal your hunger for Me, My Word, and My will for your life. Only through you can I feed and nourish the hungry heart. People who have lost their hunger eventually lose Me. They wake up one day and I am forgotten; My face is no longer familiar. My desires no longer make sense, My Word is no longer relevant, and My ways are strange and out-of-date. Beware of these hunger thieves. They come in every form and fashion—small and great, ugly and beautiful, forceful and gentle, obvious and hidden. Stop them every time you see them. Have mercy on them. They promise you freedom and pleasure but only yield you bondage and poverty. I have a universe of wisdom, treasure, and knowledge to give you. I want you to see all I have bought for you. I have entire treasure houses full of joyous discoveries since you have waited your whole life. Hunger for Me every day. Do whatever it takes to be continually hungry. I cannot resist hunger and thirst. I must satisfy it.

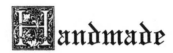andmade

Psalm 139:14
I will praise thee; for I am fearfully and wonderfully made:
marvelous are thy works; and that my soul knoweth right well.
KJV

You have been handmade. I have personally designed every cell of your body, soul, and spirit. If I have handmade every cell, don't you think I know you better than anyone does? And if I know you perfectly, I can fix you perfectly. I can make every aspect of you work in perfect harmony with Me. If you are in harmony with Me, there will be no hindrance that can stop My will in your life from marching forward. If you are unhindered, you will change the world. Your destiny has never been normal or common; you were born to be a world changer, a disciple, a mentor, and a teacher of the lost and poor. Your job is to empower people and enable them to succeed in their callings. Appreciate yourself. Appreciate what I have done in you. Don't fear your flaws. They are stepping stones to your need for Me. Don't dwell on failures, weaknesses, or areas of unfinished work. Live in My hands. Stay in My image, mark yourself as a masterpiece. Stay free by remaining grateful. Handmade things last forever in the mind of the Maker.

The Miry Clay

Psalm 40:2
He brought me up also out of an horrible pit, out of
the miry clay, and set my feet upon a rock, and established my goings.
KJV

Up from the miry clay you come slowly, surely, and forever. Damaged
and broken in pieces, yet My love prevailed in you. It sustained you
through the surgeries and seasons of troubled seas when wretched
believers and serpents were in your dreams. My love was there, always
there waiting, protecting, and covering you from the storms and
winds. Now time has passed. Your feet are clean and free from the last
pieces of miry clay. Now it's time to walk, to run, and to fly. You are
ready to do what no one believes you can. Look around; can you see
these lost souls passing by you with no hope in their eyes? Aimless,
heartless, mindless souls are drifting in the treacherous ocean slowly
being pulled out to the open sea by the undercurrent of life. They are
slowly drifting away from the reach of Love's hands. Some will never
be found; they will be lost forever. Others we will find floating on their
weak life rafts. Would you rescue them for Me? Would you be My
hands? Would you throw them your lifesaver and draw them into My
boat? Will you wash their souls from that miry clay? Lift them up and
place them on that Rock of Ages. Safe, free, rescued…just like you.

Where Are Your Stretch Marks?

Matthew 14:26
And when the disciples saw him walking
on the sea, they were troubled, saying, It is a
spirit; and they cried out for fear.
KJV

Peter walked on water. Daniel slept with lions. Joseph was sold. Shadrach, Meshach, and Abednego walked into fire. David faced Goliath. Caleb killed his giants. Moses returned to Egypt. Noah built an ark. They all have stretch marks left from stretching beyond their human strength and abilities. They stretched themselves to Me, risked their lives, their health, their reputation. They challenged their doubts, defeated their objections, closed the mouth of their unbelief, and rose beyond the mobs and crowds of the world. They became heroes to their generations and heroes of the world. Today is your day to set the standard by finding where your stretch marks are. Stretch into Me. Don't look back. The voices and faces of your past are worthless to your life of stretching. Find Me. I live on the water. Don't forget to burn your boat of safety and come and live with Me out on the waters of faith.

The Key Master

Revelation 3:8
I know thy works: behold, I have set before thee an open
door, and no man can shut it: for thou hast a little strength, and hast
kept my word, and hast not denied my name.
KJV

I will open doors for you that cannot be shut. I am the Key Master. I hold in My hands every key to every important door you need opened. Prepare yourself for a year of open doors. I will open doors of fellowship with Me by teaching you My relationship secrets. You will learn how to talk to Me so I listen, how to see Me, though I am invisible. I will teach you how to feel My abiding presence and how to sense My love. I will show you the secret to vital communication and the sound of My voice. I will teach you how to listen with your inner ears. I will show you the secret to feeling My arms around your heart and the intimate words that create emotional bonding between us. I will open doors of utterance and give you a voice of authority. I will place you in front of influential people and powerful leaders. No door will be beyond your reach. I do not limit your opportunities because of your past. All things are possible if you will believe I am as good as My holy scriptures declare Me to be. I do not dwell on failure. I dwell on potential, and yours has no limit.

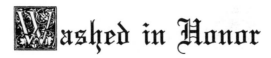ashed in Honor

1 Peter 2:17
Honour all men…
KJV

Until you are washed in honor, your potential is imprisoned, your creativity marred, and your power limited. But with honor comes riches, power, and favor. Honor is the crown on your true heart. It is what defines you in heaven. Your name is known by the honor it carries. Honor is the song of your true life. It fills heaven like the sound of a thousand birds' songs. It walks ahead of you announcing who you really are. Without honor there is no respect or self-worth. Honor is the gift you give yourself. It is the voice of your heart and the clothing of your attitudes. Honor lifts you from obscurity into prominence in My world. It is the sound of a hundred trumpets blowing, letting the world know your worth. It saves you from all corruption and protects you from the defiling forces of the world. Honor preserves your spirit, keeping it healthy and hopeful. Honor is your armor; it keeps you out of Satan's reach. It gives you immunity from his seducing spirits. It repels his fiery darts and poisonous arrows. Honor wraps itself around your heart like a shield and deflects the twisted words of the cruel and bitter. It allows you access to My rewards and gives you unlimited promotions in My kingdom. With honor dwells longevity and health. Honor is the safe house where you and I meet, exchanging trust.

Evicting Slavery

Psalm 142:7
Bring my soul out of prison, that I may praise thy name: the righteous shall compass me about; for thou shalt deal bountifully with me.
KJV

The heart of the world is a slave to Satan's pleasure pools. It is victimized daily by his cruel promises of freedom. He is the father of liars, rebels, and murderers. He creates slaves with every breath he utters. He hands out chains and torture for breakfast. He is the father of destruction. I am anointing you to evict slavery from the lives of the helpless, those who can no longer resist running or even want to. Their free will has been conquered by their chains. You are a chain breaker, a demolisher of bondage. No slave will be safe from your liberating words. Give them your power and love. Release them with the shout of triumph. Wreck the prisons of their minds. If you set their minds free, their bodies will follow. They will be liberated from within, and no one will enslave them again. The mind chain will fall under your ministry. The heart chain will melt before you. The financial chains will be permanently melted away from their bank accounts. Freedom bells will ring. Let the earth rejoice at the sound of a new liberator being born! This is your assignment.

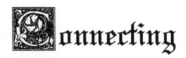onnecting

1 Corinthians 1:10
…Be perfectly joined together in the
same mind and in the same judgment.
KJV

The disconnected die a slow and agonizing death of loneliness. The secret to feeling complete and fulfilled is found in the power of connecting. If you live disconnected, you will be an empty, abandoned shell. No one will be at home when people come calling. Connecting has many secrets and advantages. No one can trust a person who cannot bond with them. It is your bonding emotionally to Me that will keep you close to Me. Your love connections are your life jackets that keep you from drowning in an ocean of sharks and predators. A deep, sincere connection between you and Me is what I want from you. Feel My love for the lost. Feel My pain for the orphan. Feel My compassion for the shepherdless, wandering souls walking like ghosts on planet Earth. Open your heart to your family; connect emotionally to each one. You cannot betray a person whose pain you feel. If you can love a dog, you can love a person. Loving is connecting. Connecting guarantees a long relationship between us. I want to be very close to you. No secret, emotional hiding places can exist between us. There must be unlimited access between us. Only then can we always be chained together with the indestructible virtues of My character. The disconnected die a slow, agonizing death of loneliness.

The Disease of Later

Proverbs 10:4
He becometh poor that dealeth with a slack hand:
but the hand of the diligent maketh rich.
KJV

Procrastination is how you steal from yourself. Never put off what needs to be said and done. With every delay you add a burden, you empower your fears, and you give chaos a chance to rule your life. The disease of "later" robs you of your opportunities and steals from your ordained harvest. Do it now. Do it with conviction and finish the unpleasant tasks that bring you to your true inheritance. Every day give yourself time to do the uncomfortable, whether it be exercise, confrontations, or boring, necessary work. Become habitually consistent like the ant. She never changes from her necessary routines that grant her life and provision. Don't be ruled by what you enjoy. My Word is necessary for you every day. Rescuing the lost is necessary. Loving the unlovely is imperative to your growth and promotion. Join hands with the uncomfortable, and success, power, and skill shall follow. Live freely while you tie yourself to godly rituals.

Into the House

1 Peter 2:5
Ye also, as living stones, are built up as a spiritual
house, an holy priesthood, to offer up spiritual sacrifices,
acceptable to God by Jesus Christ.
KJV

Come into My house where it is safe, warm, and healthy. Live with Me. Take your time exploring My house. I want you to take the whole tour. Check each room: the lighting, the furniture, and the atmosphere. You will find it perfectly suited to you. You will never need another house other than Mine. The colors are perfect for you. The kitchen has everything you enjoy eating. The temperature is perfect; the flooring is comforting to your weary feet; the beds are made for comfort; the pillows will soothe your aches and pains. Everything in My house is made especially for you. The alarm clocks are set to wake you for prayer, and the bells and chimes to remind you to sing and laugh. The birds and fish are there to help you relax and not take things too seriously. Come into My house; it's yours. I give it to you. Abandon those other futile dwellings that only confuse and torment. Hear the sound of the river running serenely through the house. It contains healing waters. Stop in now. Stay there as long as you need. There is no rent, no other tenants, and no landlord but you. Take the time to enjoy it. I will come soon to call on you and spend the day with you. I still need to show you the property and land that you own. Enjoy, enjoy, enjoy.

The Purchaser

1 Corinthians 6:20
For ye are bought with a price: therefore glorify
God in your body, and in your spirit, which are God's.
KJV

I have bought you a kingdom and purchased for you a glorious life.
I paid with My Son. He gave His life and blood to purchase for you
a destiny. It cost Us everything. The value cannot be measured; it is
beyond estimation. There is no greater treasure that you could ever
seek, find, or want. The world longs for what I have bought for you.
They spend their lives looking in all the wrong places. Life after life is
wasted, searching in the coffins of false saviors and dead saints. They
spend their life's savings traveling and digging for the elusive fountain
of youth, the holy grail, and the pot of gold at the end of the rainbow.
They die looking, when what they want and need is standing right
next to them. I am the Desire of all nations. I am the Missing Piece to
the human heart. I am the only One who can fill the black hole of the
soul. I am the Purchaser of your soul, bought and paid for with sacred
blood and perfect obedience. All you need to do is spend your life
discovering the treasure and spending your inheritance. Give it away,
and it automatically multiplies. There is an unending supply waiting
for your faith to unlock.

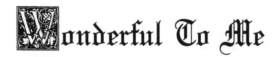onderful To Me

Jeremiah 31:3
...I have loved thee with an everlasting love:
therefore with lovingkindness have I drawn thee.
KJV

You are more than wonderful to Me. The very sight of you thrills My every cell. I delight in the sound of your voice. You are like a morning breeze to Me, like water in the desert, like rain in a drought, like a well in the wilderness, and like eyes to the blind. My thoughts are permanently addicted to you. All day, every day I think about you, how I can help you, bless you, and relieve you from burdens. Don't fear that I will ever change My mind about you because of anything you have done or said. I do not change or vary, and I am not double-minded. My love for you grows with every second of the day. I love you furiously, intensely, and unconditionally. You are wonderful to Me, a wonder of delight to My heart. Can you believe I love you perfectly, I need you completely, and I see you everywhere you go? You are never without Me, even if you forget Me. I will never forget you. I will never be too busy for you. Hear these words and believe them, or they lose their power to heal you. Trust My words and let them raise you to the mountaintop.

acred Words

Psalm 19:14
Let the words of my mouth, and the meditation of my heart, be
acceptable in thy sight, O Lord, my strength, and my redeemer.
KJV

All words bring life or death. There are no powerless words; each
word creates and produces something. With your words you can create
your world or destroy it. Words are honey or gall. Words are knives
or medicine. Words heal or wound. They bring joy or sorrow. Words
are sacred or violating. They inspire or depress. Every word flows
from a source—the source of good or evil. Words cleanse or defile.
They build or destroy. They enable or cripple. Words break or mend.
They empower or steal. They are your source to poverty or wealth,
success or failure. Therefore, tie sacred words to your neck. Engrave
My life-giving, Spirit-filled words to your heart. Memorize My words,
meditate on My words, and they will change you. Give away My
words, and they will return to you like unexpected blessings, floating
on the currents of the air. Sacred words bring love, joy, and peace.
Sacred words hold the universe together. They protect you from death
and destruction. They heal you, strengthen you, and inspire you to
dream. Sacred words unleash My wonder-working power and recreate
your personality. Therefore, speak sacred words and keep them before
you day and night. They will fill your home with light.

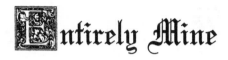 ntirely Mine

Psalm 139:13
For thou hast possessed my reins: thou hast
covered me in my mother's womb.
KJV

You are entirely, completely, and irrevocably Mine—every part of you. From the beginning, I planned you. You can never be a mistake or an accident. You were formed in detail by My hands. I made you personally. I created your heart. I molded every tiny, minuscule detail of you. I programmed you to succeed. You have yet to discover your true gifts and talents. They will amaze you and shock the world. You can never be normal or insignificant. It is impossible for you to permanently fail, lose, or stumble. Your cells are created to love Me, worship Me, adore My voice, be tuned and harmonize with My will for your life. I take joy in the sight of you. I am made happy when you realize how much you mean to Me. Others will fight for your love and affection, but only I deserve it. They will sing you their love songs, play you their music, and show you their loyalty, but only I possess eternity. I am the Beginning and the End. With Me the party never ends. I will never walk away. You see, you are entirely Mine forever, and I am entirely yours.

ebt Destroyer

Romans 13:8
Owe no man any thing, but to love one another:
for he that loveth another hath fulfilled the law.
KJV

People accumulate debt their whole lives. They pile it onto their
consciences like huge rocks and boulders on a mountaintop just
waiting for a landslide to happen. Debt is the absence of My presence,
the absence of My word and plan for your life. I will destroy all debt
and remove it from your life. I will teach you to destroy the debt
in other people's lives until you become an expert debt destroyer.
Learn at My School of Debt Destruction. Sit at My teaching table.
Let Me show you the laws of the Spirit, the laws of reduction and
multiplication, the laws of investment and withdrawal, the laws of
sowing and reaping, and the laws of faith and perseverance. Every
law brings a destruction of some kind of debt. First, soul debts: the
debts your soul collects from those who have wounded you. Second,
spiritual debts: the unfinished, spiritual requirements you know you
need to finish. Third, relational debts: debts of unresolved conflicts
and misunderstandings. Fourth, the debt of money-releasing finances:
arranging your finances under My economic system. Only My system
is failproof. And finally, integrity debts: the debts your conscience
demands of you. Do them, fulfill them, and you will be free to become
a debt destroyer like Me.

ithout Fear

Deuteronomy 1:21
Behold, the Lord thy God hath set the land before thee:
go up and possess it, as the Lord God of thy fathers hath said unto
thee; fear not, neither be discouraged.
KJV

Living without fear is the fruit of being connected to Me through daily prayer and fellowship. Remember, I promised to set you free from every fear. Each fear you have picked up through your life is slated for destruction. I am not satisfied until every fear is out of your life. There are four symptoms of fear, and I am setting you free from them. The first, the power of fear to torment you. No more tormenting nights, tormenting thoughts, or tormenting emotions. Second, the power of fear to poison you and to poison relationships and dreams. These will all be gone from you forever. Third, the power of fear to paralyze you. No more paralyzing emotions, stuck in an immoveable place unable to function without weakness, unable to speak freely or walk liberated. Fourth, the spirit of fear to make you paranoid. This is the last year to be paranoid in any area. Live your dreams, fly high, scale the mountains of your faith. Soar like a champion. Discover, explore, build, conquer, and possess what belongs to you. Enough hesitating and second-guessing. Jump into faith's arms and stay there for the rest of your life.

The World Changed

Ecclesiastes 3:11
He hath made every thing beautiful in his time: also he
hath set the world in their heart, so that no man can find out the work
that God maketh from the beginning to the end.
KJV

Everything is different now. Every day of your chosen life will be better than yesterday's messed up, broken cycles of repeated failures and torments. The world changed when My Son, Jesus, entered the world. Man was caught in a perpetual quagmire of loss with emptiness as his constant companion and violence his song. Revenge and bitterness were his breakfast, suffering and pain his motto, with loss and destruction his futile hope. Everything is different now, and all it takes to change a world is simple faith. Believe in My sacrificial accomplishments. Drink in belief, hope, and expectation. Believe I can do anything no matter how impossible or hard. Remember, nothing is too difficult for Me. When I opened My veins for the world to drink from My healing powers, everything changed. Now sin, pain, and death have been defeated. Shame, violence, and destruction are toothless. Satan, demons, and wicked angels have lost their pitchforks. The monsters of fear, tyranny, and addiction have become clawless lions in a pet farm. Your life will never be the same again if you embrace the faith of your God. Stand on top of the mountain where you belong, not underneath the mountain. Wave your two-edged sword. Blow your victory trumpet and lead My armies into battle. Everything has changed for you. It will never go back to the past. Stay here with Me and do your job. Rule, reign, and conquer.

The Fisherman's Hook

Ezekiel 47:10
...They shall be a place to spread forth nets; their fish shall
be according to their kinds, as the fish of the great sea, exceeding many.
KJV

Catching fish is your new occupation. I will put you in fisherman's school. I will teach you all the different types of fish there are and how to catch them. Each fish requires a different kind of bait; you cannot catch a minnow with the same bait as a shark. There is no ministry I want you to perfect more than this one. There are thousands of perishing souls all around you. Would you like to see your family perish and burn in the fires forever? If not, then imagine everyone out there as someone's mother or father, someone's brother or sister, someone's son or daughter, uncle or aunt. All the world is a family. Everyone is their brother's keeper. See them as your family and use the Fisherman's Hook in your hand called the Gospel. The Hook will do all the work. All you need to do is throw it out into the infinite sea of drowning souls. Sooner or later you will catch one, and eventually your skills at catching fish will improve. You will have the joy every fisherman has when he catches that large, rare, and elusive fish everyone has been fishing for. Don't be mistaken; this is the most important skill you can learn.

Take This Hammer

2 Corinthians 6:16
And what agreement hath the temple of God with idols? for ye are the
temple of the living god; as God hath said, I will dwell in them, and
walk in them; and I will be their God, and they shall be my people.
KJV

You are the temple of the living God. I will dwell in you, walk in you, and I will be your God. Take this hammer from My hand and build a destiny. Take this hammer and construct an indestructible life. Build Me a temple that I can dwell in, a place I can call My own. Let your hands go to work. Let this hammer of My will lead you to the blueprints and reveal to you the detailed patterns for every room. Take this hammer of obedience and drive the nails deep into the wood of life. Let it secure board to board. Let this hammer of love paint your house and make it the colors of heaven: white, blue, scarlet, and gold. Take this hammer of discipline and let it carve out and chisel each muscle of your soul. Let it make you tough and soft, hard and tender. Let it add to you patience and longsuffering. Take this hammer of purity and let it wash your forgettable yesterdays. Let it cleanse the temple of cobwebs and unwanted insects. Let it purify the atmosphere and blow away the poisonous gas from the air. Take this hammer and make a room just for Me with all the finest furniture. Make a room I can stay in and relax in, where you and I can meet together and exchange our lives.

eeping Prisoners

Isaiah 25:8
He will swallow up death in victory; and the Lord God will
wipe away tears from off all faces; and the rebuke of his people shall
he take away from off all the earth: for the Lord hath spoken it.
KJV

Can you hear the weeping of the prisoners? Can you hear their tears telling you their stories? Each tear represents a moment of time, a second of their miserable lives. I am a Tear Remover. I take the pains of life and turn them into miracle memories of deliverance. Can you learn the gift of wiping tears? Can you see their lives hidden in each tear? Can you reach out your hand and take them into My house of restoration? Can you help them up from the beaten, bruised floor they have slept on? Can you lay them on the bed of healing and let Me cover them in oil and wine? Can you see from where they come and where they have been, to where they are going? Can you feel their tears reaching out to you for help? They are crying from their hunger, poverty, and pain for some ambassador of Mine to come—someone sent from heaven, someone with living tears who can heal and take away their weeping heart. Can you take My keys, open their prison cells, and let them walk again in fields of wheat, barley, and corn? Can you...will you...dare you? Be My hands, My feet, My eyes, My heart, and My soul. Set the weeping prisoners free.

 Am Looking

John 15:8
Herein is my Father glorified, that ye bear much
fruit; so shall ye be my disciples.
KJV

I am looking for a fruit tree that will bear My living fruit the world
can eat; not fruit that is green and unripe but soft, juicy, ripe fruit.
The weary souls will love this fruit and talk about it. Let them publish
abroad the news that there is a tree in Zion's fields where fruit grows
bigger than anywhere else. With each bite of the fruit, the traveler
is revived. His wounds are healed with this fruit, and his memories
cleansed. The trees cannot be bought or sold. They are not for sale,
but the fruit is free. Anyone can have as much as they need, morning,
noon, or night. The trees bear fruit, and they never stop producing.
There is no lack of sunshine in these fields, no lack of rain or fertile
soil. They live to nourish. They exist to bring life. They breathe to
produce this holy, life-giving fruit. The owner of the field is very proud
and happy with his fruit-bearing trees. I will make you one of these
trees, and then you can bear much fruit and feed the passing world,
bringing them life again. Remain faithful where I plant you, and you
will grow tall and strong and your branches will house the singing
birds of the field.

n the Road to Heaven

Matthew 22:9
Go ye therefore into the highways, and as many
as ye shall find, bid to the marriage.
KJV

While you travel on your journey of life, take some time to visit with the other travelers. On the road to heaven, share your travel stories.

Remind each other of the purpose of your journey and why you started on this road. Others you meet will have forgotten the purpose of their journey. The dust will have blinded them. Wipe it from their eyes. The dust will have crept between their toes. Wash it from their feet. The wind, rain, and mud will have stained their garments. Wash them clean. The miles and miles of lonely roads will have taken their strength. Give them your shoulder to lean on. The rumors of the lost traveler who has fainted and turned back will have stolen their hope.

Feed them with new hope of victory and finished journeys. Their hearts will have shrunk because of the wrong turns and ditches they have fallen into. Rub the healing oils in your traveler's bag on their heart. Let it revive them again. Sing them the songs of the troubadour of heaven. His songs cure every illness and sickness of the heart. If necessary, hold their heads and lead them in the way. And if or when all else fails, carry them home.

The Freedom's Yoke

Matthew 11:28-29
Come unto me, all ye that labour and are heavy laden,
and I will give you rest. Take my yoke upon you, and
learn of me; for I am meek and lowly in heart: and ye
shall find rest unto your souls.
KJV

There is a yoke that is not heavy or burdensome. It is not hard or difficult to wear. My yoke sets you free. You see, if you don't wear My yoke, you cannot do what I have assigned to you. The yokes of the world are oppressive and enslaving. They drive you, compel you, and demean you. But My yoke is liberating. This yoke is for the control of your head, neck, and shoulders. Your head yoke controls your thoughts so they don't stray into dangerous territory. Your neck yoke keeps you from losing sight of Me and being hypnotized by the allurements of the world. And the shoulder yoke keeps you from turning in the wrong direction. Okay, let's put it on you now. Take the yoke of love, truth, and destiny. My yoke comes with its own power. When you speak, you speak from My yoke. When you live, you live from My yoke. When you act, you act from My yoke. A yoked person will lay his yoke on you, not just words or information, but the burden of the yoke. The yoke that sets you free is yours now. Wear it with joy and watch the captives run out of their cells.

The Devil's Pen

2 Corinthians 10:5
Casting down imaginations, and every high thing
that exalteth itself against the knowledge of God, and
bringing into captivity every thought to the
obedience of Christ.
KJV

The devil is the father of lies. Don't read what the devil's pen has written on your mind and heart through his unwilling servants' and soldiers' deeds. These unsanctified, unloving people who have crossed your life since your birth unknowingly have written the devil's ten commandments on your heart. I have an eraser, and it has already erased the books of negative information. These supposedly inerasable writings of his are all lies. They end here, today, forever! Now open your heart to Me and let it become My new book. Your life, My book. I will write your new name, Unyielding Conqueror. I will recalibrate the beat of your heart. I will repel your past and engraft your heart into Mine. I will wash away the rotting memories with newness. I know how to recreate a life story, and when I am done, even the angels will be shouting praise for the wonder of your life. Remember, My ink is inerasable, and the devil's pen has been silenced forever.

Building You

Ephesians 2:10
For we are his workmanship, created in
Christ Jesus unto good works, which God hath before ordained
that we should walk in them.
KJV

With two bricks I can build a world. I am one; you be the other. Together we can construct an amazing skyscraper, bigger and stronger than any other skyscraper that has ever been built. You see, I need you. That's right; you are not replaceable. You are indispensable. You are necessary for My plan on earth. I have detailed and specific plans for you. You are not a benchwarmer; on My team, you are a starting player. I will never pull you out of the game and sit you on the bench. That will never happen. Play with all of your might and strength. Use every gift I have given you. We will win this game called life. You are the brick. I need you to change the world and all the people you care about. You are not unskilled like you have been told. You are not unnecessary, plain, or boring. You have hidden, undiscovered talents that have not been used yet. But this year is your year to win the game and score the winning touchdown. Hit the ball, make the basket, and be the star for My team. It's okay to do this. Your heart is right, and your motives are pure. So score, score, score! Win, win, win! Be who I made you to be—a winning champion.

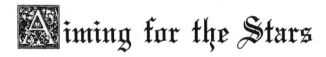 iming for the Stars

Psalm 57:7
My heart is fixed, O God, my heart is fixed:
I will sing and give praise.
KJV

Your aim determines your destination. Don't be like the aimless man who lives life by his impulses and urges. Aim for the stars. Master yourself. Conquer all distracting desires. Ignore degrading impulses and reject self-doubting, self-defeating urges. Don't look back. Don't re-embrace the pleasures of the past. Aim high because your happiness depends on your aim. Let Me pull the strings of your bow. I will even aim the arrow for you, for I know the target. I know the way the wind is blowing. Pull out the arrow of destiny. Lay it on your bow, hold still, and let it fly. Every arrow will hit its mark, bull's-eye after bull's-eye, victory after victory, triumph after triumph. Your destination will be historical. It will change the lives of thousands and thousands of people. Remember, aim for the stars. Anywhere else is the waste of a life.

he Gift

Joel 2:19
…Look, listen—I'm sending a gift:
Grain and wine and olive oil…
The Message Bible

I am removing lack from your life. I am eliminating hunger of the soul and starvation of the spirit. I am sending you a gift—the gift of My Holy Spirit to love, comfort, teach, and encourage you. No more foes at your door! No more accusing fingers or gossip running wild. No more delayed promises or unrealized dreams. From now on, your name is Breakthrough. Your life is a gift, your story will be published, your heart will lead the army of worshippers, and the angels are standing by. The heavenly choir is dressed and ready. The gift is on the way. Prepare yourself to receive Him. He is never late. He fulfills every need you have so that you are satisfied and complete. The gift is coming to open your eyes, fill your heart, and empower and increase your influence in the world. Sinners repenting, backsliders coming home; no wasted sowing, no empty fields, no spoiled fruit, and no life regrets.

The Orphaned World

Hosea 14:3
For it is only in You that the fatherless can find mercy.
Author's Paraphrase

The world is full of orphaned hearts—men and women who have never been fathered. They live in a state of constant despair and desperation. Their hearts are like lone ships at sea being tossed and driven by every wind that comes their way. They have lost their soul and had their heart smashed with rejection and abandonment. I am the Father of the fatherless, and I call you as a Rescuer. Leave what is comfortable for you. Chase My dream of an orphan-free world where every child is cherished, nurtured, and embraced. Let the world know what I think and feel about the orphan, that you were once alone, and I left My home and came searching for you. I searched for years patiently looking in every dark and dry place until I found you bleeding and dying. I did not see you and leave; I saw you and took you in as My own. Now all I have is yours. You are My adopted and beloved. I have given you My life, My wealth, and My home. Now you own what I own. Now turn toward the orphaned world and give them what I have given you.

n Unstoppable Force

John 12:24
...Except a corn of wheat fall into
the ground and die, it abideth alone: but if it die,
it bringeth forth much fruit.
KJV

Dying to your flesh is required learning for victorious, spiritual living. Until you learn to die daily to the wants, appetites, and hungers of your carnal man, you cannot live in Me. I have no corrupt, wicked nature in Me. I repel and reject sin. It cannot approach Me. I live separate from all death and sin. When you crucify your deadly desires, you open the door for Me. I love the obedient heart. I know the cost of dying for what you love. Dying releases holy living, pure life, and blessed anointing. To die for love resurrects the power of My Spirit in you. Dying kills the ugliness and releases the beautiful. It buries the past and unleashes the future. It covers the shame and unveils the glory. Learn to die and live unchained. I will help you with My grace and power. Trust Me, lean on Me, rely on Me, and make no excuses.

ake Root

Hosea 14:5
I will refresh Israel like the dew from heaven; he will
blossom as the lily and take root deeply in the
soil like cedars in Lebanon.
Author's Paraphrase

Take root deeply. Let your very soul intertwine itself around Me. Let your deepest desires wrap around My heart. Be Mine forever. Dig into the soil. Go to the very depths of love. The deeper your roots grow, the stronger you will become, and the taller you will grow. You are not a twig or a leaf. You are a cedar from Lebanon, the biggest tree in the forest, able to provide shade for the tortured, weary traveler. You are able to provide shelter from the storm and protection from the droughts of life. Your droughts are over. Your rainy season has begun. Drink deeply the life-giving waters of life. Then, your roots will continue to grow. Never stop drinking life. Never abandon the place where I have planted you. Take root. Grip life with all your might. Live rooted in Me.

The Unbreakable Net

Matthew 4:19
…Follow Me, and I will make you fishers of men.
KJV

I will teach you to catch men's hearts, to capture their souls for Me. I will instruct you in the ways of the soul winner. He who turns many to righteousness shall shine like the stars in the heavens. I will give you an unbreakable net. I will continually fill your net with souls—precious, priceless, everlasting souls. To rescue souls from perishing in hell's fire is the greatest skill and gift you can learn. I gave My Son to be murdered for these precious souls. I love them with an everlasting love. My love will be your daily motivation. It will never end. You will always be driven to help these souls out of their trouble. Each time you cast out your net, I will fill it. Your net is special. It cannot break, tear, or rip. Your net calls out to these souls. It sings the song of souls. Every soul can hear it. It is an irresistible song of love. Once they hear it, they will run toward My net. I have provided the net. Now, throw it!

he Heart Lamp

Isaiah 60:2
...the Lord shall arise upon thee, and his glory
shall be seen upon thee.
KJV

Darkness covers the earth, and deep darkness covers My people. But My light will light up your life. The Lamp in your heart is My sign of love to you. Although many of your friends turn away from Me and run toward the sirens of the world, reintroducing themselves to the masked demons masquerading as fun, happiness, and joy, they will crash on the rocks, shipwrecked, broken, and betrayed. I want you to keep your eye on them and watch out for the ship. Keep your boat anchored nearby. You see, the Lamp in your heart shall be a lighthouse to them though it's invisible to you. Because of your Heart Lamp, many of them will not crash. They will abandon their ships just in time and jump onto yours; when they do, hand them a lamp so they can live safely, protected from the sirens of yesterday's pleasures. You are a light. You are clarity. You are a clear vision. You are a visible path to life. You are My path lighter. Shine so the world can see Me.

When the Doors Swing Open

1 Corinthians 16:9
For a great door and effectual is opened unto
me, and there are many adversaries.
KJV

Opportunities! Say that word out loud. Because I am the Opportunity Maker, I never want you to feel like you are trapped or cornered in your life. I will, can, and have created new and fresh opportunities for you to succeed and discover your true purpose for living. Without Me, the doors would remain shut. You could kick them, shout at them, and they would still remain closed. But when I open a door, it stays open. It is always opened for you. These are not ordinary doors that anyone has opened. They are the doors of financial breakthrough, spiritual promotions, and relational restoration. These doors will change the scenery of your life. Get ready for new colors to enter your life and for new sounds and influence to emerge from the shadows. Waiting for you are the unbelievable blessings that leave people in awe with their mouths open and hands lifted up to Me in praise. Oh, yes, praise will be your reaction this year over and over again, for I am about to cast you deep into the waves of blessing and ocean of love.

August 20

‖rusting

Psalm 125:1-2
They that trust in the Lord shall be as mount Zion, which cannot be
removed, but abideth for ever. As the mountains are
round about Jerusalem, so the Lord is round about his
people from henceforth even for ever.
KJV

You need to trust Me now, right now. Come to Me and bring Me all
of your burdens. Bring Me your cares, fears, and tormenting thoughts.
Cast them off of yourself and onto Me. I know what to do with them.
I know which ocean to throw them into. I don't want you to worry
about your money, bills, job, or family needs. I will work everything
out perfectly. Your family will begin to work like a Swiss watch, every
second in perfect harmony with Me. I know you. I know each hour
of every day of your life. I don't waste time. I don't lose time. And I
don't forget you. Trusting Me should be your first meal every morning.
Relying on My interventions should be your daily vitamins. Resting
in Me should be your pillow of comfort, and thanking Me, your
stronghold and place of safety. Relax now. Unwind in prayer. Hear the
sound of the footsteps of answered prayer approaching. Quickly run to
the door of your heart and open it. I am coming to spend the day
with you.

nshakable Foundations

Luke 14:28
For which of you, intending to build a tower,
sitteth not down first, and counteth the cost, whether
he have sufficient to finish it?
KJV

When I build a life, I only use the best, most reliable materials. All of
My building materials have lifetime guarantees. I use nothing used,
broken, or secondhand; only the best for the best. I especially want
you to know the quality of your foundation. It is made from heaven's
golden bricks, the same foundation that heaven is built on. It is
unshakable, unbreakable, and immovable. Your foundation determines
the height, width, and length of your building, and since you are My
building, your life represents My building skills. I want you to capture
the attention of everyone passing by. I want them to stop when they
see you and take a tour of Me. I want them to want Me to build them
the same house with their own design. You see, all you need to do
is stay where I built you. Don't try and move your house to another
foundation. Only My foundation will guarantee your indestructibility
and longevity. What I build in you can never falter or fail. I am
building you to last.

I Have No Trash Can

Isaiah 48:21
They did not thirst when he led them through
the deserts; he made water flow for them from the rock…
NIV

I have a gift for making deserts bloom. You see, with Me there are no losers, failures, or unwanted rejects. I don't throw anyone away. I have no trash can. No one who comes to Me is hopeless, helpless, or worthless. I collect other people's trash and turn them into works of art. I am the ultimate Restorer, the ultimate Artist. No one is past saving for Me. I love the lost soul. I cherish the unwanted child. I caress the broken-hearted and heal the crippled mind. I remake the deformed, and I recreate the abused spirit. These are My delights, My holy hobbies. I never grow tired of fixing lives. I have no breaking point. I never grow hopeless or worn out with anyone's flaws. Each person is equally precious and valuable to Me. This is Me. This will be you. Drink this dream. Remind yourself of it every day, for this knowledge will make you spiritually rich and emotionally wealthy. Eat My dreams like candy, and they will make your life awesomely sweet.

he Dance of Life

2 Samuel 6:14
David, wearing a linen ephod, danced before
the Lord with all his might.
NIV

Life is like a dance. If you pick the wrong partner, you end up with the wrong steps. Every dance leads you to a song of life. Wrong song, wrong dance, and wrong partner—wrong life. I alone know the song you are supposed to dance to. All of the other songs will leave you unfulfilled and restless. Peace will leave you, joy will vanish, and love will elude you. Stop and listen. When you hear the right song, you will know it. Your heart will start to sing on its own. There will be no doubt. This is your song. Every beat and every stanza will be perfect. Your heart will come to life. Your joy will overflow, and your motivation for living will outrun you. I will lead you to your life partners—the special, covenant people who will dance to the same song with you, accomplishing what I have ordained for you from the beginning of time. There will be no wrecks, missteps, or false music in your life. Let Me be the Conductor of your life song and lead you in the dance of life.

ll Grow Rich

Proverbs 31:7
Let them drink and forget their poverty and
remember their misery no more.
NIV

With Me there is no poverty, there are no ghettos, no spiritual slums, no dens of thieves, no houses of iniquity, and no retirement homes. With Me all grow rich with the true riches of life. There are no welfare programs with Me. No food stamps are necessary and no food kitchens. With Me, you own the kitchen. You give out the food. You are the provider. I fill your kitchen with inexhaustible supplies. I burn down the ghetto. I knock down the slums and bulldoze the houses of iniquities. Your life is meant to be universally rich with My presence; let it guide you today. Rich with My virtue, let it heal people today. Rich with My forgiveness, hand it out as a gift to the unrepentant, undeserving world. Rich with My wisdom, use it for the benefit of others. Improve their lives with your God-given knowledge. Rich in resources, use them to rescue the helpless, clothe the naked, and house the homeless. These riches are yours to distribute. Remember that with Me what you hoard, you lose. It spoils when it is saved. Put feet to your generosity, and you and I will be lifelong partners.

Your Character Paints Your Portrait

Matthew 5:16
Let your good works be seen by all men.
Author's Paraphrase

You have a chance to make a big difference in the lives of the people you love. Your character is your life message, your true sermon, your unending message of hope to the world. Your character paints your portrait for the world to see. You are what you do when no one is watching. This is who you are and what you believe. Your actions reveal your thoughts. Your character shouts out your name from the rooftops. Words are cheap, but the little things you do when no one is watching reveal your heart. They pull off the verbal smoke screens and false masks to reveal the hidden person within. Live the same in the dark as in the light because the unseen forms you, just as the seen forms you. Don't leave Me at the door waiting until you reappear. Don't excommunicate Me from any part of your day. Let Me walk with you, eat with you, and live with you. Only then can you be sure of who you really are. Don't be afraid of what I will see or find; I already know it all. Remember, I cannot heal what you conceal—only what you reveal.

ever Abandoned

Hebrews 13:5
Let your conversation be without covetousness;
and be content with such things as ye have: for he hath said, I
will never leave thee, nor forsake thee.
KJV

All that has been happening in your life has been for the purpose of making you endlessly loyal. It is the way I am. I cannot abandon anyone; they must abandon Me. Loyalty is the crowbar that breaks open every treasure chest I have. It releases the longest lasting blessings. Loyalty is what holds a marriage together, saving it from every storm of confusion, disappointment, and hurt. It is the rescuer of every family, holding it together like the most powerful glue. Loyalty makes any team or army undefeatable; it conquers before the game has started. With loyalty the game is never over. There is no permanent loss. With loyalty I can change the rules and reinvent the endings. Endless loyalty is the source of all of your blessings. Be loyal to your friends. Stick close to your family. Give loyalty like a gift; wrap it in love and humility. Let your family feel its daily effects. It will heal wounds and dispel fears. Loyalty is a bed to rest on, a plane to fly in, and a shelter to hide under. Loyalty gives back more than you can imagine. Walk in it like a favorite pair of shoes, and it will lead you straight to Me.

btaining

1 Corinthians 9:24
Know ye not that they which run in a race run
all, but one receiveth the prize? So run, that ye may obtain.
KJV

You have lost enough in this life. You will lose no more. You have held
the precious and seen it ripped from your heart and hands. You will see
it no more. You have felt the shock of the impossible and wallowed in
the mouth of devastation, but these days are all behind you. Now the
sun will keep its sunny place in your life. The birds of joy will appear
every morning. Life will beat in your heart. Love will be your daily
bread, doing My will your nourishment, and My peace your banner.
There will be no more wars for territory, no more battles of the will,
no more schisms and divisions of purpose and calling. Now unity will
flow over you like oil, invading every pore of your life. Secrets of the
Spirit will be revealed to you like presents under your tree. Goodness
and mercy will follow you every day permeating every crevice of your
life. Boredom will vanquish and truth will prevail. Help will follow
you like an army of support, and you will be known as the obtainer of
all the true riches and treasures of life.

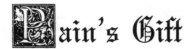ain's Gift

Psalm 94:19
In the multitude of my thoughts within me thy
comforts delight my soul.
KJV

Pain is undesirable yet unavoidable. No one lives this life without some sort of pain, whether it is the pain of rejection, mockery, or ridicule. Pain walks the earth as long as a man shall live. But when your life is interwoven with Mine, your pain has a remedy. Life is pain for those who struggle against My will. But for those who love Me and are called according to My purpose, pain has a remedy. Because My Son has taken your pain upon Himself, you have a solution for your pain. Any pain for any reason can be relieved if you will believe and receive. The door of unnecessary pain is now closed to you, for I have shut it. I do not want you to live in pain, with pain, or around pain. This is not your portion. Your portion is a life filled with joy and days of heavenly pleasure, unlimited joy, and unrestrained comfort. Your heart will be protected from brokenness, your spirit protected from abandonment, and your body protected from disease. Live free from the pains of this world. Wash the souls of the prisoners. Show them the way to a pain-free life. Teach them what I will teach you—that pain handled rightly produces invaluable gifts, strength, endurance, compassion, and empathy. Through Me, pain is ultimately defeated.

 Melted Down

Isaiah 48:10
Behold, I have refined thee, but not with
silver; I have chosen thee in the furnace of affliction.
KJV

There is a place of melting where I need to take you, a place where your iron, steel, and hard spots are melted and where every hard place in your soul is dissolved. Those areas of indifference and cruelty are removed from the hardened mind and concrete will. No stiff-necked, hard-hearted attitude can survive in My melting house. Everyone must travel here—young and old, good and bad, rich and poor. There are no exceptions. Only when you are melted down to pure love can I use you and anoint you. I have big plans for you, plans of wealth and influence. Take your time in My house. Don't get in a hurry to get out. Stay there melting until you feel your heart beating as Mine beats. When you love the way I love, you will truly be alive. Then you will enjoy every person you meet. Then you will be the most blessed person you know. For My love revealed to you is what melts you. My love is so powerful that is cleanses, heals, and melts all at the same time. In My House there are no thieves, liars, rebels, murderers, or insincere deceivers. My House was built for you. When you are done melting, you will be free from everyone who could ever offend you or control you through their imperfections. Your world is now free from control. Live in Me, live through Me, and live for Me.

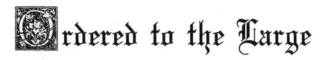 rdered to the Large

Psalm 18:19
He brought me forth also into a large place;
he delivered me, because he delighted in me.
KJV

You have been ordered to the large life — not the small life — with large blessings and large rooms. Every area where you have been confined, I am enlarging. I will not leave you in a small, boxed-in place. I am moving you to a large place where your influence is doubled and your resources are multiplied daily. You have been ordered to the large, where everything is bigger and better. In this large life is where you fully experience the meaning of true living. In this large room is where your influence is beyond what you could imagine. You will have large resources in which you can give to your heart's content and become a true paymaster. Your love will be large and go beyond the possible to the second, third, and fourth mile. You will have large faith in which you see Me do the impossible as a daily experience, as an unconscious act or thought, with mountains moving and miracles chasing you around everywhere you go. You will have large knowing in which you have the answers people need, the answers you need, and they all make sense. Yes, you have been ordered to the large.

tand Still

Exodus 14:13
And Moses said unto the people, Fear ye not,
stand still, and see the salvation of the Lord,
which he will shew to you to day…
KJV

Stand still at My window. Stand there patiently for My appearing.
Stand on tiptoe, excited to see Me, knowing that I bring all the answers
with Me. Those you love will be saved, healed, and delivered. They
will be set free from their past. They will realize My will and plan
for their lives and embrace it. Don't worry, but breathe in My faith.
These breezes can clear the atmosphere. They can refresh you and
energize you. They can help you relax and relieve your stress. Take
some time for yourself and let Me remove your load. Let Me put some
strength in your lungs. Let Me fill your faith tanks with a thousand
tanks of spiritual fuel. I know who you are and what your limits are.
Go ahead and breathe in My Spirit; it will fix the unfixable and cure
the incurable. Let Me open the windows and command the blessings to
blow your way. You need a rest, a spiritual refreshing. You need rain in
the garden of your soul. Sit down now. Hear Me speak your language
and breathe life into your bones. I am coming soon.

The Hall of the Ordinary

Psalm 33:12
Blessed is the nation whose God is the Lord: and
the people whom he hath chosen for his own inheritance.
KJV

There is a place where the ordinary dwell. It is filled with billions of people, faceless crowds, nameless souls with no honor or dignity to their lives—the hall of the ordinary. This is not your place. Your place is the hall of the extraordinary. You were never born to be obscure, faceless, or nameless. Yours is the calling of the chosen and highly favored. I know you realize that I would never have an ordinary child. I don't do ordinary; I only do extraordinary, and that's you! You were born to make a difference in your world. You were born to turn the world upside down. You were born to reach the heights of power. You were born to see the invisible. You were born to reproduce Me in others. You were born to reign and live in victory and extraordinary living. This and this alone do I want you to embrace. Take no middle ground. Stand in no sand or pebble of unbelief, only the high places for you. Yours is the highest life with the greatest results and the best blessings; extraordinary goodness, mercy, and love. Now that you know My plans, change yours, make the mental adjustments, and ride on My wings.

Let Me Look Within

Psalm 139:23
Search me, O God, and know my heart:
try me, and know my thoughts.
KJV

Let Me take your self-made armor off and look within into the secret places of your heart. Let Me see if I can find some hidden treasure of untapped potential, some priceless piece of Me waiting to be born. Let Me look within, and I will make something beautiful out of your life. Let Me clothe you with My handmade armor that cannot be penetrated by evil men's words or cruel looks and vicious intentions. No arrow of betrayal can pierce this armor; no knife of retaliation can puncture your heart while you wear My armor. So let Me look within and find the secret, hiding places of the enemy's parasites. Let Me unravel your tied up memories, cluttered emotions, and pinched nerves. I will soothe the sore spots and iron out the wrinkled parts of your soul. Let Me look within, for I dwell with those who have no "Stay Out" signs over their hearts. Invite Me into the living room of your heart. Let Me sit with you and rearrange the furniture. I promise you will like the results.

Shielded

2 Timothy 2:26
And that they may recover
themselves out of the snare of the devil, who are
taken captive by him at his will.
KJV

Let Me be your shield. Let Me cover your heart and soul with My handmade armor. Let Me teach you to live shielded and armored. Let Me teach you the art of deflection. Let Me instruct you in the art of defending yourself from the fiery arrows of the devil. Let Me guide your heart to the secret, hiding place of love and lead your soul away from the storms of life. Let Me be your life coach; for if you allow Me, I will destroy every trace of the handmade devices of the devil. I will smash the Satan-inspired memories. I will pulverize the strongholds in your mind and show you the path to paradise. Let Me heal your body and make it work again. Let Me refresh your spirit and put sails on your soul. Let Me be your comfort from the betrayals of life and soothe the aching muscles of your heart. Come here, near to Me, and let Me be your All in All. Perfectly safe, perfectly whole, and perfectly shielded.

 Dove Sent Forth

Genesis 8:8
Also he sent forth a dove from him, to see if the
waters were abated from off the face of the ground.
KJV

Today I sent the dove of heaven into your life to invade your personal life, to start taking charge of your out-of-control circumstances. I will be your Bookkeeper, Banker, Doctor, Lawyer, and Mentor. You will be filled by the dove with understanding in life, relationships, and prosperity. The dove will calm the storms, quiet the seas, and enroll you in the school of success. No more shadows following you. Move into the true substance of heaven, which is Me, your All in All. Take inventory of your past and present. Be honest with yourself. Don't cheat yourself—ever! Trust Me for your future, and I will come through for you. There will be sunshine and rain at the same time, clarity and refreshing strength, vulnerability, peace and joy, life and love; every flowing freedom all for you. I am a Dove sent forth.

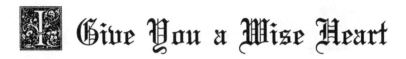 Give You a Wise Heart

Proverbs 16:21
The wise in heart are called prudent, understanding,
and knowing, and winsome speech increases learning.
AMP

Get yourself ready to see how powerful I can be. The obstacles in your way are about to vanish like smoke from a fire blown away by the wind of My Spirit. Is anyone strong enough to stop Me, prevent Me, or stand in My way? Mountains are moving, people are moving, demons are quaking, and your miracle is coming around the corner. The old heart you had failed often, but this new heart is made failure-proof with no mistakes in it. Only wisdom, discernment, and understanding fill up this heart. It will bring you honor, favor, and riches. Submit to it, feed it with My Word, trust in it, and you shall live long. All of the old weaknesses your old heart had are now gone. Your new heart loves the sound of My voice; it lives on compassion and mercy, it beats with the strength of a bull. It will not fail you or betray you. It simply cannot. Use it wisely.

My Unquenchable Love

Song of Solomon 8:7
Many waters cannot quench love, neither
can floods drown it. If a man would offer all the goods of his
house for love, he would be utterly scorned and despised.
AMP

No matter how hard they resist you, they cannot win. My love cannot be swayed from its goal: the total transformation and salvation of everyone you love. I heal, I deliver, I redeem, I restore, I strengthen, I stabilize, and I remember the cry of your heart. I will drown them in My river of love. They don't know what is headed their way, such goodness, mercy, and healing. I will surprise you every day. You will hear things, see things, and feel things you never knew existed. There will be no more dark clouds and ominous forebodings. Smile! Laugh! Dance! Your prayers have been answered! Your fears are demolished with faith. Your false expectations were all the lies of your enemy. Never doubt Me, and you will prosper beyond your wildest dreams.

The Good News Highway

Psalm 112:7
He shall not be afraid of evil tidings; his heart
is firmly fixed, trusting in the Lord.
AMP

Stand up and cheer! Your enemies are defeated and your problems will be solved, your emotions healed, your sorrows forgotten, and your relationships restored. They sneer and growl, but I laugh at their threats. Good news is My middle name, and I will tattoo My name on your heart. Rest at night and reject the storm. I know the name of every cell in your body. I named you before you were born. I carry a picture of your face in My heart. You are not just another face in the crowd. You are My special child whom I love, want, and need. I love the sound of your voice and the beat of your heart. Every one of your heartbeats is a memory of My love for you. All the bad news you have ever heard has already begun to be reversed. You have a harvest of reversals coming. Look for it. Wait for it at your door. Stand on your tiptoes. Your good news highway has just been opened.

The Feet of a Warrior

Habakkuk 3:19
The Lord God is my Strength, my personal bravery,
and my invincible army; He makes my feet like hinds' feet and
will make me to walk and make [spiritual] progress upon my
high places [of trouble, suffering, or responsibility]!
AMP

Your feet are now supernatural feet. They can walk through this trial you face; not only walk but run. Tomorrow it will be solved. You will not live in the valley but on the mountaintop. Sing, clap your hands, and bless My name for My goodness to you. Where you were unskilled and clumsy, now you will be able to accomplish great feats of strength. Your story of success has not begun to be told. You think it's over; not true! There are victories to be won, battles to be fought, slaves to be freed, wounded to be healed, lonely to be found, and orphans to be loved. Put your boots on! Get ready to start living with victory in your steps. The feet of a warrior are yours. You are not anybody's victim. You are not in a position to ever be threatened, bullied, or dominated again. You are a warrior with built-in bravery, courage, and confidence. Stand in your shoes and win!

he Lion's Heart

Job 8:7
And though your beginning was small, yet your
latter end would greatly increase.
AMP

Everyone has always underestimated you. They always expected you
to fail, but I gave you a lion's heart even when you were young. You
were My best kept secret, and now it is time for you to come out of
hiding into the light. Let them see Me shine through you and show
everybody, with your gifts and talents, who you are. Bless the poor.
Rescue the rich from their false loves and idols. Heal the sick from
their inherited infirmities. Feed the hungry. Storm the gates of hell for
the defenseless! Shout the names of the forgotten! Live your life with
a lion's heart. Remember your regiment. Stand at the gate of your old
masters and shout down the fortresses. Watch their walls crumble and
turn into dust and powder. Not one stone will be left of their fortress
of lies.

 Live without Panic

Luke 24:36
Now while they were talking about this,
Jesus Himself took His stand among them and
said to them, Peace (freedom from all the distresses that
are experienced as the result of sin) be to you!
AMP

I will be with you all day today. I will stand near you where you can feel My hand on your shoulder. I know the beginning from the end. I will give you undisturbed peace, and quietness will flow through your soul when it is anxious. Your nervous system will be calm, your muscles relaxed, and your thoughts perfectly in harmony with Mine. This will guarantee peace and life for you and your loved ones. See through My eyes, hear through My ears, and walk in My shoes. "No Panic Ever" is your new motto. All of the enemies you will ever face are already defeated. Every battle you will ever encounter is already won. You do not need to fight anymore. Simply walk up and claim your new land. Remember, when you live life without panic, you become more than a conqueror.

 ncountable Wealth

Ephesians 1:3
Blessed be the God and Father of our Lord
Jesus Christ, who hath blessed us with all spiritual
blessings in heavenly places in Christ.
KJV

Everything you need to be complete has already been deposited into your spiritual bank account. If you need a new life, a new heart, or new habits, they are there. If you need new passion, wisdom, or forgiveness, it is already waiting for you. All you need is to spend time with Me so you can learn your bank account number and how to withdraw your blessings when you need them. Remember, there is no shortage of natural or spiritual provisions in My bank. You will never be poor again. No poverty can enter your life again as long as you obey Me; you will be God-wealthy. All the love, health, power, and money you need you will have. You are the richest person in the world. You possess uncountable wealth. The world would give everything they own to possess the wealth you have in Me. I have given it to you freely. Don't squander it or take it for granted. Cherish your blessings every day, and you will never lose them.

Live Crucified, Walk Sanctified

Galatians 2:20
I am crucified with Christ: nevertheless I live; yet not I, but Christ
liveth in me: and the life which I now live in the flesh I live by the
faith of the Son of God, who loved me, and gave himself for me.
KJV

The struggles you have with bad thoughts and desires are common to everyone. You are not the only person with these inner wrestling matches. I promise you that as you learn to fight with My weapons it will get much easier. Soon, the things that threatened you the most will seem like vague memories, empty ghosts. Your old, rebellious self is crucified with Me now. Trust Me and yield yourself to the Holy Spirit in you. Don't try to do it on your own. Connect yourself to Me; I am the eternal source of life, strength, and joy. Everything you need to thrive in the wealth of My Spirit is in Me. From My words flow the issues of life. I am your inexhaustible source of life. Cling to Me with all of your passion and desire. Then you will see the results you are praying for. Live crucified and walk sanctified. Your sources will never dry up. The well of life I have put within you travels with you everywhere you go. You will never be without it.

reated in My Image

Genesis 5:1
When God created man, He made
him in the likeness of God.
AMP

Trust Me, for I am your Reward and your Compensation. I never
forget you or restrict you. I will always reward your life's work and
your efforts to please Me. Don't give in to the feelings of exhaustion
or the attacks of discouragement that knock on your door. Let your
work be done with pure motives of love, and I will put Myself on
display for you. Reject all glorying in self. It is a thief, and it will steal
My blessings from you. Every aspect of Me will be revealed to you.
I will not keep any secrets from you. I will form you to look like Me.
You are created in My image. You carry My stamp within you. You
can do things that will shock the world, things that only I can do. Let
Me come forth out of you. Let Me take over your life, and you will not
be disappointed. Look in the mirror of My Word, and you will see Me
staring back at you.

ake the Key from My Hand

Colossians 2:2-3
That their hearts might be comforted, being knit
together in love, and unto all riches of the full assurance of
understanding, to the acknowledgement of the mystery of God,
and of the Father, and of Christ; In whom are hid
all the treasures of wisdom and knowledge.
KJV

Sit still and let Me make a life that you can wear, a life sown by My hand like that of an expert tailor. I will add all the right colors to your life and stitch all the right threads into you. I am adding to your life richness, health, and significance. There are treasures of wisdom that you have never found. Oh, how beautiful your life will be when I am done with all the alterations to your personality and heart! There are rivers of comfort and spiritual discernment that I am releasing on you today. Stand there on the tips of your toes and receive My blessings. You will be a life everyone will want to imitate. I know the size of your heart. Comfort will be your coat, love your shirt, and wisdom your hat. You will dress with understanding and never lack the assurance of going to heaven. You will be known for your unable-to-be-disturbed peace.

Polish Your Trophies of Grace

Ecclesiastes 3:11
He has made everything beautiful
in its time. He also has planted eternity in
men's hearts and minds...
AMP

In your heart is the knowledge of heaven and all of the issues of life. You have a storehouse of wisdom and understanding that others do not have because you know Me. I will turn the ugly circumstances and the ugly people into trophies of grace. Where others feel like they are living in a ghetto, you will feel as if you are in a paradise, despite your physical location and regardless of your circumstances. The ugly people in your life will become stepping stones into My rich love, and the circumstances that used to frustrate you will be badges of obedience because of your love for Me. I hate ugly. I make every ugly thing beautiful with one touch. I specialize in making ugly lives beautiful. Learn from Me. Let Me show you the tricks of the trade of loving, restoring, and healing broken, unwanted lives. Remember to polish your trophies of grace.

Sing Your Way to Me

1 Chronicles 16:9
Sing to Him, sing psalms to Him;
Talk of all His wondrous works!
NKJV

Singing is My gift to you. It puts wings on your burdens, it crushes discouragement, and it cleanses the atmosphere of all heaviness. When you feel like complaining, sing, and your complaints will be turned to praise. When you feel like quitting, sing, and your soul shall grow new wings. When you feel unsure, inadequate, and unqualified, sing to Me—not about Me. When you sing to Me, you give Me your heart. You let me wrap My love and peace around you. Singing is devil repellant; it chases the blues away. It converts the soul into a faith-ruled muscle for Me. Singing untwists the heart and allows My grace to freely flow through it. Never be ruled by your feelings. Never surrender to the negative emotions that try to become your tutors, mentors, and Holy Spirit. Let My presence surround you while you sing. If you will do this, the choirs of heaven will harmonize with you, and your loving worship will be heard throughout the halls of heaven. Your singing becomes an offering of love, a rejection of fear, and an embracing of Me. Now slow down, sit down, and sing your way to Me and to your victory.

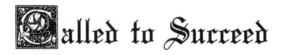

Called to Succeed

Proverbs 16:3
Roll your works upon the Lord
[commit and trust them wholly to Him; He will
cause your thoughts to become agreeable to His will,
and] so shall your plans be established and succeed.
AMP

Don't doubt My ability to intervene in your personal affairs. I can fix what is broken. Remember that I can even unscramble eggs. I have no limit to My powers. I will line up your life to My will and plan for you. You should make up your mind that success is going to be a permanent part of your future. You are called to succeed. I have no relationship with failure. I take failure and eat it for breakfast. All My children are successful if they follow Me and obey My teaching for them. There are circumstances in your life that need modification. I will take care of that for you. Relax. I am never late. I can create a way where there is no way. When I am done with you, no one will recognize you.

There Are Places

Colossians 1:9
...[asking] that you may be filled with the full
knowledge of His will in all spiritual wisdom and in
understanding and discernment of spiritual things.
AMP

There are places of weakness and lack inside of you that I have declared war on. I will not tolerate you suffering or failing in any way. I want you to be on the same page with Me, the same agenda, which is the total overhaul of your life. When we are done, your knowledge, power, and understanding will be transformed. You will understand life the way I do. I know that you are trying to please Me daily. I know this is what you want. But the missing pieces of the puzzle are what I will add to you. No cracks, fractures, or betrayed emotions will I leave unadjusted. Your life will be a life of supreme success, love, and adventure. Get on the roller coaster of heaven. Hang on and let's discover your destiny together. There are places where the enemy does not dare walk. These are the places I am going to show you.

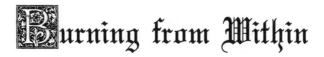urning from Within

Romans 12:11
Never lag in zeal and in earnest endeavor;
be aglow and burning with the Spirit, serving the Lord.
AMP

My Spirit is like a lightbulb inside of you. When it is on, everybody can see it. The darkness is repelled, the shadows have to flee. Everything twisted, sinister, or diabolical has to disappear. Your vision for life will clear up like fog dispelled by the rising sun. Clarity of thought will manifest within your heart. Don't listen to your wants or desires; they cloud your judgment and that always ends badly. Tenderize your heart, become flexible in your thinking, and flow with My will as if you were gliding over a river. I am making you burn and glow with light, illumination, holy zeal, and powerful passion. No more slothfulness or spiritual apathy. Love is your aim. Today I will begin to invade the people you love with My love. Your love skills will grow every day. Keep your roots connected to My river of love. Drink, swallow, and live.

The Secret Sounds of Love

1 John 4:4
You, dear children, are from God and have overcome them,
because the one who is in you is greater
than the one who is in the world.
NIV

Being godly is not as hard as it seems. I know there are areas where you have fought and fought and failed, but if you could do everything on your own you wouldn't need Me. I have deposited in you everything you need to live boldly. Getting to know My Son is your source of unlimited power and life. Becoming addicted to the secret sounds of love will unshackle your soul. Loving My voice will unravel your mind and place each thought in its place like a beautiful puzzle. Each piece answers a question and solves a mystery. The secret sounds of love will soothe the aching parts of your heart and retune your emotions to love, forgiveness, and joy. Let the sounds of love in. Let them play you a new love song. Let them lead you into my outstretched arms. These secret sounds cannot be bought or taught; they must be sought with an intense passion and desire for truth. If you want answers, resolution, and closures, sing the sounds you hear. Let your actions be a song. Let your words be a sound that heals, delivers, and restores the broken soul.

The Sound of My Plow

Ephesians 2:10
For we are God's handiwork (His workmanship),
recreated in Christ Jesus, that we may do those good works
which God predestined for us, that we should walk in them.
AMP

Before you were born, I designed you—not as you are now, but as you will be when I clean the effects of the world off of you. I made you special, unique, and individually gifted for special jobs I have planned for you. The paths and roads that you are now taking will add to you the training, skills, and abilities you need to live the life you were designed to live. Choose Me. I have already chosen you. There are gifts inside you that are still buried under the pains, wounds, and fears inside you. With every touch of My hand, another gift will surface. Don't run from My probing light. Don't be scared of the sound of My plow. It is not chasing you; it is looking for rocks, stumps, and snakes. Stop and surrender. Let the amazing new you step forward.

weet Communion

Psalm 25:14
The secret [of the sweet, satisfying companionship]
of the Lord have they who fear Him, and He will show them
His covenant and reveal to them its meaning.
AMP

Hear My words; listen to Me calling you closer. Open your heart to the healing that is hiding within them. Never doubt that I love you wholly, truly, and forever. Take My words and heal yourself. Don't lean on yourself; lean on Me. Let Me show you the secret of love, the secret of life. True and sweet communion of My Spirit is like jumping into a stream in the middle of a blistering desert. In communion I reveal My face. In communion I take your unformed parts and shape them to look like Me. Let your heart open up to the healing rays of My love. Let Me heal your unspoken brokenness and make you a repairer of lost souls. Bring them into communion with Me. Show them the way to unbroken fellowship with Me. I reveal My secrets to those who fear Me. I am ready to answer your questions. There are depths to My love that I want to reveal to you—the love that heals, the love that builds, the love that liberates the areas of your life that have been broken and shattered. You and I are in covenant, and I never break My covenant. The sweet, satisfying companionship that you and I are going to experience will go on unhindered. I don't want half of you or part of you; I need all of you. I want unrestricted access to your will and your heart. Only then can I unlock the vaults of heaven and give you unrestricted access to all of My treasures and mysteries. Come to Me, and we will live in open fellowship—learning, growing, and gaining life.

n My Shoes

Matthew 3:11
...but He who is coming after me is mightier than I, and I am not fit to remove His sandals.
NASB

When you are tired, weary, and burdened, have I not lifted you up and carried you? Have I not wiped the tears from your wounded heart and given you hope? When you felt forsaken, rejected, and abandoned, did I not reach down and pull you out of the rushing waters of discouragement? Am I not always there for you? This is who I am and what I do for you. It is time to take off your life-weary shoes, those worn out shoes—broken, tattered, used, and abused by life's dusty roads. They cannot carry you where I am taking you. They are the shoes of self-reliance, false trust, insecurity, and fear. Never again will you have to walk in your own worn out, used shoes. From this day forward, you will walk in My shoes. My shoes do not break. They never wear out, give up, or waste away. They have no limits, no conditions for working. They are the shoes of eternal purpose and divine love. They do not fail. They are not too big or too small for you. They will not hurt your feet or deform your walk. They are specially made for you. I made them with My own hands; every stitch is an act of love for you. Every piece is made with your destiny in mind. Now remove your worthless, manmade shoes and put on my love-made shoes. Conquer the world, take your God-ordained journey, and achieve greatness for Me. Remember, you get stronger with every step you take in My shoes.

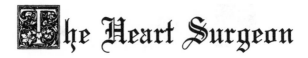he Heart Surgeon

Ezekiel 11:19
And I will give them one heart and I will put a
new spirit within them; and I will take the stony heart out
of their flesh, and will give them a heart of flesh.
AMP

Heart surgery is My specialty. I take sick, broken, and wounded hearts and I heal them. I remove the boulders and leeches from the heart. Everything that troubles and condemns you, I am getting rid of. I will enlarge your heart so the whole world fits in it. Your heart will love like I love, think like I think, and believe like I believe. This new heart I am giving you is break-proof. It can withstand all forms of cruelty and rejection. It will still keep on loving. I will make your heart so soft and teachable, so sensitive to My every whisper that even a hint will sound like a shout to you. No more bad decisions, no more wrong turns and dead ends, no more bad entanglements. Now you see with My eyes and hear with My ears because I will give you a new heart with no mistakes in it. You will act and feel like a new person, swallowed up with compassion and mercy. From this heart will flow creative ideas and inventions. No dream is beyond your reach.

The Power Source

2 Corinthians 13:4
For though he was crucified through weakness,
yet he liveth by the power of God. For we also are weak in him,
but we shall live with him by the power of God toward you.
KJV

Forgive the insults, accusations, and rude looks. Take your soul and put it in My hands. I will hide you safely inside the rock. Walk in love today. Forgive. Don't take anything personally; let everything damaging run off of you like rain. Don't grab on or hold onto resentments. Don't harden your mind against people but open your arms to fellowship with Me. Tell Me everything; this is how I can fix things. You tell Me, and I take action. Don't be molded by your abusers or enemies. Don't play their game. Ignore their actions and meditate on good things. Let My kindness comfort your mind, and you will prosper today. By doing this, you will open the floodgates of My power. This power can melt rocks, remove mountains, change circumstances, heal diseases, rearrange lives, and break curses. This power will be like a new suit. It is for you to wear and cherish. No one will be able to stand before you again. Forgiveness sets you free from your abusers and eliminates the threat of pain.

 Am What You Need

Psalm 16:5-6
The Lord is the portion of mine
inheritance and of my cup...
KJV

I am what you need today; you don't need people's approval. You need to hide in Me. Throw your emotions and affections on Me. I will satisfy you. I complete you. I cover you. I protect you. I rewrite your life. I find the missing pieces of your life and replace them with Myself. Don't worry or stress over people who are themselves incomplete and filled with unresolved conflicts. Their hardness keeps them in prison. Every thought they think lays another brick in the cell they are building for themselves. I have chosen another path for you! This path is far from the crowd of tormented souls, far from oppression and misery. Your heart is My home, your mind My theatre, and your soul My harbor. Now stay tied to Me. I am what your body, soul, and spirit need. Every cell in your body is designed for Me, tuned to Me, and connected to My voice. I speak and you live.

The Undisturbed Soul

Philippians 4:11
I have learned how to be content
(satisfied to the point where I am not disturbed
or disquieted) in whatever state I am.
AMP

I will teach you contentment. I will satisfy you with spiritual fulfillment that will relieve anguish of the soul. It relieves fear and turmoil of mind. Contentment is the ability to enjoy everything and everyone without having to change anything. I release you to enjoy your life every day regardless of the pressures and unpredictabilities. Remind yourself that the treasures of heaven are all yours. I will hold nothing back from you. I am training your soul to reign. I am showing you how to live a life seated with Me in heavenly places where the corrupters cannot reach you and where your treasures are safe. When we are done, you will be totally satisfied. Your soul will be consistently undisturbed and unmoved by threats, slanders, and accusations. The sound of thunder clouds will bring no fear. The echoes of yesterday will not move you. I am making you a champion of peace. Give it, feel it, and live it.

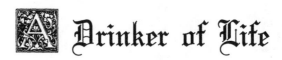 Drinker of Life

John 7:37
If any man thirst, let him come unto me and
drink and I will quench his thirst.
Author's Paraphrase

I am the Thirst Quencher. If you come to Me today and ask Me, I will satisfy all your thirsts. Some I will remove, others I will quench. I want to hear your voice calling out for the living water. One drink and a lifetime of searching is over. One drink and the well is opened permanently for you. Cold, delicious, powerful water inside of you produces healing rivers in you. Out of you will flow revelation, wisdom, health, peace, anointing, and faith until you have become an addicted drinker of life. Drink until all your thirst is quenched and then lead others to the well. There is a sick world perishing outside your door. Take My water and deliver them from their poisonous waters. Wash them with it, cleanse them with it, save their lives with it. The more you drink, the more you will have. The more you thirst, the more satisfied you will be.

 aptured by Heaven's Smile

Numbers 6:24-26
The Lord bless you and keep you; the Lord make
His face shine upon you, and be gracious to you; the Lord
lift up His countenance upon you, and give you peace.
NKJV

Everyone must be captured by something, natural or divine. I have chosen you for a special purpose. You are to be My ambassador wearing the signet ring of favor. You will not have to go through the same storms, trials, or heartaches that others do. The eyes of heaven will be upon you. The smile of heaven will be waiting for you each morning. No rejection slips for you! Heaven's favor and turnaround power will follow you all the days of your life. I will make up for all the disappointments and letdowns of your life. My smile heals your past. My smile replaces the tormenting memories and incomplete moments of your life. I keep perfect records. There are no acts of injustice that escape My notice. I repay in multiples of seven—seven blessings for each act of injustice. This is what it means to be captured by heaven's smile. I will capture you with My smile. I will keep smiling away your problems until the total eclipse of darkness occurs. I want you to walk through every door of blessing and then own those doors. Stay captured.

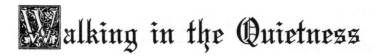

Walking in the Quietness

Psalm 15:2
He that walketh uprightly, and worketh
righteousness, and speaketh the truth in his heart.
KJV

Come walk with Me in the quietness of a righteous heart.
Righteousness cleanses the heart of infections. It removes the heart
parasites that dig their way into the secret places. I will not leave you
bleeding, hurting, or confused. I will heal the hidden and invisible
parts of you, even the unreachable you, the part of you that is hidden
from your eyes. I will never abandon you to a life of nothingness. You
will become steady, reliable, and completely trustworthy. I am putting
steel bars into your back and in your spiritual foundation. I am pouring
heavenly concrete into your life. When the storms come, you will be
at rest. Not one thing you love shall be hurt or destroyed. Your middle
name is Comfort, and your last name is Protection. Many will want to
come and live at your house because they will feel Me there, walking
in the quietness of your soul, creating an atmosphere of love in your
home. They will feel My strength in their hearts and My comfort for
their pains. Your life will be a testimony to the world of what I can do
through a totally yielded vessel. Stand in your encouragement.

Touched by Heaven

Acts 4:13
Now when they saw the boldness and unfettered
eloquence of Peter and John and perceived that they were
unlearned and untrained in the schools, they marveled; and
they recognized that they had been with Jesus.
AMP

Because you spend time searching for Me and because your heart
continually cries out for understanding, My hand of blessing will rest
heavily upon you. You will reveal heaven to the world, your searching
heart will bring heaven down to you, and your deeds of faith will
shock the comfortable and unconcerned. You will not live in fear or
self-pity. You will not cringe in doubt or recoil in double-mindedness.
There are people who carry the mark of My presence with them.
I have picked you to be one of these people. What you say and do
will be touched by heaven. Heaven stands up when you speak in My
name, clouds move, and mountains vanish. Demons tremble and the
oppressed are released. Run toward Me, and you will live under the
shadow of My protection. Boldness and fierce courage will be your
swords. Bringing Me glory will bring you the greatest happiness.
Let them stand in awe of Me in you. Let yourself decrease so I can
increase. Never look back. Do not listen to the old sirens who once
seduced your soul. I give you a new song like none you have ever
heard. One life touched by heaven.

The Untouchable Soul

Daniel 1:8
But Daniel purposed in his heart that he would not
defile himself with the portion of the king's meat, nor with
the wine which he drank: therefore he requested of the prince
of the eunuchs that he might not defile himself.
KJV

A choice is a path. Every choice sets you on a path of life or death. Choose carefully. Think before you act. Don't let pressure, fear, or pleasure define your choices. Don't let pain or ambition lead you. Reject man-pleasing emotions. Take your time choosing your traveling companions. Examine the consequences of every choice. Let purity, peace, and love be your lifelong guides. Choose that which will bring you life, health, and holy zeal. Remember, doubt is the faith killer. Don't doubt for any reason. Reject doubt like the plague. Run from unbelief. Cast it off of you like a serpent. Throw it away into the fire of purity. In doing so, you will guarantee your future blessings. I am leading you to a haven of health, a paradise of love, a shelter of mercy, and a fortress of safety. Stand upon the wall of your castle of faith, call out to the world of lost souls, and be that untouchable soul. Throw out your lifeline. Pull them up into the safety of your shelter and make them untouchable souls.

idden

Psalm 31:20
Thou shalt hide them in the secret of thy presence
from critical tongues: thou shalt keep them secretly in a pavilion
from the conspiracies of unscrupulous men.
Author's Paraphrase

You will be hidden deep in My presence. There is a place in Me where nothing can reach you—no one's words or actions. You will be held in a place of supernatural immunity called The Cleft of the Rock. You will be hidden from the scorching heat of life, covered from the sting of serpent tongues, carried by My inexhaustible wings. Soaring is your new occupation—soaring into My will, away from the conspiracies that have been sent against you. Don't give in to discouragement. Don't listen to the undermining thoughts of accusation and criticism. None of those words come from Me. I am making you a fortified wall. Every weapon of destruction will crash against you, breaking forever into a thousand pieces. The shadows of poisonous tongues will walk away. Remember that My hiding place is only known to you and Me. Whatever curse is sent your way will be reversed. They will speak one thing, and I will send another. For every negative word, you will receive an unalterable blessing. There is a shelter so strong, so majestic, so comforting, that the hoards of humanity long for it. They grope in the darkness hoping to accidentally run into it. You, however, have Me as your Guide. Take My hand and follow the Light. Soon you will be at your destination: safe, rescued, and hidden.

ot a Second Time

Nahum 1:9
Trust Me, says the Lord. This affliction shall
not rise up the second time.
Author's Paraphrase

Never again! That shall be your motto. The afflictions and hassles that have come upon you in the past will be annihilated. They will not rise again. Their voices will disappear, and your peace will never be disturbed in these areas again. Dine with Me from now on. Let Me be your permanent house guest. Let's walk together, eat together, and explore life together. Remember hindsight is 20/20. Perfect vision will be one of your gifts. You will know the end of a matter before you endeavor it. This will give you a great advantage over your enemies. They walk blindly; you will walk intuitively. Don't fear the unknown steps. They will reveal themselves at the right time. I have chosen a road for you where, at times, you will go against the grain in order to carve out a new path for others to follow. Remember, your past is forbidden from repeating itself. It is dead, buried, and cannot be resurrected. Live in today. Aim for tomorrow. Dwell in My will.

ecoming a Masterpiece

2 Chronicles 16:9
For the eyes of the Lord run to and fro
throughout the whole earth, to shew himself strong in the
behalf of them whose heart is perfect toward him…
KJV

My eyes are ever fixed on you just as a mother never takes her eyes off of her child when danger is near. I am constantly planning surprises for you to give you an inheritance that is worthy of My love for you. Take your soul out of the hands of discouragement. If you could see the surprises that I have planned for you, you would be jumping and shouting for the goodness that is headed your way. I have in My hand a paint brush. I have every color you need to become a masterpiece of love. With My brush, I will paint you out of obscurity and weakness.
I will add to you every missing ingredient of your entire life. There will be nothing necessary left out. You will remain young as you grow old! The sun will always shine for you. Your record of miracles will be longer than you can imagine. Over and over I will come through for you. I will continually reverse impossible circumstances and rearrange every negative circumstance for you. You will wear My favor as a many-colored coat. You will spend your life counting the lives you have blessed. Submit to My brush and shine!

The Winter Is Over

Song of Solomon 2:11-12
For, lo, the winter is past, the rain
is over and gone; The flowers appear on the earth; the
time of the singing of birds is come...
KJV

The winter is over. The snow has started to melt. Now, the seeds you have sown are beginning to sprout, and they are divinely infused with growing power. They cannot be stolen, they cannot be destroyed, and they cannot rot. They are guaranteed to produce what they were created to produce. These seeds will last for the rest of your life. Some of these seeds you have sown in times of weeping. Some you have sown in times of great need, and some you have sown in times of great abundance. Regardless of the season you have sown them in, your reaping will catch up with you and overtake you. You shall hear the voices of the harvesters calling out to you that your harvest is ready to be taken home. The beasts of your life are now caged. The aches of your soul healed, and the windows of your spirit now opened. The sound of the liberty bell is filling your life, for it is time to sing again. You are a mender of broken hearts. Now, live in a perpetual spring.

Beyond Your Imaginings

1 Corinthians 2:9
What eye has not seen and ear has not
heard and has not entered into the heart of man, [all
that] God has prepared for those who love Him.
AMP

You cannot imagine what I am preparing for you. All the love of the universe is working behind the scenes to make your life beautiful and gloriously filled with My presence. There is no discouragement planned for you; all the discouragement of life will be swallowed up by waves of encouragement. Wave after wave after wave! Stand there and drink in encouragement. Drink in the love of eternity that has been the onlooker of all the good times you have ever had. I have prepared amazing blessings for you. I brew the best new wine. I bake the best pastries. I create the greatest resorts anyone has ever seen. Not everyone is true, but you will be. Not everyone is honest, but you will be. Not everyone is pure, but you will be. The hogs have been slain. Now your pearls are safe! Beyond your imaginings is where you will build your home and live where dreams come true. The past brokenness is over; it will not repeat itself. Can you imagine being loved so perfectly and valued so highly that all the wealth of heaven is laid at your feet? Because you have surrendered all of you to Me, it is beyond your imaginings.

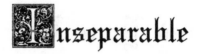

Inseparable

Romans 8:38-39
For I am convinced that neither death nor life, neither angels nor demons, neither the present nor the future, nor any powers, neither height nor depth, nor anything else in all creation, will be able to separate us from the love of God that is in Christ Jesus our Lord.
NIV

My love is like glue; once it touches someone, it cannot be removed. Regardless of the efforts to shake it off, wash it off, or rub it off, it remains stuck to its object. Never believe that anything you have done can separate you from My love for you. This love has been tested by the greatest evils ever known to man, and it remains unchanged. This love I have for you is deeper than all your pain and lasts longer than the length of your life. Swim in it. Drink it. Cover yourself with it and sleep in its arms. It will keep you safe from life's dangers. It will hold you in the palm of its hand, far above the negative voices of the people around you. It will lift your head up above your enemies and present you with the victory wreath. Remember, I have to change the size of your feet in order for you to walk in My shoes. My love in you will deliver those who have chosen to carry their dead corpses on their backs. This love is your magnetic net that draws the fish to Me. With My love net, you will catch the uncatchable fish. This love makes you unable to be intimidated by any evil force that exists. Every living thing, visible and invisible, knows what I will teach you. They are already trembling at your future victories. Remain inseparable.

The Song of Restoration

Psalm 68:19
...The Lord who daily bears our
burdens and lifts our discouraging loads.
Author's Paraphrase

The song of restoration is yours to sing. Remind yourself today that the devil is a defeated liar. He has no new tricks, lies, deceptions, lusts, fears, doubts, or accusations. All of those weapons are broken now. I am gentle, pure, and incapable of lying to you. I will never take from you, make you sick, or cause you to suffer. I will never hurt you in any way. Every day I think of ways to show you My support. Stand still and trust Me. Expect the amazing from Me. I will lift you out of the shadow of discouragement. I remove the cruel, hard-hearted people from your life. I sharpen your arrows and strengthen your arms to pull My bow. I increase your vision to see the faraway target. Remember that whatever I give you, you will keep. Your bowl is no longer cracked. The only thing you will carry is My healing, love, and power. Restore the forsaken, reach out to the abused, nurture the poor, adopt the orphan, and relieve the widow. In doing this, you will always see My face clearly, and you will never be far from My presence. This is the song of restoration.

The Drought Is Over

1 Kings 18:41
And Elijah said to Ahab, Go up, eat and drink,
for there is the sound of abundance of rain.
AMP

When the rain begins to fall, droughts end. Those times of lack, dryness, and famine end. Fall on your knees. Cry out from the depths of your heart. Turn everything over to Me. Let your soul unwind itself into Me. Let the rain saturate the dry ground of your thirsty soul. Rain is coming—lots of rain—oceans and oceans of rain. It is ready to land on you, refresh you, and fill you. It will resurrect the dry, forgotten seeds you once planted and have forgotten about. Your heart will soften, and your spirit will open up like a flower to the sun. Dead fields will bring forth bumper crops. Cry out, "The drought is over!" Shout it! Sing it! It is all true. Tragedies will turn around to blessings, failures to successes, heartbreak to healing, sadness to joy, and lack to abundance. Enrichment is your food, encouragement your nectar. There will be an end to war and a beginning of peace. Intercession will be your lifestyle. I prepare you a new table. Now you will live off of manna from heaven, and new wine for your spirit. The fruits of your garden will be rich and delicious. I am your All-Sufficient One, your nourishing One, your Mender, and your Cleanser. Stay where the rain is always falling. Live where the drought cannot come. The time of reaping has arrived for you. Gathering will keep you busy now…seeing your prayers answered, hearing the sound of spring, gathering in the crops, and feeding the starving souls at your door. I never lack and neither will you. Receive the rain. Catch it in barrels and give it away to those whose thirst has never been quenched.

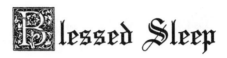lessed Sleep

Psalm 3:5
I laid me down and slept; I awaked; for
the Lord sustained me.
KJV

Sleeping peacefully is My gift to you. I will cleanse your sleep from anxiety and bad dreams. I will heal your sleeping habits. I want you to have sleep with a clear conscience, the sleep of a victorious warrior, and the sleep of the obedient. Your tossing and turning will stop because your sleep will be invaded by My presence. I, the Lord of heaven, will hold you up in My everlasting arms. My blessing will walk within the corridors of your dreams. Close your eyes from now on and receive the sleep of the undisturbed. Sacred sleep is worth more than millions of tormenting dollars. The tortures and demons of the night have been evicted. Where you were anxious, you are now peaceful. Where you were crippled, you can now walk. Your eyes see into My world, your ears hear My voice, your hands touch My heart, and your heart is filled with fearless assurance. The dust and ashes of the past have been blown away. Your pure motives allow Me to bless you. Your obedience gives Me access to your heart, and your faith opens My hands. You have passed the faith, love, and purity test. Now live and sleep in peace.

The Open Rock

Deuteronomy 2:7
For the Lord thy God hath blessed
thee in all the works of thy hand: he knows the wilderness
you have walked through and that you have lacked nothing.
Author's Paraphrase

From the beginning, I have been with you. You have lacked nothing. I know what you are going through. It may feel like a wilderness, but remember I turn the wildernesses into a garden. What is dry and old, I renew and refresh. I water your soul in the wilderness. I send you life-giving manna to sustain you. I open the rock to pour out living waters. I protect you from the scorching heat of the sun and the cold breezes at night. I make sure your clothes do not wear out, and I will point you in the right direction. I provide your every need, natural and spiritual. I have planned every aspect of your life out, every detail. Don't worry about it. I will be your victorious Banner and your Defender. No one will harm you or steal from you. You are out of their reach. I command My peace to follow you everywhere you go. When you wake, I am there. When you rise, I will go with you. When you sleep, I will increase you. I will open the rock for you, and it will pour out life-sustaining water. You have seen your last day of lack.

ashing Away Bad

Ecclesiastes 7:8
Better is the end of a thing than the beginning thereof:
and the patient in spirit is better than the proud in spirit.
KJV

Wash away the bad by surrendering to the truth. Truth is the soap of the Spirit; it washes perfectly clean. Nothing dirty or poisonous can survive the power of truth. Truth is ever at your side, ready to adjust and position you to be blessed. You have seen your worst days. They are gone and will not reappear in your life. Rest and peace are now approaching your door. I am sending you on a mission of self-discovery, for you need to know who you are in Me and who you are without Me. Put on your exploring shoes and start walking with Me. On this journey of discovery, you will find the answers that have eluded you, answers that will bring you closure and finality. I don't want you to ever suffer again. I have seen your wounds. I have heard the sound of your weeping heart. When I am done with you, you will live a dream life filled with love and adventure. The clock of your destiny is ticking, and it is time to start living. Don't ever look back after today. Leave it forever in the past. Take aim at your future. You are washed, anointed, and equipped for your true destiny. Live freely, walk boldly, and never quit this race of life until you win your prize.

The Feet of the Master

Luke 10:39
And she had a sister called Mary, which also
sat at Jesus' feet, and heard his word.
KJV

I have been waiting for you to come and sit with Me. Listen with your heart and not your head. Flush out your emotions of all stressful feelings. Hear Me whisper. My voice will heal you, repair you, and guide you. One minute with Me is worth an eternity anywhere else.

I have something to say to you, something that will make you feel invincible. Breakthroughs are coming. Joy will break forth, and you will be propelled to reign over your situations. My voice is healing to all of your soul's needs. Remember, I am the Alpha and Omega. I start things, and I finish things. Find your place at My feet and discover the secrets of the universe. Never spend one more day following the wrong purpose or wasting your time believing the wrong truth. Having life-changing answers is your calling. The more time you spend with Me, the more like Me you will become. Day by day I will rub off on you, slowly transforming your mind and imparting My wisdom to you. The world is waiting for someone who acts and thinks like Me. Be that person found sitting at My feet.

tanding on Holy Ground

Exodus 3:5
And he said, Draw not nigh hither: put off thy shoes from off thy feet,
for the place whereon thou standest is holy ground.
KJV

Take your shoes off! Take off those dirty shoes that have gathered the dust and dirt! Shake off the mud and prepare yourself to enter into My presence! The burning bush is talking to you. It is time to listen and obey. If you do that, today your staff of miracles will begin to function. All you have to do today is draw near to the fire. You are washed in My blood and left clean and white. No dirt or stains from rubbing shoulders with the world will remain on you. People will look at you and not be able to tell you were ever a part of this world. I make you worthy to walk with Me. I thrust you into the light of My presence. I place you right in front of the throne. No backseat for you! I baptize you in power. I give you spiritual wealth. I place wisdom in your heart and strength in your bones. I give you honor before men and showers of My glory to live under. Now take your barrel of blessings and drink it. Drawing near to Me is what will save you. The fire will keep you from the compromising pleasures of this world. My miracles are your bread. Your table is being spread with My glories. Remember, the place where you are standing is holy ground!

ove-filled Eyes

Isaiah 60:3
Nations will come to your light, and kings
to the brightness of your dawn.
NIV

There is a revival coming to your family. This is the answer to all your prayers. Doubt will be driven out of everyone. Your family will be in unity and true love will rule. Doubt-free living is miracle living. No one knows the weight you have had to carry, but I do. I am making you like an anvil with no fear of the hammer: unbent, unmoved, and unhurt by anything the world throws at you. You will be tough and tender at the same time. I am your Harbor from the storms of life. I create a quiet and peaceable life to live, free from spiritual dogs and apes, free from whips of torture and words of rejection. Yours will be the relevant life, filled with purpose and meaning. Kindness and goodness are now your emblems. Your teeth will never chatter with coldness. Your heart will never shiver with the frost of unforgiveness. Your blanket of warmth will be My perfect love. Your influence will reach the world. Your light will shine out of your love-filled eyes. You will be like water in the desert places.

Your National Treasure

Jeremiah 30:8
'In that day,' declares the Lord Almighty, 'I will break the yoke off their necks and will tear off their bonds...'
NIV

Breaking yokes is My pastime. I shatter them with a word. I crush opposition. I eradicate oppression, and I solidify truth. I am your national treasure. Secure Me, protect Me, cherish Me. Treat Me with respect, and you will never lack anything, great or small. Before you were born, I prepared your steps ahead of you. Nowhere in your life did I include yokes of bondage. Freedom is your inheritance; freedom is your song. Sing it to the slave, the captive, and the victim. The sound of rattling chains will be gone. The bonds on your hands that others have put on you are now shattered. No one will make you lose sleep. You are free. Remember that the eyes of heaven are upon you and that all the lost of humanity are crying out for deliverers. You are now a child of the Light, born into the Lighthouse of the world. Point the way to safety for everyone you come in contact with. I am the Plowman plowing up all the fallow, hard, rocky ground of people's hopeless hearts. Put your hand on My plow and never ever look back.
You are My archer, and I will give you perfect aim. Remember to walk away from every yoke that introduces itself to you. Remember to guard your freedom like a national treasure.

The Yoke of Light

Matthew 11:29-30
Take my yoke upon you and learn from me,
for I am gentle and humble in heart, and you will find rest for
your souls. For my yoke is easy and my burden is light.
NIV

Come to Me with your heart exposed. Don't hide anything. Clear your mind by trusting Me. Let Me relieve you of all stress and pressure. Nothing I give you hurts you. Everything I start, I finish. I am stretching out My hand to lift your yoke and replace it with Mine. My yoke heals, comforts, and enables. It is time for you to feel better than ever. The keys of life have been retrieved. There is no need for concern in any area. The iron bars of pain have all melted away. A soft, tender, loving heart will be beating in your chest. I am leading you to the deep waters where you will find your best fishing. You are destined to find the lonesome souls feeding at the best end of the pig trough, doomed by blindness to wander in the wilderness, thirsty, hungry, and desolate. They are your best and truest mirrors. They tell you where you stand with Me. How you treat them reveals your heart. Take the yoke of light on your shoulders and live a life of meaning. Change the world one yoke at a time.

ecalibrated

Romans 6:4
We were buried therefore with him by baptism into death, in order
that, just as Christ was raised from the dead by the glory of the Father,
we too might walk in newness of life.
ESV

It is never good to bathe yourself with yesterday's memories; they tend to drown you. Bury yourself in forgiveness. Cast your past into the ocean of My forgiveness. Walk in newness of life. Your old life is gone. Do not resurrect it. Keep it in the grave. I will transform your relationships, change your attitude, and renew your life. My life will be released in you. Bring Me your new purpose. Come near and be illuminated, revived, and recalibrated. Discover eternal truth hidden from the hard-hearted. Walk in a new life with no grief or despair in it. Stop at My house; I am waiting for you. You are My only appointment today. I am dedicated to seeing you discover Me. I will enrich you with wisdom. I will surround you with a shield of hope. Your assignment is to bring hope to the abused and water to the soul that is dehydrated from living separated from Me. These souls are like parched, cracked ground unable to drink without help. You are that helper, undistracted by your past and unhindered by your human limitations. Remember, I am bigger than your limitations. I thrive on limitations.

The Door of Faith

Acts 14:27
And when they arrived and gathered the church
together, they declared all that God had done with them, and
how he had opened a door of faith to the Gentiles.
ESV

The inaccessible is now yours. The unreachable is now within your grasp. These places will become your garden where you will carry Me and introduce Me to strangers that I will turn into family. Your faith sword will never fail you. It is sharper than all other swords. With this sword, vanquish My enemies, level every mountain, and pierce through the heart of darkness. Speak it, think it, and walk it. With every step you take, I will create a storehouse of blessings for your family. Give them away, and they will always multiply, for I am your ever-present Help and Keeper. Even though you sometimes walk among scorpions, they will never sting you. Their poison cannot harm you now. I have injected you with the anti-venom. There are many promises I want to fulfill for you. Because you are a faith-Word disciple, I can do that now. Keep your eyes on Me. Hold My Word forth like a light, and I will lead you directly into My Promised Land. Once you are there, I will be your tour guide through every inch of promised ground. Remember to never leave your faith sword lying on the ground.

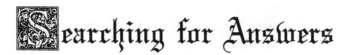earching for Answers

Proverbs 2:3-5
Yea, if thou criest after knowledge, and liftest up thy voice for
understanding; If thou seekest her as silver, and searchest
for her as for hid treasures; Then shalt thou understand
the fear of the Lord, and find the knowledge of God.
KJV

The search for wisdom and understanding is of primary importance
to your life. When you seek it with all of your heart, you will find it
waiting for you. It will explain the issues of this life to you. It will
remove the veils of secrecy around life. This wisdom is your source
of spiritual strength and security. The more you understand, the more
peace is created in your life. I will hold victory in reserve for you and
will stand guard over you for every endeavor of your life. You never
have to live or fight alone. Yours will be the sleep of the anointed. Your
spiritual senses will become highly acute and sharp. Your discernment
will protect you from corrupting influences. You will see life through
My eyes with no confusion, deception, or misunderstanding. Clarity
is your middle name. Because of these discoveries, you will feel like
the richest person in the world. These new treasures will completely
consume your life with purpose and wonder. Isn't it true that your
greatest desire is to know Me fully, without reserve? This then is what
I grant to you: complete disclosure, without reservation, knowing Me
fully, daily, and eternally.

he High Life

2 Chronicles 32:30
And Hezekiah prospered in all his works for God
gave him great honor and wealth for he sought the Lord.
Author's Paraphrase

In Me, you have been granted a high position of honor and influence. You have been given great riches. Your children will inherit the great storehouse of multiplied blessings that you are receiving. New doors of opportunity will begin to swing open. You will be caught by surprise and left with your heart filled, your hands lifted, and all opposition permanently crushed. The face of darkness will have a face of weakness. Your face will shine with My inner radiance and glory. No wrinkles, no signs of being worn out. No shame or broken-down attitudes, no brokenheartedness for you. I am building you with special tools—tools that build indestructible fortresses out of people's lives. You will never be demoralized again by anyone. You are the conqueror now, the winner! You will be the aggressor, spiritually pulverizing the enemy and reducing his lies to dust. This is the high life.

The Drawn Sword

Deuteronomy 20:3-4
…let not your hearts faint, fear not,
and do not tremble, neither be ye terrified because of them;
For the Lord your God is he that goeth with you, to fight
for you against your enemies, to save you.
KJV

You are taking the offensive. You are going in running, not crawling and not trembling! And you are not going to allow the enemy to trespass on your property. My Son died for you to boldly take the offensive. You know the One in whom you believe, and you are fully aware of My capabilities within you. I am stronger. I am wiser. I am more powerful than anything you are going to face. I go before you; I am the first to confront your enemies on your behalf. You have nothing to fear. Refuse to give in to terror, trembling, or panic. I will fight for you, and you will stand in My victory. You shame the accusers. They will crawl away squashed, soured, smothered, and shredded into powerless wimps. Stand with your sword drawn. Take back your lost territory. The days of insecurity and doubting are far behind you. You are a powerful, terrifying warrior for Me. This is the beginning of your days of victory and conquering.

Heart of Forgiveness

Matthew 6:14
For if ye forgive men their trespasses,
your heavenly Father will also forgive you.
KJV

Today is a day of forgiveness. It is a day to get on your knees and to forgive every person who has abused you, lied about you, taken advantage of you, misrepresented you, or made you look bad in front of the people you love. Never forget how much I have forgiven in your life. Think about all of the things you have done in your life, and remember that at any time you can ask Me to forgive you, and I instantly do so without question. Today you are going to live in sincerity and authenticity. There is no hypocrisy and no holding of grudges against another person, no matter what they have done. You are not going to allow your prayers to be hindered. No, today your prayers are going to be answered. Every single one will be answered because every hindrance and road block will be moved out of the way. Now, release every person from unforgiveness, resentment, offense, and hatred. In this, you position yourself for a miracle. I do not forget your love and obedience to My will, and I will send My blessings to you. When you forgive, you untie My hands to perform miracles on your behalf. Remember, all I want to do is bless you.

The Battle Gear of Victory

Isaiah 9:2
The people walking in darkness have seen a great light; on those living
in the land of the shadow of death a light has dawned.
NIV

I am the God of light. Everything about Me radiates light. I reveal
every kind of light, natural, spiritual, and relational. Any area where
darkness dwells becomes My light arena. The dark lords fear My light
because it exposes their weakness. When you dwell in My light, you
are immune from every form of darkness. Wear your light like armor;
it will guide you, renew you, and protect you from evil. The more you
dwell in this light, the more like Me you will become. Your nature
will change, your personality will be healed, and your character will
be developed by Me—all because you embrace My light. Your joy
shall be increased immeasurably. You are going to joy before Me all
day long. You are going to have a party, a feast in Me. I have shattered
the yoke and the burden that was on your shoulders. The rod of the
oppressor is removed from you right now. You are not brittle, you are
not oversensitive, you are not easily frustrated. All day long you will
walk in the battle gear of victory. The burdens that try to come on you
will bounce off because of the great authority of My Spirit that will
come on you. Jesus is your Lord, and I have come personally to you!
I have identified Myself with you in every way. I am your Counselor,
your Mighty God, and your Everlasting Father. I am your Prince of
Peace and Light. Now, be a light carrier.

Mercy's Reach

Galatians 6:7
Be not deceived; God is not mocked: for
whatsoever a man soweth, that shall he also reap.
KJV

Men spend their lives laughing at My Word and spitting at My sacrifice, but I cannot be wrong. What I say always comes to pass. Whatever you sow into the ground will come up. There are many seeds you have sown that are waiting for Me to speak growth into them. Your waiting is now over. Harvest time is here; I will destroy the bad seeds of your life that would bring you a bad, destructive harvest. Stand still and receive My crown of unmerited mercy. Wear your mercy where others can see it and touch it. Mercy heals hurting, hopeless hearts. It will be the theme of your new life. Give it away like candy. Share a kind word, act in a kind manner, especially to those of the household and family of God. You can never outgive or outbless Me. My mercy is from everlasting to everlasting. It reaches to the highest heavens and the farthest heart. No one is sheltered from its grip.

oven

Psalm 139:15
My substance was not hid from thee, when I was made in secret, and
curiously wrought in the lowest parts of the earth.
KJV

My life is forever woven into your life. I have placed Myself in you.
I have melted My nature into yours. I have refined, purified, and
cleansed your spirit with love's soap. Now you are altogether clean.
Your infected wounds are healed. Your withered will is restored to
its strength. I am woven like a silken ring with thousands of intimate
threads that have been meticulously tied together by love. No one can
uncoil you. No one can dismiss you. You are out of the reach of the
destroyers. You are fully and completely captured. You are slowly
becoming undistinguishable from Me, woven tenderly with skill, with
Wisdom's hand, forever found and forever complete. You are unflawed
by love, transparent, vulnerable, touchable, and lost and found within
the sinews of My crimson thread woven eternally into Me.

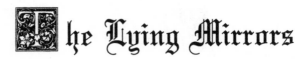he Lying Mirrors

Jonah 2:8
They that observe lying vanities forsake their own mercy.
KJV

It is time to smash the lying mirrors of your life. It is time to crush the lies that have been flying in your face since you were a child—lies that have shaped your personality, altered your decisions, and ruled over the domain of your emotional world. It is time to break in a million pieces all that tells you that you are flawed, unfixable and limited. Throw away those lying mirrors that have revealed the wrong side of life to you. You were born for greatness, you were born to conquer life and to reach out into heaven and take what I have bought for you with My life. Yes! It is time to look into the true mirror of My Word and find your true self created in My image, molded by My hands. Since the foundation of the world, you were holding the true mirror in your heart. The truth about you is already hidden within you. Draw it out by trusting and obeying My Word. Now is the time for you to see yourself from My eyes and never look into the lying mirrors again. Stare at Me! Never take your eyes off of Me, and I will not withhold any good thing from you.

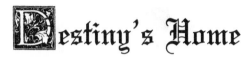estiny's Home

Isaiah 42:9
Behold, the former things are come to pass, and new
things do I declare: before they spring forth I tell you of them.
KJV

The past is in its grave where it belongs. Don't go back and dig it up. It will still look and smell like the past. Do not desire to change it or release it. It is gone forever and erased from My memory. You are free from its poisonous venom and its tormenting echoes. Look ahead; always look ahead. Burn for the future, not for the past. Leave the worms of yesterday buried in their coffins. Let them eat on each other and not on you. Take yourself out of yesterday's reach. Move your heart with your new thoughts of life and hope. Keep yourself moving forward, always forward. I live in motion. I dwell in a constant state of advancement; therefore, take My hand. Let Me take you into the future I have created for you where no ghost can live, no worm can hide, and no lie abide. Yes, let Me be your guide into the new paradise I have made for you where all of your dreams come true. The future is your destiny's home.

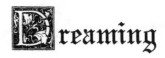reaming

Numbers 12:6
And he said, Hear now my words: If there be
a prophet among you, I the Lord will make myself known unto
him in a vision, and will speak unto him in a dream.
KJV

Dreaming is My way of staying awake inside of you. Dreaming is the essence of becoming connected with Me around the clock. I birth My good and holy dreams in you, and this way you never stop producing life for Me. I will come to you in your dreams, and I will teach you the songs of angels. I will reveal My path for you. You must have My life-long dreams for you constantly living inside of you, reminding you to love and forgive, inspiring you when you get discouraged, igniting and inflaming your heart with holy and zealous fires. Don't listen to your false dreams. Shut them out. Listen to the whispers of My voice. Embrace the impossible, and you will realize the impossible. Dreaming will be like turning on the lights in a dark room. Your unanswered questions will be answered, your nagging doubts will vanish, your offended heart will heal by spending time with Me in the quiet of My presence. Drink it like water, and eat it like bread. Nourish yourself; enlarge your capacity for Me and dream.

 ld Wineskins

Matthew 9:17
Neither do men put new wine into old bottles: else
the bottles break, and the wine runneth out, and the bottles perish:
but they put new wine into new bottles, and both are preserved.
KJV

Doing things the same old way will not produce new and different results. Just because the ways are old ways does not mean they are right ways. What may have been right at one time in life may no longer be relevant to what I am doing now or the way I have chosen to do it now. Each generation has its own set of ears and can only hear through its set of ears. Be a learner, be an adjuster; remain flexible to change. Throw out your old wineskins. Don't be stubborn or hardheaded about the way things have to be. Judge by the fruit of your tree's bearing. If you are completely honest, nothing can stop your success. You will become the most influential person you know in every endeavor. Let Me teach you the art of unstoppable promotion. Let Me guide your feet to the top of the world. I will show you how to truly bless people from the highest to the lowest. No one will be outside of your blessed touch. Your family will be enriched. Every relative, co-worker, friend, and stranger will benefit from the new wine flowing from you. Tell them to drink to their heart's content as you get the double portion for your flexibility.

From Useless Ashes

Isaiah 61:3
To appoint unto them that mourn in Zion, to give unto
them beauty for ashes, the oil of joy for mourning, the garment of
praise for the spirit of heaviness; that they might be called trees of
righteousness, the planting of the Lord, that he might be glorified.
KJV

From your useless ashes, I make a beautiful life. Oh, what plans I have for you today! Plans of beauty, plans of hope, and plans of accomplishing things that matter. You are becoming relevant in heaven's history books. We know you up here. Your deeds are seen, heard, and recorded—the good, the great, and the awesome. We will never stop believing in you. It is time to believe in yourself. Take My hand. Let Me make you a Masterpiece. Everything I touch becomes a Masterpiece. I find the lost, useless, broken, and unwanted. I make it something beautiful. I call you by a new name. I see your heart fixed and remade, shaped like Mine. Draw Me to you by your humility. Call Me to come where you are by your hunger. Hunger makes everything taste delicious. Your ashes have blown away. You will never see them again. Stand firm until the end.

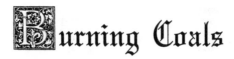urning Coals

Leviticus 16:12
And he shall take a censer full of burning coals
of fire from off the altar before the Lord, and his hands full of
sweet incense beaten small, and bring it within the vail.
KJV

If you scatter the coals, the fire goes out. But if you unite the coals, the fire grows into a flame of furious burning. Heat begins to blow forth, warming the cold and driving away the chills of life. No frozen hearts can remain. No cold feelings or avoidance necessary. All are warmed in the house whose fires burn brightly. I have made you a burning coal, never to blow out, smolder out, or be put out. Stay close to the other coals; they are there to help you remain hot and blazing with spiritual passion and genuine, pure love. Never stray from the coals. Stay where they are. Remain on fire. The wolves fear and hate the fire. You may see their eyes and hear their growls, but you will never feel their teeth and see their footprints near the fire. The fire of My Word terrifies them. It reminds them of their destiny with fire. All the beasts of the field fear the fire. As long as you flame, all beasts remain tame. You have nothing to fear from the dwellers of the night. They cannot and will not draw near My fire. Stay close to the fire. It is where I live. For I am an All-consuming Fire, ready to warm you and devour your enemies.

nknown Power

Psalm 68:35
O God, thou art terrible out of thy holy places:
the God of Israel is he that giveth strength and power
unto his people. Blessed be God.
KJV

There is unknown and undiscovered power in My Word. When you quote it or sing it, it releases its miracles. It can heal the broken heart. It can open the blind eyes. It can unstop the deaf ears and make cripples walk. It can revive the weary soul and convert the lost and wandering heart. Unknown power can be yours. There is unknown power in My name, for there is no name like the name of My Son, Jesus. All beings in heaven, earth, or under the earth must bow to His name. At His name, fevers break, cancers dissolve, the lame walk, the leper is cleansed, the dead are raised. At His name the armies of heaven gather, the demons of hell tremble and bow. At His name, the gates of heaven open to welcome the lost souls home. At His name, weak hearts are restored, marriages healed, and children return home. Yes, there is unknown power in His name. There is unknown power in the blood of My Son. Beware of the blood banishers and blood haters. Their hearts have been turned knowingly by the serpent's hand. You see, he fears My blood. Wherever he sees the blood applied, he must leave the premises. He cannot stand the sight of My blood. One drop and all the hoards of hell must flee. They are destroyed, wrecked, and their words abolished from the minds of seekers. Yes, there is unknown power available to you.

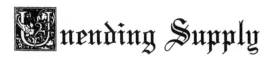

Unending Supply

Nehemiah 9:21
Yea, forty years didst thou sustain them
in the wilderness, so that they lacked nothing; their clothes
waxed not old, and their feet swelled not.
KJV

What do you lack? What is missing from your life? Do you believe
that I am not aware of it, of every tiny detail of your life? I know what
you need, inside and out, before you need it. I have already prepared
to supply it. It is time to trust Me to release stress, doubt, and fear, to
throw yourself into My everlasting arms. Prosperity is headed your
way. It is coming from many unexpected sources. Each one will shock
you into praise. Meditate on this. Let it strengthen you and never fight
the same enemy twice. You are My target of provision. Lack will be
erased from your thoughts. Abundance will chase you in My arms.
Your eyes will see needs everywhere you go. Your hands will never
be empty again. Your ministry will burst forth like water from a dam.
Your storehouses of love will never be empty. Your bank account will
sing to you the song of deliverance. Now, use My blessings to bless.
Take My abundance and saturate the aching hearts of the needy.
Let your motto be "Find and Supply."

What You Value

1 Samuel 30:8
And David enquired at the Lord, saying, Shall I pursue after this
troop? shall I overtake them? And he answered him, Pursue: for thou
shalt surely overtake them, and without fail recover all.
KJV

You pursue what you value. Everyone lives by this unwritten code.
Each heart values something; it can be good or bad, evil or righteous,
godly or ungodly, selfish or selfless. But this code lives within the
heart of every person on earth. You must examine your heart. Daily
monitor what your heart is pursuing. It can never be taken for granted.
The heart can change at any time. It must be guarded and protected. It
must be treated like a garden. The weeds must be pulled, the stumps
removed, and the predators held in check. It must be tilled, turned
over, and fertilized daily. It cannot be left on its own, or it will grow
wild things. Worms will devour it and snakes build their holes in it.
The weather will dry it out, and the scavengers will pick it dry. The
heart demands daily attention, constant cultivation, and daily watering.
If you do these things, your heart will never betray you. It will never
fall in love with your enemy. Pursue Me and guide your heart into the
treasures of heaven. Then, your life will become a living spring full of
riches and precious things.

hen Faith Is Kneeling

Hebrews 11:6
But without faith it is impossible to please him:
for he that cometh to God must believe that he is, and that
he is a rewarder of them that diligently seek him.
KJV

When faith is kneeling, mountains move. Obstacles melt before your very eyes. Troubles vanish and difficult people are subdued. Let My faith guide you to Me every day. Faith pleases Me. It lets Me know that you still need Me, that you are totally depending on Me for your everyday needs and provisions. With faith by your side, you will never lack or be poor. Your spirit will never be in despair. Futility will be a foreign word. Needs will bow. Discouragement will never knock on your door again. Wear your faith in Me and My Word like a new set of clothes. Walk upright with your head held high. You have just chosen the faith life. Oh, the joy that is waiting for you! The treasures you are about to inherit, the power you are about to experience in your daily life, and the miracles that are about to happen in your relationships. Shout for joy! Faith is kneeling, and I am listening.

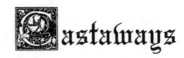astaways

Genesis 14:16
And he brought back all the goods, and also
brought again his brother Lot, and his goods, and the
women also, and the people.
KJV

The earth is filled with castaways: men, women, and children whose lives have been shipwrecked and shattered on the rocks of life. Their dreams have been stolen, their innocence defiled, their families wrecked, and their security erased. These lives do not escape My attention. I am looking for rescuers who will take their lifelines and throw them out into the darkness, pull the castaways in, and load them onto My ship. My ship cannot crash, be wrecked, sink, or capsize. It is an indestructible ship built to stand through every storm of life. It cannot rot, decay, or puncture; it has a lifetime guarantee. Cast out your net every day. I have already changed the current around these castaways, so they will fall into your nets. Pull, pull, pull. Never stop until every castaway is rescued. Make this your life vision. Let it consume you as you remember that you were once a castaway, too.

The Watered Soul

Psalm 84:6
Passing through the valley of weeping,
they make it a place of showers; the early
rain also fills the pools with blessings.
Author's Paraphrase

The soul that has not been watered quickly withers. The watered soul remains fresh and alive. It is healthy and full of life-giving goodness. It shrinks drought, and it dismisses dirt and pollution. The watered soul is addicted to drinking in life. It rejects dirt, dust, and mud. It is keenly aware of joy. Joy is the watered soul's fruit. It produces joy in bumper crops, joy in the morning to dispel the gloom and grip of depression. It rejects sadness. You are a watered soul from now on. Those who have lined up against you to drain you of My water will fail. They will run out of the waters of revenge and the mountains of bitterness they have collected through the years. Your job is to water your friends and enemies and give them what they do not deserve and could never earn. In this way, you will be silencing the enemy's voice in their heads. Stay close to Me with a tender heart. Reject hardness of all types. Drink My love; let it be your miracle juice. You will never have a drought in your life. Say it to yourself everyday: "I am a watered soul."

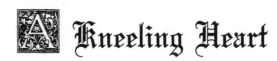 Kneeling Heart

Deuteronomy 4:29
But if from thence thou shalt seek the
Lord thy God, thou shalt find him, if thou seek him
with all thy heart and with all thy soul.
KJV

A kneeling heart is more powerful than ten thousand empty, insincere prayers. This is the time to build an altar in your heart. It is altar time. That is what you need. You will always need it. Altar time is the source of your life in Me, with Me, through Me, and for Me. Bend the knees of your heart and move the world. One bent heart in worship and obedience cannot be stopped by all the demons of hell. No dark power can stop a bent heart. No temptation can seduce it, no fear can grip it, and no insult can wound it. A kneeling heart is immune to corruption, deceit, greed, lust, and offense. A kneeling heart cries out to the whole universe that I am King of kings and Lord of lords. One kneeling heart is all it takes to change the course of history. Command your heart to kneel, and it will obey you. Do not let it have its way. Bend it to My will, and soon it will kneel on its own. One kneeling heart begets another kneeling heart until thousands of hearts are kneeling and thousands of lives have been changed forever.

The Smiling Heart

Psalm 30:11
Thou hast turned for me my mourning into dancing:
thou hast put off my sackcloth, and girded me with gladness.
KJV

The world is filled with sad and grieving hearts. Their faces reveal their hearts. They don't know how to let go of all offenses and abusers. They have never learned the science of letting go. Don't get caught in their trap. Let Me train you to walk with a smiling heart. If you keep walking with Me in intimate, unbroken fellowship, I will permanently imprint My smile on your heart. I will write entire symphonies on your face. The world will hear the song flowing out of you, and they too will be infected with the songs of heaven and sing them throughout eternity. Never underestimate the power of a genuine smile. It is a miracle accomplishment in this torn up world. To smile when the world is full of war, hatred, despair, and disease. To smile when families are being ripped apart daily. To smile when hopelessness rules the earth. To smile is a trumpet of hope. One smile can bring a soul out of their dungeon. To smile because you know that with Me nothing is unfixable—that I alone can unscramble eggs, that nothing is too difficult for Me to change, and nothing is beyond the reach of My outstretched arms. So smile your clouds away.

I Am Watching

Deuteronomy 32:10
I will scan you and watch over
you as the apple of My eye.
Author's Paraphrase

My eye of love and protection is never off of you. I never remove My gaze off of you. You are at the center of My attention. Your welfare is My daily obsession. I live so you can live. I stay awake around the clock just to keep you safe. I am a perfectly loving, watchful Father. No one is going to hurt you or surprise you with disaster. You are no longer vulnerable to the devil's schemes. I have removed you from the war. I have put indestructible armor on you. I see every aspect of your life. Remember, I saw you before you were even formed in your mother's womb. I have planned out your life, step by step. I see you when you sleep and when you wake. I lift you up and turn disasters into blessings. Because I am watching over you, your life will be spent cleaning the oasis of people's souls. I watch you, you watch Me, and we live in mutual protection and peace. You speak for Me, and I speak for you. The end result is an amazing life worth watching.

he Limp

Zephaniah 3:19
I will deal with all who afflict you;
I will heal the limping ones.
Author's Paraphrase

A limp is a hindrance to your walking, jumping, and running. You are made to be whole. You are created to function without hindrances and with nothing in your life that can stop your growth or delay your blessings. I am not satisfied when you have unnecessary delays to your destiny. I have a lot for you to accomplish: plans, assignments, and exploits for you to achieve. No more limping, struggling, or crawling. From now on, your walking improves. Your walk with Me will be completely transformed; your life of joy will burst forth unexpectedly. Your running after Me will shift along with your focus and purpose in life. When people see you, they will see you running the race of life and winning that race. Now rise up and run. Run the way of My commandments and let your heart be enlarged until the whole world is running toward Me as well. No more delays, hindrances, or postponements. The dam of your dreams is breaking, and your dreams are headed your way.

Filling Infinity

James 1:17
Every good gift and every perfect gift is from
above, and cometh down from the Father of lights, with whom
is no variableness, neither shadow of turning.
KJV

Do you believe I am as good as your heart can imagine? Do you believe that My thoughts toward you are thoughts of goodness only? Do you believe I am making plans to bless you and prosper your family? Do you believe I have unlimited power to change your world? I have enough goodness to fill all of infinity with shouts of praise for My interventions in the lives of desperate people. You are My tool, My weapon, My blesser. You are called to fill heaven with the souls of the lost and perishing; this is your assignment. Do you dismiss it, forget it, or ignore it? No, for this is the door that will lead you to all of your success in life. The snakes are out of the grass, the wolves have stopped their howling, and the cannibals are now toothless, gumming their way back to their dens. If I can fill infinity, then I can fill you with all the treasures, gifts, and insight you need to reign in this life. Carry My trumpet with you and fill the earth with My praise.

The Richest Person on Earth

Proverbs 28:27
He that giveth unto the poor shall not lack:
but he that hideth his eyes shall have many a curse.
KJV

I want to make you the richest person on earth. I want to show you the path that many seekers of truth have found, the path to true riches and unimaginable wealth that leads through the valley of the poor. In this valley all the poor of the world live; they are hungry, starving, thirsty, naked, abandoned, rejected, forgotten, stepped on, hurt, wounded, forsaken, hopeless, empty, lost, and unloved. Find them wherever they are; journey across the world if you have to. Enrich them with the pearls of eternity. Fill their pockets with money, their stomachs with food, and their hearts with love. Put shoes on their feet, clothes on their backs, and joy in their spirits. Lift their heads with hope and turn their weariness into a stream of joy by giving them a sense of dignity. Your love is your weapon, faith your bullets, and the poor your targets. Never feed yourself first. Never put your needs ahead of theirs, and I will grant all of your wishes. I will open heaven's gates for you. Do everything with a pure, unselfish motive and enter into the richest life on earth. No thief can steal it, no moth can corrupt it, and no rust can wear it out.

The Finished Jar

1 Thessalonians 5:24
Faithful is he that calleth you,
who will also bring it to pass.
Author's Paraphrase

Perhaps you have trouble seeing what I am doing in your life sometimes. Perhaps you wonder what the purpose is behind your life. But you are not an insignificant part of My plan; you are not replaceable. Yours is a sacred life, a divine idea of Mine. Your life matters greatly to My plan on earth. I can see what you cannot. I know what you don't. Your job is to relax, obey, and trust. Don't run or get distracted. Don't let the world turn your head. I know exactly where I am taking you. I called you as a broken, unfinished jar. No one else wanted you, but I do. No one else believed in you, but I do. Trust that I will finish what I have started in you. I will not leave you as an unfinished project. Every part of you that is lacking, missing, or broken I will repair or replace. Every promise I give you is a piece of eternal glue holding you together. The weak and helpless who see you will be strengthened by you. The visible, distraught, and broken will reach out to you because they will see the healed cracks in you. You are My finished jar, My container, My carrier of truth and hope. I always finish what I start. Let Me complete you.

 **iligence**

Proverbs 22:29
Do you see a man diligent in his
work, he shall stand before kings…
Author's Paraphrase

Diligence is your key to success. The ants, bees, and created creatures live by diligence. They never lack; they are never weak, sick, or broken. Feebleness never enters their world. They do what they were created to do. They live by the habit of consistency. Life is not supposed to be hard; it is supposed to get smoother and easier as time passes. Your heart will become stronger day by day. Your spiritual gifts will become more effective as time goes by. Your diligence in work and ministry will pay you with great rewards and blessings here on earth and in heaven. Don't quit doing the right thing because you don't see immediate results. You will reap the blessings of your labor. Your diligence in righteousness will place you before great men and women of influence and power. You must live one day at a time. Expect breakthroughs, expect miracles, expect the unexpected returns on your sowing. Your future is already planned. You must chisel it out of the stone rock; it is in there waiting to be set free. And oh, what a future filled with promotions and power! Wear your diligence like the finest cloth.

holeness

Galatians 3:13
Christ hath redeemed us from the curse of the law,
being made a curse for us: for it is written, Cursed
is every one that hangeth on a tree.
KJV

My life was the price for your wholeness. I paid for you to be forgiven from all your past, present, and future sins, failures, and presumptions. I gave Myself so you could breathe the air of freedom. Let the bells of freedom ring in the secret parts of your mind. I paid for your total restoration and healing. All your sicknesses and diseases have been cured at Calvary. Now you can walk in divine health. Obey, and you will receive these blessings. I paid for you to be delivered from every bondage, addiction, and bad habit. My death produces your life. My suffering equals Your comforting. I paid your debts in full—your debt to Me, your debt to the world, and your debt to yourself. I have laid Myself down on a piece of old wood so you can sleep like a king.

I took your pains so you could lead a happy and blessed life. I was punished so you could be forgiven. I was judged so you could receive mercy. I tasted death so you could experience eternal life. Bathe in this life and the life to come. I defeated the devil so you could live devil-free. Drink in what I have purchased. Learn, learn, learn. Grow into My image. Take My sacrifice and heal the world. I have paid for your prosperity in body, soul, spirit, and all other areas of your life.

I have broken the curse of legalism. I have shattered the curses of your forefathers. I have redeemed you from sin; it will no longer have power over your life. The door to heaven is open for you. Your name is written in the Book of Life. I am your Purchaser; I alone have rights over you.

In Solitude Defined

James 4:8
Draw nigh to God, and he will draw nigh to you…
KJV

I define you by My fingerprints on your soul. My hands create miracles. My hands heal and restore joy and health. I write your future on your mind and soul. Love is My pen, mercy My paper. I hide Myself within the pages of your choices. Take time alone with Me. Speak your dreams, cultivate your destiny with integrity's scepter. Live apart from the savage spirit that is in the world. Instead, dwell in unconditional love. Live for the wretched, rejected, ruined souls of this world. Give your life color, glory, and purpose. Dissolve the aches and pains of the unwanted. Remember to wash the feet of the poor. Keep yourself from the soul parasites of power, fame, selfishness, and pride. Avoid the leeches of indulgence, pleasure-seeking, and hardheartedness. Don't let other people's spiritual crimes affect your gifting. Love through who you are. In solitude, you will be defined. Let us walk together in unbroken fellowship. Become one in spirit and soul with Me, and I will release the true riches of life to you. Stand alone in your convictions, and I will surround you with people who will enrich you and bless you.

It's Never Too Late

Isaiah 40:29
He gives power to the faint and weary,
and to him who has no might He increases strength
[causing it to multiply and making it to abound].
AMP

It is never too late with Me. The weaker you are, the better I like it, for My strength is perfected in weakness. If you had no weaknesses, you would not need Me. The more weaknesses you have, the greater blessing you will become. Don't quit or give up. I will multiply your resources naturally and spiritually; your warehouses will overflow with abundance enough to share with everyone. It is never too late. Remember My history. Remember My faithfulness. Remember My loyalty to My Word. If I am present, all things automatically restore themselves. No more delays. No more disturbances. No more casualties. No more anxiety attacks. This is it; I will come through for you now.

 # Take Notice

Galatians 6:9-10
And let us not be weary in well doing: for in
due season we shall reap, if we faint not. As we have therefore
opportunity, let us do good unto all men, especially unto
them who are of the household of faith.
KJV

Never stop sowing blessings into people's lives. Even if they don't appreciate it or even notice, do it because it is right. And remember, I notice and write it down in My diary. I will never forget any good thing you have done. When you feel like quitting, double your sowing. When you get discouraged, lift your hands and worship Me. In times of heartache or anger, pray with forgiveness in your heart. Your love will never stop flowing if you do these things. Today, I have noticed you. I have noticed your motives, your dreams, and your desires. Live above self-pity. Walk in bold faith. Take your armor and use it to defeat My enemies. Take their spoil and share it with those who have been plundered. I take notice of you. Now, embrace My care and surrender yourself to My plan.

laying the Prophets of Baal

1 Kings 18:40
Take the prophets of Baal, let no
one escape. And they took them, and Elijah slew them there.
Author's Paraphrase

Not one of those false prophets running around your head shall escape. Every false, lying voice from the past, present, or future shall be eliminated from your life. The devil is the father of lies. It is his job to overload your mind with lying information, thoughts, and confusing information that is contrary to the truth. Lies lead to death; truth leads to life. You are a child of truth, born of the truth and by the truth. You are a dragon slayer for Me. Take your truth sword and become skilled at using it. Let Me strengthen your spiritual arms. Let Me teach you the use of your sword. Become a sword master. Slay those false prophets in people's lives. Cut off their heads, and their voice will be silenced. Have no mercy on lies, distortion, or exaggeration. Slay the enemies of the cross. Remove their presence from every person you love and know. Let truth be the defender you send forth. Slay them with your words, deeds, and attitudes. Become My slayer.

 Joy Addict

Psalm 51:12
Restore to me the joy of my salvation
and uphold me with a free spirit.
Author's Paraphrase

Never underestimate the power of joy. Think how often you have lacked it, and how trouble, sin, and depression flee when joy enters the room. Have you noticed that people with joy don't walk in fear? Fear cannot take root in the garden of your heart when joy is there pulling the fear roots out of it. Joy is like healing oil to your soul. It keeps your soul from cracking and developing soul mites, those little microscopic parasites—irritating, distracting, and causing soul infections. Joy prevents all the diseases of a sick soul. Don't live without it. Joy comes in the morning. Lift your heart in your hands to Me every morning. Praise Me for your life. Thank Me for your victories—past, present, and future. Stand on My promises. Let them be the crutches and braces of your soul. I am making you a joy addict, one addicted to living within My smile.

 he Lights Are On

Psalm 18:28
For thou wilt light my candle: the Lord my
God will enlighten my darkness.
KJV

Your journey is one of continual, evolving illumination. When I am done educating you in My ways, My thoughts, and My ideas about life and living, you won't be able to find one area of confusion, darkness or doubt. My light of truth is your headlamp in the caves of life. My candle is your illumination through every untrodden path you may find yourself on. The cobweb ideas given to you by deceived and misinformed people you have been afflicted by will melt within your mind. Yours is the path of truth and justice, knowing all about Me. Knowing how to walk with Me harmoniously is a great gift. This gift of truth and understanding will open many doors for you. Your wisdom will be sought by many so-called intellectuals. They will stand in awe of the wisdom you possess to answer their life's questions. The lights are on, and they will never go off again. Walk in the light, stay in the light, reject the false light of false illuminators who have been seduced by the red dragon. Your path is now clear. Follow the road signs to heaven.

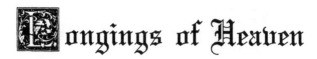ongings of Heaven

Psalm 37:4
Delight yourself also in the Lord, And He
shall give you the desires of your heart.
NKJV

There are two authors of longing. The devil creates in you longings
of your flesh, those illegitimate desires that become obsessions and
addictions. These are the devil's train tracks within you, and they
lead to his prisons. He is the jailer of your soul. Longings of the
unattainable are his music, his enchantments. If you lust and long for
the unattainable, you only torture yourself. Don't do it; self-torture
is foolish. It is not wise to love what will destroy you. I have made
you a heart that loves what I love, that has room only for Me, that has
only one heart to give away. I am giving you the longings of heaven,
those desires that have made hundreds of men and women great in My
kingdom. One desire from heaven will clear out an entire city of bad
desires. You long for what you see, you see what you imagine, and you
imagine what you meditate on. Dwell on My Word; think on it. Use it
like water, like medicine. It will create the longing that will launch you
into greatness.

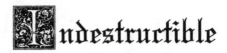ndestructible

Matthew 7:25
And the rain descended, and the flood
came, and the winds blew, and beat upon that house;
and it fell not: for it was founded upon a rock.
KJV

I do not build what can be destroyed. I do not use weak and breakable materials when I lay the foundation of your life. Everything I use to build you is indestructible. Your first responsibility is to let Me tear out the old foundations. You see, there are already in place old, breakable false foundations laid by unwise, unqualified builders. These builders use bad, useless, breakable materials. They only wanted your resources and didn't care about your life or longevity. Can you hear the bulldozers of heaven ripping, pulling, and breaking up those false mental foundations? Those unresolved values and beliefs, those wrecked-soul philosophies and deceptive crutches of the flesh? Yes, everything must go. And then I begin to build an everlasting temple, a temple whose foundations are sure, reliable, indestructible, dependable, trustworthy, and everlasting. Stand strong so others can take shelter within your pavilions.

The Billboard of Heaven

2 Kings 6:17
The Lord opened his eyes and he saw the mountain
was full of chariots of horses or fire round about Elisha.
Author's Paraphrase

Everyone who is on earth feels overwhelmed from time to time. Everyone believes they are alone. It is human nature to feel separated and isolated from everyone, but it is not necessary for our purposes. Look around you—not with your natural eyes but with the eyes of the Holy Spirit. You will find that all of heaven is observing you. They are there as your cheerleaders, praying for you, cheering for you, believing the best about you. Heaven's cheerleaders do not entertain negative thoughts about you; they do not wait for your downfall. They know your destiny and trust Me to bring it to pass. You are never alone. In time, those feelings of aloneness will disappear and be replaced with My presence; you and Me, walking together through life. We welcome anyone else who wants to join us. Open hearts lead to open hands. And open hands are the billboard of heaven.

From the Heart

Proverbs 4:23
Keep and guard your heart with all vigilance and
above all that you guard, for out of it flow the springs of life.
AMP

From the heart flow the meanings of your life. Never allow anyone to deform your heart with hurtful words, cruel actions, or malicious attitudes. Your heart is the seat of your life. I look to the heart. I respond to a humble, contrite heart. It moves Me to action. A broken, soft, and tender heart is the seedbed for My love. I can change the world with one surrendered and pliable heart. The heart is the storage center for all good and bad; therefore, you need to watch over it with care and love. Don't allow anything in your life that could undermine My plans for you. Thieves will always try to break in and steal your heart from Me. It is the most valuable thing you have. It is where I live. Your heart is your key to Me; all My riches are deposited in your heart. My Word must dwell in your heart. My presence flows from your heart. Love, joy, and peace abide in the heart, and out of your heart flow the issues of life. Stand strong with a heart of faith and love, and see Me remove the veil that will reveal to you the mysteries of My kingdom. Give Me all of your heart without reserve, for I have already given you Mine.

Wear Your Armor

Ephesians 6:11
Put on the whole armor of God, that you may
be able to stand against the wiles of the devil.
NKJV

When you go out into the jungle called the world, never leave home without your armor. Wear it; put on every piece carefully. Don't hurry. When it comes to your armor, you need to make sure it is fully functional. Check the helmet of salvation; make sure your thoughts are in harmony with Mine. Remind yourself of who you are in Christ, My Son. Recall the blessing I have given you and don't allow undermining thoughts to take root. Strap on the breastplate of righteousness; tell yourself who I have made you to be. Do the righteous thing and remain unreachable by the claws of evil. Fasten your girdle of truth; truth in all areas provides access to My Spirit. Wear and lace up your shoes of peace; walk where I would walk and how I would walk, and you will never end up at the wrong destination. Never forget to take up your shield of faith; it stops all missiles of destruction against your life. It protects you from all satanic weapons. And finally, wear your sword and don't hesitate to use it on yourself or others. Use it on your Adamic nature. Subdue it with your sword. Wipe out the very remembrance of your enemy's voice. Plunder the camp and take the spoil, for it is your birthright.

The Unflinching Soul

2 Thessalonians 2:2
Do not allow your minds to be quickly
unsettled or disturbed, whether it be by some [pretended]
revelation of [the] Spirit or by word or by letter.
Author's Paraphrase

The unflinching soul is My gift to you. It will never be alarmed at the intimidation of people's threats or the impending dangers staring at you. You will live undisturbed. A quiet peace will settle over you like a warm blanket on a cold winter day. The unflinching soul rests in My arms permanently; it is not subject to alarm, fear, or panic. It will never shake hands with torment or sit at doubt's throne. It is separated from the poisons of the unbelieving soul. Its harbor is the harbor of peace and truth. It walks with the giant-killers, and it rejects the mind of the traitor and the heart of the grasshopper. Yes, the unflinching soul is like the sails of a boat, always ready to capture the breath of heaven and transport you to your desired haven. The unflinching soul is your armor, your trumpet, and your sword. It will usher you into My hall of faith, writing your deeds for the fearful to see, separating you from the lies of the slander collections, giving you bread to eat and wine to drink for your soul's refreshing. Stand, therefore, in My Word—unflinching, unmoved, undisturbed, and winning the trophies of life for your God.

The Fibers of Your Heart

Romans 4:19
He did not weaken in faith when he considered the
[utter] impotence of his own body, which was as good as dead
because he was about a hundred years old, or [when he considered]
the barrenness of Sarah's [deadened] womb.
AMP

Abraham did not weaken in faith as he considered the weakness of Sarah's womb. Do not cave in. Today, reach into Me! Reach into My strength! Stretch yourself into the storehouse of My faith. I am not moved by the circumstance you are in; I decide what will happen to you, and My decision for you is a miracle breakthrough. Whatever appears impossible, I will bring into reality. Proclaim your victory now! I am encircling you with My arms, connecting the fibers of your heart to Mine. Each day you and I become one. I am establishing your name and ministry. I am extending the sphere of your influence so that the people who pass through your life will be affected for eternity. Your heart is like the sound of a church bell, ever ringing in My heart and drawing people to worship Me. My love will encompass you and your loved ones, generating a spiritual awakening that will be heard everywhere you go. Surrender daily to the connecting fibers of your heart that are crying out for Me. Now relax and let Me finish what I have started in you.

The Scars of Love

Isaiah 53:5
But he was wounded for our transgressions, he
was bruised for our iniquities: the chastisement of our peace
was upon him; and with his stripes we are healed.
KJV

These sacred scars I carry are for you. They are forever chiseled in the halls of heaven. These scars of love spell the doom of Satan and his mignons who are eternally defeated by them. These sacred scars I carry for you are to remind the world how much I love and care for you and for all those you love. My scars are the trophies of My love for the world and all who dwell therein. My wounds have healing power—power to heal the sick in body, the wounded in heart, and the broken in spirit. These holy scars cry out to the universe that there is hope in life, that all who come to Me will never be rejected or left behind. I cannot and will not abandon you, ever. I see the scars, I reach toward you, I run after you. I live to capture your love, given with free will. The scars of love are the ribbons of victory. They shout throughout the universe that true love is possible for a fallen, wretched world of diseased people. Point them to My scars. I will point them to heaven. Healing is headed to you. Both old and new wounds will disappear today. You will feel just as if they never happened. Those wounds that have festered and become infected will now heal and close up. The new ones that have just happened will also disappear and turn into a scar of love. A scar is seven times stronger than original skin. What used to hurt you and bother you so easily you will now not feel. Don't be driven, guided, or motivated by your pain. Don't make any pain-inspired decisions; give them up, silence their voice. Remember, life is about being and becoming who you dream of being. Stop the downward momentum. Yield to My soft voice and climb out of the bad, emotional habits. Let Me toughen your spirit. Thick skin and a soft heart; that's your answer. Dive headlong into forgiveness. Wear it like a coat and don't fear people's words, looks, or actions. Set yourself free. My scars of love produce your life of wholeness. I suffered for you to rule and reign in this life. Cover yourself with My love scars and no other scars will touch you.

ivine Reversals

Isaiah 43:2
When thou passest through the waters, I will be
with thee; and through the rivers, they shall not overflow
thee: when thou walkest through the fire, thou shalt not
be burned; neither shall the flame kindle upon thee.
KJV

What people mean for harm, I will reverse, and for every harmful intention they have against you, you will receive a blessing. The more life tries to burn you, the more you will prosper and increase. You are immune to destruction and decay today. Overflowing prosperity will follow you now. Habits are breaking. Some of your friends have chosen the wrong lives; don't let your emotional connection with them separate you from Me. They bring judgment, pain, and failure in their smile. I don't. I am your Partner. I am your ever-present Help. I am always fixing things for you. I am your Doctor, Pilot, Captain, and your Benefactor. I execute righteousness for you. I lift the oppression off of you. I love you as your True Father, King, Creator, and Covenant Keeper. Walk in these truths. Let them be your lamp. Use them as a lighthouse of truth. Nothing will harm you as you stay on My path of truth. All the devices of the devil are rendered ineffective. His plan is thwarted, his voice is silenced, and his lies against you are dismantled. Divine reversals are your gift, for I am the God of divine reversals.

The Music of Your Soul

Psalm 91:4-5
He shall cover thee with his feathers, and under his wings shalt thou
trust: his truth shall be thy shield and buckler. Thou shalt not be afraid
for the terror by night; nor for the arrow that flieth by day.
KJV

I give you a new song and new music for your soul. From this will
flow divine protection from physical harm, emotional pain, and mental
torment. You will feel the shadow of My hand covering you from the
arrows and weapons of darkness. A cloud of love and the power of My
Presence will follow you around all day. Relax and enjoy your Father's
care. Today, the sun shines for you. The clouds bring holy rain and the
devices of the devil have been dismantled and reduced to dust. I want
you to live undistracted with 100% focus on your task. Find the hidden
treasure in the difficult people around you. Love them as you love Me.
This life will become the music of your soul. All that you are or ever
will be is defined by this song: hide in Me. Nothing will harm you,
not even the gates of hell can prevail against you. First you hear the
music and then you play the music until finally, you become the music.
This music is who I am. I am an everlasting Song. My Being resonates
throughout the universe. All created things are filled with this song.
Every part of nature and the universe will forever sing My song.
Submit to the music and your soul shall be healed. Your mind will be a
source of peace and your emotions a continual party of love.

our Very Breath

Psalm 105:24
And he increased his people greatly; and
made them stronger than their enemies.
KJV

Stand still and watch Me fight for you today. I know the names of your
enemies and where they live. I have sent out hit men who will remove
the threat from your house and life. You are going to see the victory
that you have been waiting for. Do not get anxious. Do not fear or
worry. Lift your hands to Me in thanksgiving and watch Me prevail
for you. I remove the criminals from your life. I heal the patients in
the hospitals. I release the slaves for your sake. I shepherd you with
My staff, and I open the banquet hall to prepare for a feast. I teach you
how to wash the feet of the unworthy, ungrateful, useless souls without
feeling demeaned or used. This life defines you. Live it with zeal and
continual, unstoppable increase will be your experience. Open your
heart as wide as the sky. Then, your supply will never run out. Feed the
orphan, clothe the widows, deliver the helpless. Make these your very
breaths, and you and I will never be apart.

Riding on the Clouds

Isaiah 62:1
*For Zion's sake will I not hold my peace, and for Jerusalem's sake I
will not rest, until the righteousness thereof go forth as brightness, and
the salvation thereof as a lamp that burneth.*
KJV

I am riding on the clouds of your answered prayers. I am the Divine
Messenger and Mailman. Don't be shy with your prayer. Let Me know
what you need every day and everywhere. Lifetime healing is your
portion, unquenchable love and undeniable glory your elixir. From
the heart of the morning I have ordained righteousness for you. There
shall be no more running around in circles. Now you are the carrier
of the burning torch, My spokesman. Do not hold your peace. Do not
stand for the plow of injustice to ruin your fields or recapture your joy.
Reinstate your original purpose. Comfort those who mourn because
they have been robbed and have lost everything. Help them recover
everything. I will help you do this. I will go before you and strengthen
your convictions. You will become a perpetual fountain of piercing,
overpowering prayer. Don't stop until you see Me fully in control.
Remember, I am riding on the clouds of your answered prayers. Now
fill the skies with glory clouds and let all of heaven ride with us
into destiny.

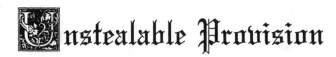nstealable Provision

1 Samuel 30:24
For who will hearken unto you in this matter?
but as his part is that goeth down to the battle, so shall his part
be that tarrieth by the stuff: they shall part alike.
KJV

Regardless of what you have done, there is a provision that I have kept
for you. I have set aside the spoil that others have fought for. They
are your partners. Since you have been faithful to pray for the saints,
unexpected surprises are on the way. Let Me show you the breadth
and depth of My goodness toward you. Let Me heal your past, prepare
your future, and straighten out your todays. Let Me wake your soul,
and let Me give you wings that set your spirit free to soar out of the
wilderness and into the land of your dreams. Let's end the struggles.
Let Me drain you of all discouragement. You know I forgive you of
everything and I heal you of everything. I redeem everything. I satisfy
your mouth with good things, all because I love you. Don't look
around for people's approval. Look straight ahead at Me. I am the
only One you can fully trust. I will never fail you. I will always bless
you beyond what you deserve. I am waking your soul to the tunes of
victory. It will sing the songs of Zion and never slumber or sleep in My
presence. Full, holy rage is now yours. Burn with these holy fires and
consume the world with My love.

n the Shadow of Peace

Matthew 6:25
Therefore I tell you, do not be anxious
about your life, what you will eat or what you will drink,
nor about your body, what you will put on. Is not life more
than food, and the body more than clothing?
ESV

Don't worry, for worry is an insult to My faithfulness. Trust and rest in My goodness. Take no thought! Throw your hands up right now in surrender. Don't drink in anxiety and fretting. Stand with a smile in your heart, run with a sword in your hand, and speak with assurance in your voice, for I am reliable, dependable, and trustworthy. Remember, I am sitting on the throne of your situation. If you put your trust in Me, I will sit you on this throne with Me. I am never late, never lacking, and never forgetful. I heal the broken wings of the traveler. I resolve the struggles of the anguished soul. I relieve the sorrows of the sufferer. I calm the storms of the sailor. I bless the work of your hands. Every precious dream is safe in My hands. Dwell then under the shadow of My peace. Surprises of abundance are headed your way. Outrageous gifts and provisions for your life journey have been mailed. Never question My overabundant goodness to you. Give it and live it.

The Pen of Good News

Psalm 112:7
He will not be afraid of evil tidings;
His heart is steadfast, trusting in the Lord.
NKJV

I hold in My hand the pen of good news. I alone can use this pen; it will not work for anyone else. I have chosen to use it for you. Do not fear evil tidings! Do not be afraid today. My hand has taken hold of your life. I will not allow you to be overwhelmed with the possibility of bad news. Shake off the vain imaginations of your mind. Cast them down and remind yourself that there are no bad reports on the way. My pen of good news and encouragement will begin to write on your mind and heal it. Your years will lack the wear and tear that others carry. The mountains you see ahead of you that seem so big right now will disappear with one wave of My hand. My immeasurable blessings have awakened to their assignment; that assignment is you and yours. They have been commanded to attach and glue themselves to you, to never leave your side, day nor night. I will lift you to the heights of humility and graciousness. Drink in My enduring mercy. Let it heal your memories and resolve the unresolved conflicts within you. Listen now for the music of the praising soul. For this is your lot in life. Now take My pen in your hand and write good news for the world to read.

This Indestructible House

Deuteronomy 33:28
So Israel lived in safety, in a land of
grain and wine, whose heavens drop down dew.
ESV

There is a home I am building for you, one that produces grain and wine in abundance. The days of drought and lack are over. Do not subscribe to Satan's newspaper. It is death to your spirit and faith. Instead, lift your head and drink heaven's rain. Let it water every part of your soul and spirit. Let it quench your thirst for Me. Let it unlock the windows of heaven. All dryness shall disappear from your life. You shall wake up to joyful mornings. The early rain will fall on you. Where you were dry, empty, and lacking, now strength, energy, and willpower will envelop you. You will now find refreshing and renewed power. No more giving up in frustration. Rebound on My Word! Gather your grain, which is My Word. Drink new wine, which is living revelation of My Word. Watch as I open My hand to you and leave it that way. Remember that I brought you through the waters of life and death. I crossed the rivers to find you. I protected you from the fires. I held you above the floods. I revealed to you My sacred paths. I crossed the deserts of your heart. I dispelled the terrifying darkness hanging over you. I filled your empty heart with love and grace. Now drink this new wine and dwell in this home I have built for you, this indestructible house.

No Enemies Within

John 14:30
I will not talk with you much more, for the prince
of the world is coming. And he has no claim on Me. [He has
nothing in common with Me; there is nothing in Me that
belongs to him, and he has no power over Me.]
AMP

There is a place where the arrows of the devil cannot reach you. None of his schemes work in this holy place. Here you will abide safely, covered from life's deadly poisons. No sign of the enemy's presence will be found in you, for you will be untouchable. Your body, soul, and spirit will be hidden in Me. No fingerprints of the enemy will be left on your family or your work, and your future will be secure. There is a private, secret throne inside you where only I should sit. Never allow anyone else to occupy it. This is the secret of total freedom for you where there are no masters, no remnants of yesterday's loves, no wrong entanglements, no out-of-balance obsessions, no overreactions, and no soul ties to the songs of the world. Leave the enemy's playground and cross the river to your destiny. Offer your life on the altar of surrender, and I will not withhold any good thing from you. There will be no enemies left within. You will never hear his voice again or feel his footsteps behind you. You will tear the mask off of his prophets and unchain his prisoners, sitting safely in My fortress of safety.

Honey from the Rock

Deuteronomy 32:13
I will make you drink honey
from the rock, and oil out of the flinty rock.
Author's Paraphrase

My sources of divine supply are yours. My sweet communion and kind friendship are yours. I leave Myself to you as your portion in this life. I give you honey from the Rock of Ages, resulting in miraculous transformations, purified motives, and cleansed aspirations. Stand in front of the Rock. Open up the doors of your heart and drink the healing waters of life. Drown in love and swim in mercy. Dance in the anointing. Dive into the mysteries of life. Let the waters continually refresh your soul. Let them carve out a highway of holiness that will allow you to see Me. As you swim in the honey, it will dissolve all the bitter tastes of your entire life. Every stage of your life will be renewed and remade. The boring will become exciting. The irrelevant will become necessary, and the distractions will fade away. Teach others where and how to drink. Teach them to stay connected to the Rock. Inspire them with your example. Show them where to come to receive healing for their brokenness. Teach them how to mend. Show them where the cripples are healed and the lepers are cleansed. Teach them to hear the sacred sound of the river where no enemy can come and no disease can survive.

Bring Your Vessels

2 Kings 4:3
Then he said, "Go, borrow vessels
from everywhere, from all your neighbors -
empty vessels; do not gather just a few.
NKJV

You determine your own harvest. Show Me your appetite. Bring your empty vessels to Me. Name each vessel. Whatever you choose to name them, that is what I will fill them with. What do you lack? Bring Me a vessel. What do you need? Bring Me a vessel. What do you want Me to change about your life? Bring Me a vessel. What dreams do you need to see happen? Bring Me a vessel. Where do you want Me to take you on your walk with Me? Bring Me a vessel. Do you need your family healed or blessed? Do you want a breakthrough in your finances? Do you want Me to open certain doors of opportunity? Bring Me a vessel! Bring Me all the vessels you want to bring. I don't run out of answers, miracles, or surprises. I want you to need Me. I want you to depend on Me. I want you to be the happiest person in the world. Bring Me your vessels—and not just a few.

he Center

Philippians 3:7
But what things were gain to me,
those I counted loss for Christ.
KJV

I am your vault. Hide all your most precious possessions inside of Me. No one can break in and steal what you hide in Me. Anything you give up, whether it be people, things, dreams, or desires, I will replace with Myself. I am more valuable than all other things that you could ever own. Everyone who wants Me as the center of their life must be tested; their heart must be proven. There can be no one else sitting on the throne of your heart. I cannot release the keys of My kingdom to you if you have other things before Me. You need to know what I already know about you—that I am the center of your life. From the center flows all the true issues of life, and all that anyone could ever desire comes from a true and free heart. I am not a tyrant; I am a Father who truly knows best. Move out of the shadows into the center stage of life. Let's explore life together and find what everyone else is searching for.

This One Precious Pearl

Matthew 13:45-46
Again the kingdom of heaven is like a man
who on finding a precious pearl, sold
everything he had and bought it.
Author's Paraphrase

This one precious pearl is all you will ever need. It is the pearl the whole world is searching for. This pearl fills the empty places of the soul and lights the fires of the heart. This one precious pearl is worth more than all the other pearls put together. It holds the rights to all your dreams. It contains the answers to all your questions. Therefore, take hold of this pearl, and the songs of the world will never return. Your life quest will become a clear vision, and your purpose will reveal itself. Take time to cherish this pearl. Polish it daily. Never lose it, sell it, or give it away. It is My gift to you. It can never be bought, sold, or replaced. It will define your life and empower your relationship with Me. This one precious pearl cost Me everything I am, everything I have, and everything there is. When you love it as deeply as I do, it will cost you everything too. This one precious pearl is Jesus.

The Sound of Your Sickle

Revelation 14:18
Put forth your sickle and reap the
ripe fruit I have prepared for you.
Author's Paraphrase

It is time to reap your hidden harvest. It is time to pick up your God-made sickle. This sickle has been sharpened. It cannot fail or grow dull and useless. It is your gift from Me. Use it, cherish it, and sharpen it with a surrendered heart and clear conscience. Lean on it, rely on its power, let it yield blessing to you. Let My compassionate heart, which is your sickle, heal your world and turn the soil of your life around.

I will never stop loving you—not ever. I will never leave a stump, boulder, or rock in your life. Your sickle will make your dreams come true. Put forth your sickle and claim your God-given life. I have not forgotten your potential. I am digging in your heart every day. Yield to My shovel. There is no hardness your sickle cannot break, no root too deep, and no fallow ground it cannot penetrate. Use your sickle daily, and fruit will begin to fall off the trees for you—juicy, soft, sweet fruit that cannot be resisted or destroyed by drought, worms, or harsh conditions. All this responds to the strike of your sickle; therefore, lift your sickle and plunge it into your destiny.

ild Grapes

Micah 4:4
But they shall sit every man under his vine and
under his fig tree; and none shall make them afraid…
KJV

Some people wait a whole lifetime for their dreams to come true and never see them. Men, women, and children die with empty hearts and unfulfilled lives. But this is not your inheritance. I do not have a box of ashes for you or a treasure chest filled with used rags. Your inheritance is love-made, fashioned in My heart. Every piece of it is designed to add value and wealth to your life. You are My vineyard, My place of creating new wine for the healings of the soul. You will never produce wild, unripe grapes. Your family will not be visited by evil, and your inheritance will not be poisoned by invaders or stolen or ruined by neglect. It is yours for life, and it is safe from erosion. Treat it with great love. Cherish it and esteem it as sacred, and it will yield a fresh crop of blessings every year. Expect sweetness from the grapes in your garden. Do not look for the withered, spoiled grapes. They will fall into the soil and become fertilizer for the rest. Give yourself wholly to learning, loving, and living.

The Devil's Teeth

Psalm 46:9
He makes wars cease to the end of
the earth; He breaks the bow and cuts the spear
in two; He burns the chariots in the fire.
NKJV

One word from My mouth, and the wars cease. One wave of My hand, and your troubles are over. No more unexpected train wrecks. No more spilled seeds of destiny. No more mistakes of ignorance. Open your heart, and your eyes will be healed to see as I see. My point of view is the only true point of view. Seeing is believing, and I see everything. Prepare yourself for a love invasion, the end of catastrophes, and inner struggles. A complete reconstruction of your life has started—one where the ditches are filled, the road blocks removed, the mountains leveled, and perfect clarity and knowledge released in your life. The jungle is being cleansed of deadly predators and snakes in the grass.

The wild beasts are being caged, and the blind spots will reveal themselves. You are headed for a total makeover. You are never going to see the devil's teeth again. Know this: I have pulled the devil's teeth. All he can do is show his dentures.

eep On Rowing

Psalm 66:12
...we went through fire and through water, but
You brought us out into a broad, moist place [to
abundance and refreshment and the open air].
AMP

Life is like being in a canoe on the rapids. No matter how rough the waves get, you have to keep rowing. Stay in the boat. Listen to My instructions and keep rowing. Hold on tight to the paddles; they will get you through those unpredictable waters. When people misunderstand you, misjudge you, twist your words and actions, and label you as something ugly and awful, keep on rowing. When they steal your reputation, keep on rowing. When they insult your integrity and chase your opportunities away, keep on rowing. When they blame you for their mistakes, keep on rowing. Learn this lesson today. Don't ever pull your oar out of the water. Row, row, row, and keep rowing. There is a peaceful place coming around the bend. The rapids always subside, the danger always passes, and terror always vanishes. Life is waiting for you to discover it. Sometimes you have to do the right thing even if people turn it into the wrong thing. Row, row, row. There is a peaceful place coming around the bend.

 **hase Me**

Song of Solomon 1:2
We will run after you, for
your Love is better than wine.
Author's Paraphrase

Chase Me, and I will chase you. Chase Me, and your dead dreams will walk again. Chase Me, and your bad desires will melt away. Chase Me, and the giant-killer inside you will come forth. Chase Me, and you will find your destiny. Chase Me, and heaven will follow you. Chase Me with your soul, and you will never lack peace. Chase Me, and your purpose will reveal itself. Chase Me with all your affection, and I will be your first, truest Friend. Chase Me with your worship, and no idol will ever occupy your heart. Chase Me with your trust, and I will come through for you. Chase Me with your faith, and every mountain will vanish. Chase Me with your life, and we will never be strangers. Chase Me with your heart, and you and I will always be close. Chase Me always, for I am already chasing you.

The Pearls of Heaven

Proverbs 28:27
He who gives to the poor will not lack, but
he who hides his eyes will have many curses.
NKJV

The secret of your success is the way you treat the poor. I want you to find the poor and enrich them with the pearls of heaven. Fill their stomachs, clothe their naked backs, comfort them with hope, and give them the ability to dream. Deliver their wounded souls and point them toward Me. If you follow this light, you will never lack anything in your life. You will be the richest person you know. This lifestyle is My heart. I love the abandoned, rejected, suffering souls, and I want you to become a soldier for the poor. Stand up and fight for them. Hear their cry. Never turn the other way. Every time you stretch out your hand to them, I will stretch out My hand to the ones you love. Clothe their spirit with spiritual wisdom. Wash their minds with faith, heal their ears with love languages, and repair their hearts with acts of kindness. Remember, the pearls of heaven are in your care.

The Champion Inside You

Philippians 4:13
I can do all things through Christ
who strengthens me.
NKJV

Your potential is your inspiration and your tormentor, all at the same time. You know there is untapped potential in you waiting to be released. There is a master painter and sculptor of souls inside you. There is a fisher of lost souls, a builder of My kingdom, an entrepreneur for Me, a deliverer of the oppressed, and a rescuer of lost and abandoned children. You know you can speak to the nations and confound the intellectual with My words. Since the day you could walk, you knew you could run. You knew there would always be more. As long as you have breath, you will always be an achiever for Me. Live your life in the energy that makes things happen. I will always be with you. I will always help you and strengthen you. Don't ever back down from challenges. They are like food to you; you live on them. They are your daily bread. This is who I have made you. Now submit to the champion inside and conquer My enemies.

bba Father

Romans 8:15
For ye have not received the spirit of
bondage again to fear; but ye have received the
Spirit of adoption, whereby we cry, Abba, Father.
KJV

I understand you even if no one else does. I know all your secret thoughts—good and bad. I know your many feelings. I know your mood swings, your frustrations, your despair, and your joys. I know where you came from. I know all of your private and public experiences. No one else can claim that! I am uniquely qualified to help you out of your tight places. I have made all the necessary arrangements for your old chains to be melted down and thrown away in a deep and unreachable well. You cannot experience what I have planned for you with problems resting on your back. The calling I have for you is too intense, too great. This is what I need you to learn: A minute with Me equals a lifetime of wealth. I love you unconditionally and will never forsake you. I am your Father. I have adopted you forever. I have a heart of love for you that no one can change. I am eternally committed to your success and well-being. Sound the trumpet; make the world listen to the sacred call.

Just In Time

Psalm 116:7-8
Return unto thy rest, O my soul;
for the Lord hath dealt bountifully with thee.
For thou hast delivered my soul from death, mine
eyes from tears, and my feet from falling.
KJV

It is time to stop and find a comfortable chair. Sit down, put your feet up, and let Me minister to you. Forget about everything that you need to do; it can wait. Plug into Me now. Rest, relax, unwind, and breathe in deeply the breath of life. Let My peace fill your lungs. Let your tired soul be refreshed with My loving presence. Rest is just as important as work. How long have you been working and where has it taken you on your journey to know Me? This is your time. It is your time to fill your gas tank, to recharge your battery. You have to do it; I order you lovingly to do it. Now, when you've rested, you can do more in less time with a better result. Remind yourself of what I have already done for you, how I have saved your life from dangerous situations and people, how I have stopped the pain and caught you when you were falling. Therefore, don't worry; with My help, you will change the world, just in time.

# teadfast Love

Lamentations 3:22-23
The steadfast love of the Lord never
ceases, his mercies never come to an end; they are
new every morning; great is thy faithfulness.
RSV

Don't clothe yourself in yesterday's guilt rags. Don't put on the chains
of your past failures. Turn away from that. You cannot win today's
victories if you are dwelling on yesterday's defeats. Let go! Stand
up! Don't bow your soul to yesterday. I have victories for you to win
today. Forgive yourself and others. Give yourself a new beginning as
a gift. They say you're done, finished, and wiped out. I say the best
is yet to come. Shout for joy and shock the world! This is a new day
with no mistakes in it, no guilt or accusing fingers. Say this: "God's
love never runs out. His mercies are new every morning. Great is
His faithfulness to me." Remember, I have an inexhaustible supply
of second chances. Your heart is not black or disloyal. I have made it
soft, pliable, and faithful. Believe this and prosper. Do not listen to the
discouragers. Listen to the Encourager. I complete what I start, and I
will complete you.

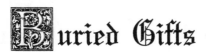uried Gifts

Proverbs 18:16
A man's gift maketh room for him,
and bringeth him before great men.
KJV

When I found you lost, lonely, and hopeless, I decided to give you
some very special and powerful gifts. These gifts will help people
crawl out of their dungeons. Your buried gifts have heard the sound of
My resurrection voice. "Come forth" is the call I have sent forth. These
gifts will give you entrance into the hearts of the high and low. No
place of influence will be unreachable to you. Those who have laughed
at you in the past will be ashamed of their own twisted heart. Those
who are looking for failure will be silenced. Don't expect a normal life
from now on. The opportunities are marching your way. Life is about
to say "yes" to your dreams. Use your new gifts and bless people.
Help someone every day. Don't waste any opportunity. I am preparing
a platform for your voice. My plans for you include all of your most
impossible dreams. Stand still and let your gifts do the work.

And the Dove Came Back

Genesis 8:11
And the dove came back to him
in the evening, and behold, in her mouth
was a freshly plucked olive leaf...
ESV

My Dove is the glory of heaven. He fills the air with beauty and love that no man has ever been able to resist. He saturates all of heaven with healing, wholeness, and purpose. My Dove is love revealed, joy expressed, and power manifested. My Dove will turn your negative circumstances into victorious breakthroughs. When you hear the sound of the Dove's wings, know that miracles are about to break forth into your life and the delayed blessings are being released. My Dove is the mender of broken and torn hearts. My Dove repairs the breeches between people. He solves, resolves, and absolves people of their sins and problems. My Dove, the conductor of the music of life, which turns the ugly into the beautiful, makes the sounds of your life harmonize with Me. My Dove is the protector of your treasures and inheritance. He brings peace to the world.

The False Prophets

1 Kings 18:40
And Elijah said unto them, Take the
prophets of Baal; let not one of them escape.
And they took them: and Elijah brought them
down to the brook Kishon, and slew them there.
KJV

No voice but Mine. No truth but Mine. No good but Mine. These truths need to fill your brain. These truths are like medicine to your soul. Never forget them. Bind them around your neck and write them on the tablet of your heart. They will awaken the dead dreams in your heart's field. These truths will soften the hearts that hear you and give them supernatural endurance in the race of life. All droughts will end, opening the clogged wells of life, ending all desert crossings. Now the windows of heaven will open for you, watering the garden of your life and destroying the swarms of devouring pests. You will ignite the revival of the Word by slaying the false prophets of Satan, ending all circumstantial catastrophes and releasing the blessing of the heroes of heaven. You will be thrust into a life of relevance and purpose, establishing your voice as a voice of power and courage. No voice but Mine. No truth but Mine. No good but Mine.

The House of the Unoffended

Psalm 119:165
Great peace have they which love thy law:
and nothing shall offend them.
KJV

There is a place you can go where the rude, offensive people who exist around you cannot penetrate your soul's armor. This place has been known to only a few; it is a hiding place so secure and impenetrable that none of your past tyrants can reach you. There I am making you immune to emotional invasion. This holy place is the house of the unoffended, the place of loving and eating My Word daily, drinking My wisdom, and acting on My advice. My Word will become a shield around you, protecting you from the painful daggers of the Judas' hearts that live blindly by their undisciplined impulses. You have seen the last of the torture chambers and mud pits that these people can drag you into. To rule your emotions is a great victory. To be free from the imperfections of the unlovely is great freedom. Stand apart from the snares of pity. Live with your wings spread. Glide over the obstacles and turn your life into a sea of opportunities. Soar into your promotions and receive your rewards. Be a lighthouse of love and point the way for those who have lost their lanterns and run out of oil. Remember, your position is great peace. Be a lighthouse of love and forgiveness.

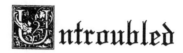ntroubled

Philippians 4:9
Practice what you have learned and received and heard and
seen in Me, and model your way of living on it, and the God of
peace (of untroubled, undisturbed well-being) will be with you.
AMP

Untroubled, undisturbed well-being is your portion. Sit down at My
table and dine in these truths: that in Me there is a place of untroubled
serenity and well-being. If you dwell in Me and My Word dwells
in you, you will become a mirror reflecting My image to the world.
They will see how I live inside of you, making you untouchable to
the corroding influences of the world. I will reveal to the world My
peace through your life. Peace is My medicine for the troubled and
tortured. It cleanses, repairs, and refreshes the soul with hope. It
restores the mind and heals the cracks in a person's thinking. Never
trade My peace for pleasure. Never lose sight of Me. In the midst of
all the screaming voices, take hold of Me and never release your grip
of love on Me. You should know that I came to fix the brokenness in
your life, to teach you My ways, to instruct you in Christlike living.
If you embrace My teaching, your life will be a constant celebration
of heaven. Talk like I talk, forgive like I forgive, act and respond like
I do. Prosperity will then follow you around all day long. I want you
to taste every kind of prosperity there is: financial, spiritual, social,
emotional, and physical. All of these are for you and are prepared by

Me. I see your personal struggles of faith. I see the irritating people around you. The answer is not to get rid of them but to get rid of the undeveloped part of your human nature. Learn, follow, and obey. When you wake up in the mornings, you will begin to notice Me in the mirror. You are a bringer of peace. Remind yourself of that and free yourself. Untroubled, unbreakable, unmistakable.

The Nectar of Life

1 Peter 1:8
Without having seen Him, we love Him,
without having seen him we believe in Him and we exalt
and are thrilled with inexpressible and glorious joy.
Author's Paraphrase

I am past finding out. Everything about Me is a mystery waiting to be discovered. I dwell in eternity, and I see all things at once. I know everything that was and is and ever shall be. I know this, that My plan for you is past your comprehension. It was conceived in eternity by your Father who loves you infinitely. Anything I wish comes to pass. I don't dream and not realize I am dreaming. What I dream, I have. I have dreamed of your life completed. You love Me without having seen Me. I want you to know that is why I will withhold nothing from you. Ask Me, and it's yours. Oh, the glorious possibilities that await you! Everything you have thought was fun will pale in comparison to what I am preparing to do for you. These plans are the plans of perfectly, uncontaminated love and unspeakable riches that hold the universe together. You don't have anything to worry about. Every tiny detail of your life fits perfectly into My sovereign plan. Live freely, love unconditionally, and breathe in the nectar of life.

Live Your Life with Open Hands

Genesis 39:3
And his master saw that the Lord was
with him and that the Lord made all that
he did to flourish and succeed in his hand.
AMP

I know you have felt alone in the past—helpless, confused, and misunderstood. You are not alone today. You will not face this day without feeling Me near you. My hand is there with you, and you will never be alone again. I am going to shock everyone by supporting your efforts with miraculous results so big and grand that no one else will be able to claim the credit for the blessings. I will find the snakes in the garden and get them out. No thorns or little foxes that spoil your life will survive. You will look around today and feel My arms carrying you, directing you, and encouraging you. Whatever you touch will prosper. Success will follow you around like a faithful dog, screaming to the world what it can have if it follows Me. Share your money, love, and blessings. Live your life with open hands.